The "I Don't Know How to Cook" Book

-2ND EDITION-

300 GREAT RECIPES

You Can't Mess Up!

MARY-LANE KAMBERG

adamsmedia
Avon, Massachusetts

For my daughters, Rebekka and Johanna
My gratitude to the Kansas City Writers Group

𝔔

Published by Adams Media, an F+W Publications Company
57 Littlefield Street
Avon, MA 02322
www.adamsmedia.com

ISBN-13: 978-1-59869-703-2
ISBN-10: 1-59869-703-X

Library of Congress Cataloging-in-Publication Data is available from the publisher.

Printed in the United States of America.

J I H G F E D C B A

This publication is designed to provide accurate and authoritative information with regard to the subject matter covered. It is sold with the understanding that the publisher is not engaged in rendering legal, accounting, or other professional advice. If legal advice or other expert assistance is required, the services of a competent professional person should be sought.

—From a *Declaration of Principles* jointly adopted by a Committee of the American Bar Association and a Committee of Publishers and Associations

Many of the designations used by manufacturers and sellers to distinguish their product are claimed as trademarks. Where those designations appear in this book and Adams Media was aware of a trademark claim, the designations have been printed with initial capital letters.

This book is available at quantity discounts for bulk purchases.
For information, please call 1-800-289-0963.

Contents

Introduction v

Recipe for New Cooks vii

Chapter 1: Breakfast Foods to Start Your Day 1

Chapter 2: Sandwiches 29

Chapter 3: Soups and Stews 53

Chapter 4: Salads 79

Chapter 5: Main Dishes—Beef and Pork 106

Chapter 6: Main Dishes—Poultry 145

Chapter 7: Main Dishes—Seafood 165

Chapter 8: Main Dishes—Vegetarian and Vegan 187

Chapter 9: Side Dishes 209

Chapter 10: Snacks and Appetizers 233

Chapter 11: Desserts 264

Appendix A: Equipping the Kitchen 305

Appendix B: Glossary of Cooking Terms 309

Appendix C: Cooking Vegetables 315

Index of Cooking Questions 319

Index 321

Acknowledgments

From the first instant I shared the idea for a cookbook for people who can't cook, dozens of friends and family members encouraged and assisted me in the effort. Special thanks to my mother and research assistant, Jessie Ladewig; my husband, Ken Kamberg; my daughters, Rebekka Kamberg and Johanna Kamberg; my siblings, Brock Ladewig, Amy Phillips, and Ann Nelson; and the rest of my extended family: cousins, in-laws, nieces, nephews, my dear friends, and the clerks at Dillons Store No. 69, my favorite supermarket.

Particular thanks go to Michelle Langenberg, Lucy Lauer, Chalise, Candy Schock, and Robin Silverman for their help. And to these friends and family who offered their favorite easy-to-make recipes: Melody Aldrich, Beth Bailey, Barbara Bartocci, Marsha Bartsch, Josh Baze, Nina Bertilsdotter, Deborah Bundy, Kerri Fivecoat-Campbell, Ginger Carter, Meri Carter, Judith Choice, Lance Clenard, Maril Crabtree, Alberta Daw, Ruth Ann Falls, Jeannine Fox, Ricki Gilbert, Lisa Waterman Gray, Jacqueline Guidry, Madeline Guidry, Carolyn Hall, Greg Hockett, Ann Ingalls, Sally Jadlow, Judith Bader Jones, Ken Kamberg, Joe Karroll, Heather Kiepura, Tami Kohler, Betsy Krusen, Hank Krusen, Lindsey Krusen, Mary Ladewig, Julie Laird, Amelia Mendus, Sophia Myers, Joan Nietzchke, Jon Phillips, Jane Rogers, Nate Rogers, Rex Rogers, Larry Schilb, Marsha Schilb, Corrine Russell, Susan Shanaman, Niki Shepherd, Deborah Shouse, Patty Sullivan, Janet Sunderland, Polly Swafford, Vicki Swartz, Denise Tiller, Pat Walkenhorst, Toni Watson, and Bette Willmeth. Thanks, too, to my able, efficient agents Mike and Susan Farris and my editors Danielle Chiotti and Chelsea King.

Introduction

Response to the first edition of The "I Don't Know How To Cook" Book has been gratifying. Friends who bought it tell me they "use it all the time," and I get e-mails from other readers complimenting particular dishes and asking for more recipes. So, by popular request, here's a new, improved version of the original. This book contains my favorites from the first book, along with many exciting new dishes.

When I wrote the first edition of this book, my goal was to create a hands-on learning experience for new cooks. I wanted to provide recipes so tasty and easy to make that new cooks would enjoy a successful cooking experience. My philosophy is if you can read (and follow directions), you can cook.

For this new and improved version, I stuck to the original premise and philosophy. Here are more recipes you can make, even if you've never cooked anything before. I purposely omitted fancy cooking terms that might scare you away. (You can find them in the glossary if you need them to understand traditional cookbooks.)

All recipes in this cookbook were chosen because they're easy to make; some just need a little cooking practice. They're grouped according to difficulty within each chapter and identified by these symbols:

LEVEL **E**
SERVINGS **4**

Easy: **E**
Medium: **M**
Hard: **H**

Vegetarian recipes are identified with a "**v**" right after the recipe title, and the serving size is indicated below the "easy" level.

Try the recipes marked "easy" first to ease into the cooking game. After that, challenge yourself with those marked "medium" and "hard." You'll gain cooking skills while you build your cooking repertoire. After you've tried a few recipes for yourself, invite some friends and cook for them. (Note: Always fix recipes that you've made before. The night of the party is no time to try something new!)

Welcome to the kitchen!

Recipe for New Cooks

1. Before you begin, read the recipe all the way through. Assemble all ingredients. (The ingredients in *The "I Don't Know How to Cook" Book* are listed in the order of their appearance in the directions. If you like order you can line them up in a row—but you don't have to!)

2. Always wash your hands before and after handling food, especially meats and poultry, which may contain harmful bacteria that proper cooking kills.

3. Ovens and microwaves vary, so many recipes give a range of cooking times. In recipes that give a range of cooking times, such as 15 to 20 minutes, check the food after the first time listed. If the dish is not done, return to the heat source for the additional time.

4. No recipe is cast in stone. After you try a recipe for the first time, make notes to yourself in the cookbook's margin. Note cooking times for your oven or microwave, as well as measurements you would like to adjust to your personal taste.

5. Sometimes you'll want to prepare fewer or more servings of a recipe. All you have to do is a little math. You can double a recipe by multiplying the measurement of each ingredient by two. You can cut a recipe in half by dividing the measurement of each ingredient. But be careful. Cooking times may vary—especially in microwaves that need more time to cook larger quantities of food. If you're doubling a recipe, do *not* double the cooking time. Cook it according to directions, but be aware that you may need a little more cooking

time. The reverse may be true when cooking smaller amounts.

6. Plan menus. Eat different types of foods so you get a variety of nutrients. If you're new at meal planning, follow the school lunch menu, which often appears in local papers. Qualified dietitians plan the menus. Do what they do.

7. Nothing will dampen your enthusiasm for cooking more than a kitchen full of dirty pots, pans, and utensils when the food is done. Whenever possible, clean as you go. When you are finished with a pot, measuring cup, or mixing bowl, wash it while you're waiting for noodles to boil or during baking times. You can let the cooking utensils drip dry. Or, if you're really a neat freak, you can also dry them and put them away. (Nah!)

Bon Appétit!

These common measurements will help you for this cookbook and any other!

3 teaspoons = 1 tablespoon

4 tablespoons = ¼ cup

5 tablespoons plus 1 teaspoon = ⅓ cup

1 cup = ½ pint

2 cups = 1 pint

2 pints = 1 quart

2 quarts = ½ gallon

4 quarts = 1 gallon

Chapter 1
Breakfast Foods to Start Your Day

Easy

Orange-Banana Smoothie 2
Orange-Glazed Biscuits 3
Easy Coffee Cake 4
Makin' Bacon 5
Poached Egg 6
Fried Egg 7
Variation: Fried Egg & Cheese 7
Boiled Egg 8
Scrambled Eggs 9
Apple Oatmeal 10
Honey-Banana Bagel Spread 11
Peaches & Cream Spread 11
Strawberry Bagel Spread 12
Honey Butter 12

Medium

Blueberry Muffins 13
Home-Fried Potatoes 14
French Toast 15
Vegan French Toast 16
Scrambled French Toast 17
Nutty Banana Pancakes 18
Huevos Rancheros 19
Popovers 20

Hard

Pumpkin-Nut Bread 21
Sausage Soufflé 22
Apple & Sausage Pancakes 23
Breakfast Burrito 24
Quiche Lorraine 25
Mushroom Quiche 26
Banana Bread 27
Bacon & Egg Casserole 28

Orange-Banana Smoothie   v

Wake up to this delicious breakfast in a glass, and get ready for a great day!

Bananas are known to calm the mind and oranges are said to clear the mind. You'll be prepared to take on the world in just a few minutes.

Use an electric blender or electric mixer.

What You Need

1 banana

1 (6-ounce) can frozen orange juice concentrate

1 (6-ounce) can water

Ice, as needed (about 2 cups)

What You Do

1. Peel and slice banana. Place the orange juice, water, and banana in an electric blender. Add enough ice to fill the blender. Blend until smooth.

2. If you don't have a blender, place orange juice, water, and banana in a medium-size mixing bowl. Use a spoon or electric mixer to stir rapidly until well blended. Place ice in glasses. Pour the banana mixture over the ice.

LEVEL **E**

SERVINGS **10**

Orange-Glazed Biscuits   v

Sweet and tangy, these breakfast biscuits will start your day with sunshine.

Make orange juice from the leftover orange juice concentrate.

Measure remaining concentrate and add 3 times as much water, then stir.

What You Need

½ cup butter or margarine

1 cup white granulated sugar

3 tablespoons frozen orange juice concentrate

1 (12-ounce) can refrigerated biscuits

What You Do

1. Preheat oven to 375°F. Melt the butter (or margarine) in a saucepan over low heat. Stir in the sugar and orange juice concentrate. Dip the top of each biscuit in this mixture and place glazed-side down, side by side and touching the other biscuits in a greased tube pan, Bundt pan, or round cake pan.

2. Pour the remaining sauce over the biscuits in the pan. Bake, uncovered, for 15 minutes. During baking, the glaze works its way to the bottom of the pan, so when serving, turn biscuits upside down on serving plate so the glaze will drizzle over the top for an attractive presentation. Serve warm.

The aroma of cinnamon and freshly baked biscuit dough is an inviting way to start the day.

You can substitute chopped walnuts for the pecans.

Easy Coffee Cake v

What You Need

½ cup butter or margarine

½ cup brown sugar, firmly packed

1 teaspoon cinnamon

1 (12-ounce) can refrigerator biscuits

2 tablespoons chopped pecans or walnuts

What You Do

1. Preheat oven to 350°F. Melt the butter (or margarine) in a saucepan over low heat. Stir in the brown sugar and cinnamon.

2. Grease a 9" round cake pan or spray with nonstick cooking spray. One at a time, dip the top of each biscuit into the butter mixture. Place butter-side down in the pan, starting on the outer edge and overlapping the biscuits in a circle. Use remaining biscuits to fill the middle of the pan.

3. Add nuts to remaining butter mixture. Spoon the mixture onto the biscuits. Bake uncovered for 10 minutes.

?

How Should I Measure Brown Sugar?

Some recipes that call for brown sugar specify the measurement should be "firmly packed." To measure that way, put the brown sugar in the measuring cup and use the back of a spoon to pack it down. Keep tightly pressing it into the measuring cup until you have the amount asked for. This method results in more brown sugar than you would get using the usual measuring method—and that's what the recipe writer intends.

Makin' Bacon

There's nothing like the sound and smell of bacon sizzling in the pan to start your day.

Bacon is a favorite with eggs, pancakes, and French Toast (page 15).

You can also use cooked bacon in tossed salads and on sandwiches.

Method 1: Pan-Fried

1. One at a time, lay strips of bacon side-by-side in a cold skillet. Turn on heat to medium-high. As the bacon cooks, use a fork to move the slices often to avoid sticking. When each slice is brown on the first side, use a fork or tongs to turn it over.

2. Cook on the second side until the bacon is as crisp as you like it. Use a fork or tongs to move each slice from the pan to several sheets of paper towel.

Method 2: Microwaved

1. Place 2 thicknesses of paper towels on a microwave-safe plate. Place strips of bacon on the paper towels. Cover with another layer of 2 paper towels.

2. Microwave for 5 to 10 minutes. Check after 5 minutes and again every 2 minutes until done.

Method 3: Baked

Preheat oven to 400°F. Separate pieces of bacon and lay across the rack of a broiler pan. The slots in the broiler lid will let bacon fat drip into the lower part of the pan. If you don't have a broiler pan, use a shallow ovenproof baking dish. Bake on a middle oven rack for about 10 minutes. No need to turn.

What Do I Do with Bacon Fat?

Bacon fat is often used to add flavor to eggs, vegetables, or other foods. After cooking bacon, pour the fat into an ovenproof glass container. (The fat will be hot and could crack containers not designed to hold hot food.) Cool to room temperature. Cover and store in refrigerator until ready to use. If you don't plan to use it to add flavor to other foods, do not pour it down the sink. You'll clog your drain pipes. Instead, pour it into a used can, chill in refrigerator until solid, and discard.

Poached Egg   v

Poached eggs are cooked in steam.

You can make them in a frying pan that has a lid, or use a poaching pan, an electric egg poacher, or a microwave egg poacher.

Poached eggs are especially good served on toast, with a somewhat runny yolk soaking into the bread. Yum.

?

What You Need

About 1 teaspoon butter, margarine, vegetable oil, or nonstick cooking spray

1 egg

Water

What You Do

1. Lightly coat a frying pan with butter (or alternative).

2. Break the egg into the pan. Add ½ teaspoon water (for each egg). Cover tightly.

3. Cook for about 5 minutes or until the egg is as firm as you like.

Oops! What Do I Do If There's Eggshell in My Eggs?

If a bit of eggshell ends up in your mixture, the best way to get hold of it is with another piece of eggshell. (That's why you don't want to be too quick to toss the shells into the trash or stuff them down the garbage disposal.) Pick up a big piece of shell and use it to scoop out its offending cousin. The substance inside the shell helps the pieces stick to each other for easy removal.

Fried Egg

What You Need

2–3 tablespoons butter, margarine, bacon fat, or vegetable oil

1 egg

What You Do

1. Melt the butter (or alternative) in a frying pan over medium heat. When melted, crack the egg into the frying pan.

2. For "sunny-side up," cook until the yolk is done according to your preference. For "over easy," let cook until the white is almost done. Flip with a pancake turner. Immediately flip over onto serving plate. "Basted" eggs look like "over easy" eggs, but you don't flip them over. Instead, as the egg cooks, spoon hot fat from the frying pan on top of the egg. The top will cook, but you won't risk breaking the yolk during the flipping process.

Variation: Fried Egg & Cheese

When the egg white is cooked, or immediately after flipping over the egg, add a slice of your favorite cheese. Cook until the cheese melts.

Boiled Egg v

Both soft-boiled and hard-boiled eggs are cooked the same way. The only difference is the cooking time.

Start with an egg at room temperature.

What You Need

1 egg

Water as needed to cover the egg

What You Do

1. Place the egg in a saucepan (for many eggs at once, you can use a Dutch oven but don't stack on top of each other). Cover with water. Bring to a boil over medium-high to high heat.

2. When the water boils, cover tightly. Remove from heat. For a soft-boiled egg, let cook for 2 to 4 minutes, depending on your preferred firmness. For a hard-boiled egg, let stand 20 minutes.

3. Rinse the egg in cold water to stop the cooking process and to make it easier to remove the shell.

?

OK, So How *Do* I Boil Water?

Boiling water means heating it enough that it turns to steam. All you do is pour the water into a saucepan or microwave-safe dish and heat over high heat on the stovetop or on high in a microwave oven until big bubbles break on the surface. Boiling water is an important cooking method used for cooking eggs, hot dogs, vegetables, and even some meat. Water boils faster if you cover the pan with a lid. Be careful not to let the pan boil dry. As water boils, it evaporates as steam. So if you heat it too long, all the water will disappear and your food will burn.

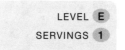

LEVEL **E**
SERVINGS **1**

You can eat scrambled eggs alone or with cheese or other added ingredients, such as chopped bell pepper, chopped onion (or dried onion flakes), sliced olives, mushrooms, bacon bits, diced ham, or crumbled cooked sausage.

Scrambled Eggs v

What You Need

1–2 tablespoons butter, margarine, bacon fat, or vegetable oil

2–3 eggs

2–3 tablespoons milk (optional)

What You Do

1. Melt fat over medium heat. (If using butter, don't let it turn dark brown. Reduce heat if necessary.)

2. Crack the eggs into a small mixing bowl. Add 1 tablespoon milk for each egg. Quickly stir with a fork to break the yolks and blend in the milk. Add any optional ingredients. Pour into frying pan.

3. Stir they eggs so they cook evenly, about 5 minutes. When the eggs are still a bit runnier than you like, remove from heat and let sit for 1 or 2 minutes. (Eggs will continue to cook.) Fluff with a fork.

This is not your mother's oatmeal. With the fragrant aroma of apples and cinnamon, this oatmeal has the zing and spice of apple pie.

Serve with milk. Enjoy!

Apple Oatmeal v

What You Need

1 apple

⅓ cup oats (uncooked oatmeal; not instant)

¼ cup raisins (optional)

¼ teaspoon cinnamon

⅔ cup milk

About 2 tablespoons brown sugar

What You Do

1. Peel, core, and chop the apple. Place in a saucepan with the oats, raisins, and cinnamon. Stir in the milk and cook over medium heat until bubbly. Reduce heat to low. Simmer for 5 minutes, stirring occasionally.

2. Spoon into serving bowls. Sprinkle each with about 1½ teaspoons brown sugar.

Honey-Banana Bagel Spread   v

What You Need

3 ounces cream cheese

3 tablespoons butter or margarine

1 banana

3 tablespoons honey

What You Do

1. Set out the cream cheese and butter to soften at room temperature for 10 to 15 minutes. Place in a small mixing bowl.

2. Peel the banana and slice crosswise. Add to the mixing bowl. Add the honey. Use a potato masher or electric mixer to stir together until smooth.

Peaches & Cream Spread   v

What You Need

4 tablespoons cream cheese

2 tablespoons peach preserves

What You Do

Set out the cream cheese for about 10 minutes. In a small bowl, mash cream cheese until smooth. Stir in preserves until well blended.

Strawberry Bagel Spread v

Strawberries and cream on a toasted bagel—yum!

What You Need

4 ounces cream cheese

½ cup fresh strawberries or 3 tablespoons strawberry jam

⅓ cup white granulated sugar

1 tablespoon orange juice

What You Do

Set out the cream cheese to soften for 10 to 15 minutes. Place in a small bowl. Clean the strawberries (see "How Should I Clean Strawberries?" on page 274), and cut into slices. Mash with a fork. Add the sugar and orange juice to the cream cheese. Use a spoon or electric mixer to blend until smooth.

Honey Butter v

Try this melt-in-your-mouth spread on biscuits or dinner rolls.

What You Need

½ cup butter or margarine

1 tablespoon honey

What You Do

Set out butter for 10 to 15 minutes until soft. Place in a small mixing bowl. Use a fork or mixer to blend until smooth. Stir in the honey until well blended.

Blueberry Muffins v

Don't pay for a box of muffin mix. You'll be proud to serve these muffins you make from scratch!

You'll need paper muffin cups, or grease 9 cups of a muffin tin for baking.

For a different flavor, replace the blueberries with 1 cup of cranberries or ¾ cup raisins or chopped nuts.

What You Need

1¾ cups flour

¼ cup sugar

2½ teaspoons baking powder

1 egg

¾ cup milk

⅓ cup vegetable oil

1 cup blueberries

What You Do

1. Preheat the oven to 400°. In a medium mixing bowl, combine the flour, sugar, and baking powder. Set aside.

2. In a separate, small bowl, use a fork to beat the egg. Still using the fork, stir in the milk and vegetable oil.

3. Pour the egg mixture into the flour mixture. Stir slowly just until blended into a slightly lumpy mixture. Stir in the blueberries.

4. Place paper muffin cups into a muffin pan, and pour the batter almost to the top. Bake 20 to 25 minutes. Test for doneness by inserting a toothpick into the center of one of the muffins. Muffins are done when the toothpick comes out clean.

Home-Fried Potatoes v

Here's a way to enjoy cottage fries without the trouble of peeling and deep-frying.

Serve with Fried Egg (page 7).

What You Need

1 tablespoon butter, margarine, or vegetable oil

1 (15-ounce) can sliced potatoes

¼ teaspoon garlic powder

¼ teaspoon onion powder

Salt and pepper, to taste

What You Do

1. Melt the butter, margarine, or vegetable oil in a frying pan over medium heat.

2. Drain the potatoes. Add to the frying pan. Gently stir until potatoes are well coated with butter. Sprinkle with garlic powder, onion powder, salt, and pepper. Continue stirring until thoroughly heated and golden brown.

?

What Do I Do If My Potatoes Sprout in Storage?

If your potatoes sprout while you're storing them, you can still use them. Just break off the sprouts before peeling the potatoes. Potatoes are native to the Americas. When they were introduced to Europe about 500 years ago, people were afraid they caused leprosy. However, 200 years later, the Irish recognized potatoes' food value. Potatoes are a good source of potassium and are high in vitamin C.

You can top this breakfast favorite with maple syrup, your favorite flavor of jam or jelly, honey, or confectioners' sugar.

You can use slightly stale white or wheat bread that has become dry (but not moldy!) or 1" thick slices of French bread left over from another meal.

French Toast   v

What You Need

2 eggs

½ cup milk

2 tablespoons butter or margarine

6 slices bread

What You Do

1. Crack the eggs into a medium-size mixing bowl. Add the milk and stir with a fork until well blended.

2. Melt the butter or margarine in a frying pan over medium heat. Dip each slice of bread into the egg mixture so it is coated on both sides. Place in the frying pan. Heat until bottom side is golden brown. Use a pancake turner to flip to the other side. Heat until golden brown. Serve immediately.

Here's a tasty variation you might enjoy, even if you're not a vegetarian.

Serve with warm maple syrup, confectioners' sugar, or fresh fruit.

Vegan French Toast   v

What You Need

2 bananas

¾ cup vanilla soymilk or rice milk

1 teaspoon cinnamon

1 teaspoon vegetable oil

8 slices bread

What You Do

1. Peel the bananas and slice crosswise. Place in a medium-size mixing bowl. Mash with a potato masher or electric mixer. Stir in the soymilk and cinnamon. Mash or mix until smooth.

2. Pour the oil into a frying pan. Heat over medium heat.

3. Dip the bread slices one at a time in the banana mixture. Flip over once to coat both sides. Scrape off any excess mixture. Place the coated bread in the frying pan. Cook until lightly browned on the bottom. Use a pancake turner to flip to the other side. Cook until lightly browned. Serve immediately.

Scrambled French Toast v

Can't decide between scrambled eggs and French toast? Make both!

Serve with butter and maple syrup. You can use slightly stale bread in this recipe.

What You Need

4 slices bread (white or wheat)

2 eggs

½ cup milk

½ teaspoon cinnamon

1 teaspoon sugar

1 teaspoon vanilla extract (or imitation)

2 tablespoons butter or bacon fat

What You Do

1. Cut bread (including crust) into ¾" cubes and place in a medium-size mixing bowl.

2. In a separate small mixing bowl, beat together eggs, milk, cinnamon, sugar, and vanilla extract. Pour over bread cubes. Lightly toss until bread is well coated.

3. Melt bacon fat in a small frying pan over medium heat. Pour bread mixture into the frying pan. Cook until brown on the bottom side. Use a pancake turner to flip the mixture as a single unit. Continue cooking until second side is well browned, yet still moist. Cut in pie-shaped wedges. Serve immediately.

Nutty Banana Pancakes v

If you like Apple and Sausage Pancakes (page 23), you might also like this similar dish with a different fruit and without the sausage. Serve with maple syrup and butter.

What You Need

2 eggs

1 cup all-purpose flour

1 cup milk

2 tablespoons vegetable oil

1 teaspoon cinnamon

1 teaspoon vanilla extract (or imitation)

2 tablespoons chopped pecans

⅛ teaspoon salt

1 banana

What You Do

1. Preheat oven to 375°F. In a large mixing bowl, combine the eggs, flour, milk, and vegetable oil. Stir until well blended, but still a bit lumpy. Stir in the cinnamon, vanilla extract, pecans, and salt.

2. Pour batter into a greased 8" × 8" ovenproof baking pan. Slice the banana and place on top of the batter. Bake for 20 to 25 minutes, until puffy on the edges and golden brown on top.

Huevos Rancheros v

Here's a *muy bien* dish to give your breakfast a spicy flavor.

Serve with sour cream and your favorite picante sauce or salsa—chunky salsa works well.

What You Need

½ cup vegetable oil

4 (6") corn tortillas

⅔ cup shredded Monterey jack cheese

⅔ cup shredded sharp Cheddar cheese

4 eggs

What You Do

1. Pour the oil into a large frying pan to about ⅛" deep. Heat the oil on medium-high. One at a time, cook the tortillas in the oil until soft. Drain on paper towels or on a wire rack with a paper towel under it. Cover with paper towel to keep warm.

2. Mix the cheeses in a small mixing bowl and set aside.

3. Fry the eggs (see page 7). Place each tortilla on a serving plate. Place a cooked egg on top of each tortilla. Top with the cheese mixture.

These warm, crusty muffins puff up and brown, leaving a hollow center.

Serve with butter or margarine and warm maple syrup.

Bake popovers in ovenproof custard cups or in a deep muffin tin.

Popovers v

What You Need

Shortening

1½ teaspoons butter or margarine

1 egg

½ cup milk

½ cup all-purpose flour

⅛ teaspoon salt

What You Do

1. Preheat oven to 450°F. Use solid shortening to grease ovenproof custard cups or deep muffin tins. Melt the butter (or margarine) in a small saucepan over low heat.

2. In a medium-size mixing bowl, beat the egg. Stir in the milk and melted butter. Add the flour and salt. Beat just until smooth. Do not overbeat.

3. Fill the custard cups ⅓ full. If you're using a deep muffin tin, fill about ¾ full. Bake for 40 to 45 minutes, until golden brown. (Do not open the oven door to check on the muffins for the first 30 minutes.)

This tasty bread brings the pumpkin flavor of fall holidays to the breakfast table any time of year.

You can omit the nuts if you prefer.

Pumpkin-Nut Bread v

What You Need

Shortening, as needed

2 cups all-purpose flour

2 teaspoons baking powder

½ teaspoon salt

½ teaspoon pumpkin pie spice

¼ teaspoon baking soda

1 firmly packed cup brown sugar

⅓ cup vegetable oil

2 eggs

1 cup canned pumpkin

¼ cup milk

½ cup chopped walnuts

What You Do

1. Preheat oven to 350°F. Use solid shortening to grease the bottom (not the sides) of a 9½" × 5¼" × 2¾" or 8½" × 4½" × 2½" loaf pan.

2. Combine the flour, baking powder, salt, pumpkin pie spice, and baking soda in a medium-size mixing bowl; stir until well mixed.

3. In a separate, large mixing bowl, use a portable hand mixer to beat together the brown sugar, vegetable oil, and eggs until well blended. With a spoon, stir in the pumpkin and milk.

4. Add the flour mixture about ¼ cup at a time, stirring until the batter is just smooth. Gently stir in the nuts. Pour the batter into the loaf pan. Bake for 1 hour. Let cool for 10 minutes; then remove from pan and place on a wire rack until cooled.

Sausage Soufflé

A soufflé is a fluffy baked egg dish with a wide variety of other ingredients.

Prepare the night before.

Some of the fat necessary in this recipe comes from the milk. So, if you use skim milk, add 1½ teaspoons of butter or margarine.

What You Need

1 pound hot pork sausage (in a tube)

18 eggs

2½ cups whole milk

7 slices white bread

1½ cups shredded sharp Cheddar cheese

1½ teaspoons dry mustard

¾ teaspoon salt

What You Do

1. In a frying pan, cook the sausage until browned. Drain off grease and set aside the sausage.

2. In a medium-size mixing bowl, beat together the eggs and milk. Cut the bread (including crust) into 1" cubes. Stir into the egg mixture, along with sausage, cheese, dry mustard, and salt until well mixed. Pour into an ungreased 9" × 13" ovenproof baking pan. Cover and refrigerate overnight so the bread can absorb the flavors.

3. Preheat oven to 325°F. Cover and bake for 45 minutes. Remove cover and bake for another 15 minutes.

These special pancakes are easier to make than regular pancakes and tastier, too.

You can substitute ¾ cup blueberries for the apples.

Serve with maple syrup and butter.

Apple & Sausage Pancakes

What You Need

Shortening, as needed

½ (12-ounce) package medium or spicy ground pork sausage

1 cup pancake mix

⅔ cup milk

2 eggs

2 tablespoons vegetable oil

1 apple

1½ teaspoons cinnamon

1½ teaspoons white granulated sugar

What You Do

1. Preheat oven to 375°F. Use the shortening to grease a 9" × 13" ovenproof baking pan.

2. Brown the sausage in a frying pan. Drain off fat and set aside the sausage.

3. In a large mixing bowl, combine the pancake mix, milk, eggs, and vegetable oil; stir until well blended but still a bit lumpy. Add drained sausage.

4. Pour the batter into the greased baking pan.

5. Peel the apple and remove the core. Slice the apple lengthwise and layer the slices on top of the batter. Sprinkle lightly with the cinnamon and sugar. Bake for 25 to 30 minutes, until puffy on the edges and golden brown on top. Serve warm.

Breakfast Burrito

Buenos días! Start your morning with a flavor from south of the border.

Serve with salsa and sour cream.

What You Need

4 medium-size red russet potatoes

1 pound lean ground beef

8 eggs

¼ cup milk

2 cups shredded Cheddar cheese

10 (8") flour tortillas

What You Do

1. Rinse the potatoes under cold, running water. Peel and cut into 1" cubes. Place the potatoes in a large frying pan with the ground beef. Brown the beef and potatoes (see "How Do I Brown Ground Beef?" on page 111). Drain off the fat.

2. Preheat oven to 350°F. In a medium-size mixing bowl, beat together the eggs and milk with a fork, wire whisk, or electric mixer until well blended. Pour into the beef mixture. Stirring, cook until the eggs are done.

3. Place about ⅓ cup of the mixture onto the middle of a tortilla and sprinkle with cheese. Fold the bottom ¼ of the tortilla over the mixture. Fold one side over the mixture. Fold the other side over the first side. Gently roll the tortilla over and place seam side down in a 9" × 13" ovenproof baking pan that has been sprayed with cooking spray. Continue until all the tortillas are filled.

4. Cover with aluminum foil and bake for 25 to 30 minutes, until heated through. Or, cover with a paper towel and microwave on high until hot. (Do not use aluminum foil in a microwave.)

Quiche is a pie that tastes like an omelet in a pie crust.

Serve it as an appetizer or use it as an entrée.

Quiche Lorraine

What You Need

1 (9") frozen pie crust

1 large onion

¼ pound bacon

1 cup grated Swiss cheese

4 eggs

¼ teaspoon salt

¼ teaspoon nutmeg

Dash cayenne pepper

2 cups milk

What You Do

1. Preheat oven to 375°F. Bake the empty pie crust for 10 minutes, until lightly browned.

2. While the pie crust is baking, chop the onion; set aside. Fry the bacon (see Makin' Bacon on page 5). Remove the cooked bacon from the pan and drain the fat, leaving about 2 tablespoons in the frying pan. When the bacon has cooled, break the slices into crumbles; set aside.

3. Cook the onion in the bacon fat over medium-high heat, stirring constantly until tender.

4. Spread the cheese in an even layer in the bottom of the pie crust. Sprinkle the bacon and onion over the cheese.

5. In a medium-size mixing bowl, beat the eggs with a whisk or fork. Beat in the salt, nutmeg, and cayenne pepper until well mixed. Stir in the milk until well blended. Pour the egg mixture over the cheese, onions, and bacon in the pie crust. Bake for 30 minutes or until golden brown.

Here's an easy quiche for veggie lovers.

You can use all one kind of mushroom or a combination of different varieties.

Mushroom Quiche v

What You Need

1 (9") frozen pie crust

1 pound fresh mushrooms (any type)

1 clove garlic (or ⅛ teaspoon dried)

1 tablespoon butter or margarine

Salt and pepper, to taste

2 tablespoons chopped fresh parsley (or 2 teaspoons dried)

3 eggs

1½ cups whipping cream

½ cup grated Parmesan cheese

What You Do

1. Preheat oven to 375°F. Bake empty pie crust for 10 minutes, until lightly browned.

2. While the pie crust is baking, wipe the mushrooms with a slightly damp paper towel. Slice the mushrooms and chop the garlic (if using fresh).

3. Melt the butter (or margarine) in a large frying pan over medium-high heat. Stir in the mushrooms and garlic. Season with salt and pepper. Cook, stirring constantly, until all the liquid is cooked out of the mushrooms. Stir in the parsley.

4. In a medium-size mixing bowl, beat together the eggs, whipping cream, and Parmesan cheese. Gently stir in the mushrooms and garlic. Pour the mixture into the pie crust. Bake for 30 minutes or until golden brown.

Banana Bread v

Moist and aromatic, this banana bread will become a family tradition.

When serving, sprinkle with confectioners' sugar.

If you're going to make 1 loaf, why not make 3 loaves at once? Purchase foil loaf pans you can give away. Leave loaves in the pans. Let cool. Cover with plastic wrap and tie with ribbons to give as gifts.

What You Need

1 cup solid vegetable shortening, plus extra for greasing

2½ cups cake flour, plus 3 tablespoons for flouring

2 cups white granulated sugar

4 eggs

6 ripe bananas

1 teaspoon baking soda

1 teaspoon salt

What You Do

1. Grease 3 loaf pans with shortening. Add 1 tablespoon flour to each. Tilt, tapping gently until the pans are lightly coated. Preheat oven to 350°F.

2. In a large mixing bowl, use a spoon or electric mixer to beat together the 1 cup shortening and sugar until soft and smooth; set aside.

3. In a mixing bowl, use a potato masher or mixer to mash together the eggs and bananas; set aside.

4. Measure the 2½ cups flour, baking soda, and salt into a sifter or strainer. Sift 3 times over waxed paper or into another mixing bowl. If using a strainer, shake the dry ingredients through the strainer 9 times.

5. Add about ½ cup of the banana mixture to the sugar and shortening mixture; beat. Add about ½ cup of the flour mixture; beat. Continue alternating the mixtures until well blended. Do not overbeat.

6. Pour into the greased and floured loaf pans. Bake for 45 minutes. Let cool. To freeze, wrap loaves in waxed paper, then wrap again in aluminum foil. Use directly from the freezer, slicing off ¾" slices as needed.

Bacon & Egg Casserole

Here's another casserole that you prepare the night before and pop into the oven in the morning.

Some of the fat necessary in this recipe comes from the milk. So, if you use skim milk, add 1½ teaspoons of butter or margarine.

You can also serve this dish for dinner as an inexpensive main course; make it in the morning and cook it at dinnertime.

What You Need

8 slices bacon

8 eggs

1 quart milk (2% or whole)

1 cup shredded American cheese

1 teaspoon salt

1 (6-ounce) box herb-seasoned croutons

What You Do

1. Fry the bacon (see Makin' Bacon on page 5). Remove the cooked bacon from the pan and drain on paper towels. When the bacon is cooked, crumble it with your hands. Place in a cup or small bowl. Cover and refrigerate overnight.

2. In a large mixing bowl, beat together the eggs and milk. Stir in the cheese, salt, and croutons. Pour into an ungreased 9" × 13" ovenproof baking pan. Cover and refrigerate overnight.

3. Preheat oven to 350°F. Sprinkle the crumbled bacon over the egg mixture. Cover and bake for 45 minutes.

Chapter 2
Sandwiches

Easy

Grilled Cheese Sandwich 30
BLT 31
Grilled PB&J 32
Bacon & Cheese Sandwich 33
Egg Sandwich 34
Variation: Open-Face Sandwich 34
Hot Ham & Turkey Sandwich 35
Broiled Cheese Sandwich 36
Hot Turkey-Crab Croissant 37
Fried Bologna Sandwich 38
Open-Face Ham Sandwich 39

Medium

Tuna Salad Sandwich 40
Variation: Chicken Salad Sandwich 40
Egg Salad Sandwich 41
Hot Cheese Toast 42
Grilled Reuben Sandwich 43
Variation: Grilled Rachel Sandwich 43
Mini Pepperoni Pizza 44
Broiled Tuna Puffs 45
Open-Face Crab Sandwiches 46
Hummus Pocket Sandwiches 47
Hoagies for a Crowd 48
Cucumber Sandwiches 49

Hard

Saucy Ham & Cheese Sandwiches 50
Sloppy Joes 51
Variation: Vegetarian Sloppy Joes 51
Artichoke-Feta Wraps 52

Grilled Cheese Sandwich v

Golden brown bread and melted cheese is a well-known kid favorite.

For variety, add a slice of lunchmeat and/or a slice of tomato before grilling.

You can substitute margarine for the butter.

What You Need

2 tablespoons butter, divided

2 slices bread

1 slice American cheese

What You Do

1. In a frying pan or on a griddle, melt 1 tablespoon of the butter over medium heat.

2. Butter one side of one piece of bread and place in the frying pan, buttered-side down. Place a slice of cheese on top. Butter one side of the remaining slice of bread and place on top of the cheese, buttered-side up.

3. Cook for 2 to 3 minutes, until the bottom is golden brown. Use a pancake turner to flip the sandwich. Cook another 1 to 2 minutes or until the second side is golden brown. Serve warm.

? How Can I Customize a Grilled Cheese Sandwich?

If you like grilled cheese but are ready for a more grown-up taste, try adding an extra slice of a different type of cheese. Or, add one of these ingredient combinations before grilling: dried Italian seasoning and grated Parmesan cheese; thinly sliced tomato and luncheon ham or bologna; cooked bacon slices, sun-dried tomatoes, and basil; sliced jalapeño peppers (from a jar) and bean dip; thinly sliced tomato, thinly sliced avocado, Dijon mustard, and mayonnaise.

BLT

Here's a traditional American favorite.

You can use freshly cooked bacon or leftover bacon that you have covered and stored in the refrigerator.

If you like, add a slice of your favorite cheese.

What You Need

2 slices bacon

1 leaf lettuce

1–2 slices fresh tomato

2 slices bread

1–2 tablespoons mayonnaise or mayonnaise-like salad dressing

What You Do

1. Fry bacon (see Makin' Bacon on page 5). Drain on paper towels. When cool, break each slice in half crosswise to make 4 strips about the width of the bread.

2. Rinse the lettuce under cold, running water and pat dry with a paper towel. Slice the tomato.

3. Toast the bread. Spread mayonnaise on one side of each piece. On one slice, stack lettuce, bacon, and tomato. Top with second slice (mayonnaise-side down).

Here's a new twist on an old favorite.

Try it with other peanut butter sandwich variations, using pickles, raisins, bananas, or other ingredients.

Serve with fresh fruit or raw, sliced carrots.

Grilled PB&J v

What You Need

2 tablespoons peanut butter

2 pieces bread

2 tablespoons jam or jelly (any flavor)

2 tablespoons butter or margarine, divided

What You Do

1. Spread the peanut butter on a slice of bread. Spread jam or jelly on the other. Put the 2 slices together. Spread 1½ teaspoons of the margarine on the top slice.

2. Melt 1 tablespoon of the margarine in a large frying pan or griddle. Place the sandwich in the frying pan, margarine-side down. Spread the remaining 1½ teaspoons of margarine on the outside of the bread slice that is now on top. Cook until the bottom slice is slightly browned and crusty. Use a pancake turner to flip once. Cook until the second side is slightly browned.

Bacon & Cheese Sandwich

This sandwich is quite tasty, especially when the bacon is freshly fried.

You can make this with toast, but also try it on untoasted bread, which soaks up the bacon fat and melted cheese. Yum!

What You Need

2 slices bacon

1 slice white onion

1 slice American cheese

Mayonnaise or mayonnaise-like salad dressing, as needed (about 1 tablespoon)

2 slices bread

What You Do

1. Cut the bacon slices in half horizontally and fry (see Makin' Bacon on page 5). When you have turned the bacon the final time, arrange the 4 halves of bacon slices in a row in the bottom of the frying pan. Reduce heat to low.

2. While the bacon continues to cook, place the onion slice on top. Place the cheese on top of the onion. Heat until the cheese melts.

3. Spread the mayonnaise on one side of each slice of bread. Use a pancake turner to remove the bacon, onion, and cheese from the pan as one unit. Place on bottom slice of bread. Top with the second slice.

Egg Sandwich v

Egg sandwiches aren't just for breakfast. You can eat them for lunch— or even for dinner.

Here are a couple of delicious versions.

What You Need

1 egg

2 tablespoons butter, margarine, or bacon fat plus 1 pat butter or margarine

1 slice American cheese (or your favorite cheese)

2 slices bread

What You Do

1. Fry the egg (see Fried Egg on page 7) in the 2 tablespoons butter, margarine, or bacon fat. Break the yolk in the pan. Flip the egg once.

2. While the egg is cooking on the second side, place the cheese on top. Heat until the cheese melts.

3. Butter one side of each slice of bread. Use a pancake turner to remove the egg from the pan and place on buttered side of one piece of bread. Top with the second slice of bread (buttered-side down).

Variation: Open-Face Sandwich v

Soft-boil the egg (see Boiled Egg on page 8). Toast and butter a slice of bread. When the egg is done, gently crack the shell. Use a knife or spoon to scoop the egg onto the toast. Use a knife to cut up the egg and spread it in an even layer on the toast. Eat with a knife and fork.

Hot Ham & Turkey Sandwich

Here's a quick way to serve a hot lunch in the time it takes to make a sandwich. Hot and yummy.

What You Need

1 slice dark rye bread

1 slice luncheon turkey

1 slice luncheon ham

1 slice tomato

½ cup shredded mozzarella cheese

What You Do

1. Toast the bread. Stack the turkey, ham, tomato, and cheese on top. Place on an ungreased baking sheet.

2. Broil 4" to 6" from the heat until the cheese melts.

Broiled Cheese Sandwich v

This zesty blend of flavors is easy to prepare and quick to heat.

Serve with fresh fruit or raw vegetables.

What You Need

3 English muffins

¼ cup green onions

½ cup sliced black olives

¾ cup shredded Cheddar cheese

2 tablespoons mayonnaise

¼ teaspoon chili powder

¼ teaspoon salt

What You Do

1. Slice English muffins in halves horizontally. Toast muffins.

2. Chop green onions, including green tops. Place in a medium-size mixing bowl. Drain olives and add to bowl. Add cheese, mayonnaise, chili powder, and salt. Stir until well blended.

3. Spread on English muffins. Place muffins on an ungreased cookie sheet. Broil until cheese melts and bubbles.

Hot Turkey-Crab Croissant

One pound of imitation crab meat equals about 8 sticks or 2 cups of the shredded type.

To prepare ahead, cover sandwiches with plastic wrap before cooking, and store in refrigerator until ready to heat and eat.

What You Need

8 slices bacon

4 croissant rolls

8 slices deli turkey lunchmeat

1 pound imitation crabmeat

4 slices cheddar cheese

What You Do

1. Fry bacon (see Makin' Bacon on page 5). Drain on paper towel. Slice croissants in half lengthwise. If crab is used in stick form, cut in half lengthwise.

2. Preheat oven to 400°F. Layer 2 slices of the turkey, 2 slices bacon, and ¼ pound crab on bottom half of each croissant. Top with one slice of cheese. Replace the top of croissant. Bake uncovered for 5 to 8 minutes until cheese melts.

Fried Bologna Sandwich

Here's a new twist on bologna and cheese that will remind you of a hot ham and cheese sandwich.

Serve with a fresh apple or Waldorf Salad (page 95).

What You Need

1 tablespoon butter

1 slice bologna

1 slice American or Swiss cheese

2 slices bread

1 tablespoon mayonnaise

1½ teaspoons prepared mustard

1 slice tomato

What You Do

1. Melt butter over medium heat in a frying pan. Add bologna and heat until it puffs up. Leave the bologna in the pan, but remove from heat. Place cheese on top until it melts.

2. While bologna is cooking, toast bread. Spread mayonnaise and mustard on the toast. When bologna and cheese are ready, place on one piece of toast. Add tomato slice. Top with second piece of toast.

Easy, crunchy, and tasty, this hot sandwich takes only 15 minutes to make—and even less time to eat.

Broil in the oven, or heat in a microwave or toaster oven.

Open-Face Ham Sandwich

What You Need

1 cup fresh bean sprouts

4 slices pumpernickel bread

4 teaspoons Dijon mustard

6 ounces thinly sliced deli ham

4 thin slices red onion

1 cup shredded mozzarella cheese, divided

What You Do

1. Rinse and drain the bean sprouts. Pat dry with a paper towel. Set aside.

2. Toast the bread. Spread 1 teaspoon mustard on each slice. Stack ham, bean sprouts, an onion slice, and one-fourth of the cheese on each piece of bread.

3. Broil 4" to 6" from the heat, or microwave 2 sandwiches at a time on high, or toast in a toaster oven for 2 to 3 minutes until cheese melts and ingredients are heated through.

Tuna Salad Sandwich

LEVEL **M**

SERVINGS **4**

Eat the salad by itself, or serve on bread or toast with a leaf of lettuce.

Because tuna salad contains mayonnaise, you should keep it cold until ready to eat.

It's not a good choice for a trip to the beach on a hot day.

For a slightly different flavor, you can substitute mayonnaise-like salad dressing for the mayonnaise.

What You Need

2 eggs (optional)

1 (12-ounce) can tuna

1 stalk fresh celery

⅔ cup mayonnaise or mayonnaise-like salad dressing

2 slices bread or 1 hamburger bun

What You Do

1. Hard-boil the eggs (see Boiled Egg on page 8). Remove the shells. Chop the eggs and place them in medium-size mixing bowl.

2. Drain the tuna. Use a fork to flake it into the bowl. Chop the celery and add it to the bowl.

3. Stir in the mayonnaise until blended. Chill for at least 1 hour before serving. Spread on bread or bun.

LEVEL **M**

SERVINGS **4**

Variation: Chicken Salad Sandwich

Follow the directions for Tuna Salad Sandwich, but substitute 1½ cups of precooked chicken (see "How Should I Save Cooked Chicken for Other Recipes?" on page 153) or 1 (10-ounce) can drained chunk chicken for the tuna.

?

How Do I Use an Egg Slicer?

An egg slicer is a handy kitchen tool that makes slicing and chopping eggs easier than with a knife. For slices, open the slicer, and place a peeled hard-boiled egg lengthwise in the bottom. Pull down the top. Remove the slices. For chopped eggs, carefully lift the sliced egg, holding the slices together as if the egg were still whole. Lift top of the slicer. Lay the sliced egg crosswise in the slicer. Pull down the top.

Serve egg salad by itself or as a sandwich filling.

Keep cold until ready to eat.

Egg Salad Sandwich v

What You Need

4 eggs

1½ stalks fresh celery

2 tablespoons mayonnaise or mayonnaise-like salad dressing

½ teaspoon prepared mustard

1 teaspoon white granulated sugar

Salt and pepper, to taste

4 slices bread or 2 hamburger buns

What You Do

1. Hard-boil the eggs (see Boiled Egg on page 8). Gently crack the shell and remove the shell from each egg. Chop the eggs and place them in a medium-size mixing bowl.

2. Chop the celery and add it to the bowl. Add the mayonnaise, mustard, sugar, salt, and pepper; stir until well blended. Cover and refrigerate until ready to serve.

3. Spread on bread or buns.

What Does "To Taste" Mean?

Recipes sometimes include ingredients without specific measurements followed by the words "to taste." Most often this phrase applies to salt or pepper. It means to add an amount that tastes good to you. Just pretend you are adding the ingredient to your own serving plate.

Hot Cheese Toast   v

You can serve this toast for lunch, as a snack, or as a side dish with Peachy Beef-Zucchini Stew (page 57) or The Best Chili Ever (page 54).

You can make this in a toaster oven or under a broiler in a conventional oven.

Do not substitute mayonnaise-like salad dressing.

What You Need

½ green onion

¼ cup shredded sharp Cheddar cheese

¼ cup shredded Monterey jack cheese

¼ cup mayonnaise

Garlic powder, to taste (less than ⅛ teaspoon)

Cayenne pepper, to taste

¾ teaspoon dried parsley flakes

4 slices French bread, about 1½" thick

1 tablespoon grated Parmesan cheese

What You Do

1. Chop the green onion, including part of the dark green top. Place in a medium-size mixing bowl. Stir in Cheddar cheese, Monterey jack cheese, mayonnaise, garlic powder, cayenne pepper, and parsley until well blended.

2. Spread the cheese mixture on one side of each slice of bread. Sprinkle the Parmesan cheese on top. Place face up on an ungreased baking sheet or on the rack of a toaster oven. Broil until the cheeses melt and bubble. Serve hot.

This grilled sandwich is a deli favorite.

Use slices of corned beef left over from Boiled Corned Beef and Cabbage (page 119).

Serve with a dill pickle and frozen French fries cooked according to package directions.

Grilled Reuben Sandwich

What You Need

2 tablespoons bottled Thousand Island salad dressing

2 slices pumpernickel rye bread

1 tablespoon butter or margarine

2–4 thin slices corned beef

1 slice Swiss cheese

¼ cup canned sauerkraut

What You Do

1. Spread one-fourth of the salad dressing on one side of each slice of bread.

2. Stack the thinly sliced corned beef on the bread. Layer the Swiss cheese on top. Drain the sauerkraut and use a fork to scoop it on top of the cheese. Top with the other piece of bread.

3. Melt the butter or margarine in a frying pan over medium heat. Place the sandwich in the frying pan. Cook for about 1 minute, until the bottom side of the bread is browned. (It will be hard and crisp.) Use a pancake turner to flip the sandwich to the other side; cook until the second side is browned.

Variation: Grilled Rachel Sandwich

Follow the directions for Grilled Reuben Sandwich, but substitute pastrami for the corned beef, and coleslaw for the sauerkraut.

Mini Pepperoni Pizza

Pizza flavor without the work. No long wait. And no need to tip for delivery!

If you're a cheese lover, top with grated Parmesan cheese.

What You Need

1 English muffin

¼ cup canned spaghetti sauce

Sliced pepperoni, as needed

1 green onion

½ cup shredded mozzarella cheese

What You Do

1. Preheat oven to 350°F. Slice the English muffin in half. Spread ½ of the spaghetti sauce on each half. Arrange the pepperoni slices on top of the sauce.

2. Chop the onion, including the green top. Sprinkle half of the onion on each mini pizza. Top with cheese.

3. Place on a baking sheet. Bake for 10 to 12 minutes, until the cheese melts and bubbles.

Broiled Tuna Puffs

Bubbly and cheesy, this yummy open-face tuna sandwich with a slightly tangy flavor will satisfy your hunger.

The ingredient list may seem long, but this tasty recipe is easy to prepare— and worth the effort.

You can substitute hamburger buns for the English muffins.

Cover and store one-half of the green bell pepper in the refrigerator for another use. Depending on your preference, you may want to limit the amount of this ingredient to about 2 tablespoons.

To prepare ahead, loosely cover the prepared muffins with aluminum foil or plastic wrap (toothpicks stuck in the muffins help keep the covering from touching the tuna mixture). Store in refrigerator until ready to broil.

What You Need

2 English muffins

1 fresh tomato

½ fresh green bell pepper (optional)

1 (6-ounce) can tuna

1½ teaspoons prepared mustard

¼ teaspoon Worcestershire sauce

½ teaspoon dried minced onion

¾ cup mayonnaise, divided

½ cup shredded Cheddar cheese

What You Do

1. Preheat oven broiler. Cut the English muffins in half horizontally.

2. Slice the tomato into 4 slices about ¼" thick. Set aside. Clean the green pepper and remove the seeds. Cut the pepper in half. Chop the remaining half and place in a medium-size mixing bowl.

3. Drain tuna and add to bowl. Add the mustard, Worcestershire sauce, onion, and ¼ cup of the mayonnaise. (You'll use the rest in step 5.) Stir until blended.

4. Toast the muffins, and heap ¼ of the tuna mixture on each slice. Spread the mixture to the edges to prevent burning. Place a tomato slice on each muffin.

5. In a separate bowl, mix the remaining ½ cup mayonnaise with the cheese. Top each muffin slice with ¼ of the cheese mixture. Place the muffins on a baking sheet and broil in the oven on the second rack from the top for 3 to 5 minutes until mixture "puffs" and the sandwich is heated through.

Open-Face Crab Sandwiches

If you love crabmeat, this hot and tasty sandwich is for you.

Serve with fresh fruit or Waldorf Salad (page 95).

What You Need

1 (8-ounce) package cream cheese

1 (6-ounce) can crabmeat (or flaked imitation crabmeat)

2 tablespoons dried parsley flakes

Garlic salt, to taste

Seasoned salt, to taste

4 (1½" thick) slices French bread

What You Do

1. Let the cream cheese soften at room temperature for 10 or 15 minutes. Place in a medium-size mixing bowl. Add the crabmeat, parsley, garlic salt, and seasoned salt. Stir until well blended.

2. Preheat oven to 400°F. Spread on one side of each French bread slice. Place on an ungreased baking sheet. Bake for 5 to 10 minutes.

?

How Do I Grate Cheese?

To grate hard cheese, start with a block of cheese rather than cheese slices. Place a cheese grater across the top of a small mixing bowl (or stand it on one end in the bottom of the bowl) with the sharp-edged bumps facing up. Unwrap cheese and hold it by one end. Pull across the grater so the sharp edges on the bumps "grab" the cheese and cut it into strings. Continue until you have the amount you need.

Hummus Pocket Sandwiches v

Tired of ordinary sandwiches on ordinary white bread? Try this high-protein vegetarian sandwich instead.

Serve with spicy pickles.

What You Need

12 ripe cherry tomatoes

4 (7") pita bread rounds

2 cups Hummus (see Hummus on page 257)

1 (¾-ounce) package alfalfa sprouts

Olive oil, as needed

What You Do

1. Rinse the cherry tomatoes under cold, running water and cut into halves.

2. Slice an opening at the top of each pita. Spread the hummus on the inside of each side. Stuff alfalfa sprouts and 6 cherry tomato halves into the opening of each pita.

3. Drizzle olive oil over the sandwich filling. Serve.

Hoagies for a Crowd

Serve a crowd in the time it takes to make a sandwich! After heating and slicing, reassemble on a serving tray and let guests serve themselves.

Place any remaining salad dressing and mustard mixture in a small serving bowl for guests who want more.

What You Need

1 to 1½ cups mayonnaise-like salad dressing

1 to 3 teaspoons prepared mustard

1 loaf French bread

½ head iceberg lettuce

2 tomatoes

1 red onion (about 3½" diameter)

3 types of sliced lunchmeat

2 types sliced process cheese

What You Do

1. Start with 1 cup salad dressing and ½ teaspoon mustard. Add mustard as needed to make a golden color. (If it gets too yellow, add more salad dressing.) Set aside.

2. Cut bread in half horizontally (as if it were a hamburger bun). Spread mustard mixture on each half. Shred lettuce using the large holes on a grater or by cutting into thin strips.

3. Rinse tomatoes under cold running water. Pat dry with paper towels. Thinly slice tomatoes and onion. Alternate layers of lunchmeat, cheese, shredded lettuce, onion slices, and tomato slices on the bottom half of bread. Replace top of loaf, and cover entire sandwich in aluminum foil. Store in refrigerator until about an hour before ready to serve.

4. Preheat oven to 350°. Remove sandwich from refrigerator. Heat in the wrapper for 30 to 40 minutes or until warm. Unwrap and place on cutting board. Cut slices about 2" wide, or let guests cut their own. Serve warm.

These are especially great for summer, while the cucumbers are fresh.

Serve as a sandwich or snack or use party rye or crackers topped with 1 cucumber slice and serve as an appetizer.

Refrigerate leftovers.

Cucumber Sandwiches

What You Need

1 (8-ounce) package cream cheese

½ cup mayonnaise

1 package dry Italian salad dressing

1 cucumber

2 slices bread per sandwich

What You Do

1. Place the cream cheese and mayonnaise in a small mixing bowl. Stir together until well blended.

2. Sprinkle the dry Italian salad dressing into the bowl, stirring until well blended.

3. Rinse the cucumber. Peel and slice crosswise about ¼" thick.

4. Spread the dressing on a slice of bread. Top with cucumber slices. Add another piece of bread.

Saucy Ham & Cheese Sandwiches

Here's hot ham and cheese with extra flair and flavor.

For a spicy variation, substitute your favorite bottled barbecue sauce for the Mustard Sauce.

What You Need

½ pound precooked ham

½ pound block processed cheese

1 recipe Mustard Sauce (see below)

4 hamburger buns

What You Do

1. Preheat oven to 400°F. Cut the ham and cheese into ¾" cubes and place in a medium-size mixing bowl. Add the Mustard Sauce and stir until well coated.

2. Spoon the mixture onto the hamburger bun bottoms. Replace the bun tops. Tightly wrap each sandwich in aluminum foil.

3. Bake for 10 to 15 minutes or until heated through.

?

How Do I Make Mustard Sauce?

For mustard sauce that goes well with Saucy Ham and Cheese Sandwiches (above) or other ham recipes, chop ¼ cup fresh green bell pepper, 2 sweet pickles, and 3 hard-boiled eggs (see Boiled Egg on page 8). Stir together in a small mixing bowl. Add 1½ teaspoons minced onion, ¼ cup mayonnaise, and 2 tablespoons prepared mustard. Stir until well blended. For extra zip, substitute prepared horseradish mustard for the prepared mustard. You can omit the green bell pepper from the sauce, if you prefer.

Sloppy Joes

LEVEL **H**

SERVINGS **12**

Here's an easy make-ahead dinner for a crowd.

To serve, spoon about ⅓ cup of the beef mixture onto hamburger buns.

For an open-face version, spoon onto buttered English muffin halves.

Top with some shredded Cheddar and broil until the cheese bubbles.

What You Need

¼ medium-size white or yellow onion

1 tablespoon vegetable oil

2 pounds ground beef

2 stalks celery

⅔ cup ketchup

½ cup water

2 tablespoons lemon juice

1 tablespoon brown sugar

1½ teaspoons Worcestershire sauce

1½ teaspoons salt

1 teaspoon vinegar

¼ teaspoon dry mustard

What You Do

1. Chop onion. Heat the vegetable oil in frying pan over medium-high heat. Add onion and stir until tender. Crumble in ground beef and brown (see "How Do I Brown Ground Beef?" on page 111). Drain off fat.

2. Rinse the celery. Chop and add to the beef mixture. Reduce heat to low. Stir in the ketchup, water, lemon juice, brown sugar, Worcestershire sauce, salt, vinegar, and dry mustard until mixed. Cover. Cook for 30 minutes, stirring occasionally. Serve hot.

LEVEL **H**

SERVINGS **12**

Variation: Vegetarian Sloppy Joes v

Follow the directions for Sloppy Joes, except substitute 2 pounds of veggie burgers for the beef.

Artichoke-Feta Wraps   v

To serve, garnish with plain yogurt and cilantro leaves.

This prize-winning original recipe was created by Judith Bader Jones after her son asked, "Why don't you ever make anything with feta cheese?" It is reprinted here with her permission.

What You Need

1 (14-ounce) can artichoke hearts

3 green onions

3 tablespoons prepared pesto sauce (or homemade Pesto on page 217)

¼ cup crumbled Feta cheese

2 tablespoons grated Parmesan cheese

2 tablespoons grated Romano cheese

8 (8") flour tortillas

What You Do

1. Preheat oven to 350°F. Rinse the artichoke hearts. Drain. Chop into small pieces. Place in a medium-size mixing bowl. Slice the green onions. Add to the bowl.

2. Stir in the pesto sauce, Feta, Parmesan, and Romano.

3. Spoon ¼ cup of the mixture onto the center of each tortilla. Fold one side of the tortilla to cover the mixture. Fold the second side to overlap. Secure with toothpicks. Arrange in a rectangular, ovenproof baking dish that has been sprayed with nonstick cooking spray. Bake uncovered for 25 minutes.

Chapter 3

Soups and Stews

Easy

The Best Chili Ever 54
Tomato Soup 55
French Onion Soup 56
Peachy Beef-Zucchini Stew 57
Miners' Stew 58

Medium

Fiesta Bean Soup 59
Gazpacho 60
Cold Avocado Soup 61
Veggie Lovers' Chili 62
Curried Vegetable Stew 63
Beef Barley Soup 64
Chicken Veggie Stew 65
Potato Soup 66
Taco Soup 67
Pepperoni with Bean Soup 68

Hard

Black Bean Soup 69
Veggie Beef Soup 70
Variation: Vegan Veggie Soup 71
Chili Blue 72
Black-Eyed Peas 73
Italian Sausage Soup 74
Mulligatawny Soup 75
Minestrone 76
Italian Sausage & Noodles Stew 77
Spinach Soup 78

If you like spicy chili, this recipe is for you!

Serve with saltine crackers, shredded Cheddar cheese, and sour cream if you can't take the "heat."

The Best Chili Ever

What You Need

½ large onion

2 pounds ground beef

1 (1¼-ounce package) chili seasoning mix

¼ teaspoon garlic salt

salt and pepper, to taste

chili power, to taste (1-3) teaspoons

1 (15½ ounce) can kidney beans

2 (15¾ ounce) cans hot chili beans

1 (15 ounce) can diced tomatoes

1 (15 ounce) can tomato sauce for chili

1 (12 ounce) can tomato paste

What You Do

1. Chop the onion. In a large frying pan, brown the ground beef (see "How Do I Brown Ground Beef?" on page 111) along with the chopped onion, chili seasoning mix, garlic salt, salt, pepper and chili powder. Drain off the fat. Place the mixture in Dutch oven, stew pot, or 2-quart slow cooler.

2. Drain the kidney beans and chili beans. Stir into the ground beef mixture. Stir in the diced tomatoes, tomatoes sauce, and tomato paste. Cover and cook over low heat on the stovetop to high heat in the slow cooker until warmed through. For best flavor, cook at least 1 hour longer to let seasonings mingle.

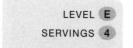
You can make tomato soup out of a can, but if you're in the mood to try an easy soup recipe, give this a try.

Serve with a Grilled Cheese Sandwich (page 30) or Cheese Biscuits (page 236).

Tomato Soup

What You Need

1 slice onion

1 (46-ounce) can tomato juice

1 (10¾-ounce) can tomato purée

2 cups water

1 beef or vegetable bouillon cube

1 bay leaf

4 whole cloves

2 teaspoons white granulated sugar

1 teaspoon salt

What You Do

Separate the rings of the onion slice. Combine all the ingredients in a Dutch oven and stir to mix. Bring to a boil. Reduce heat to low and simmer for 5 minutes. Remove and discard the bay leaf. Serve warm.

French Onion Soup

If you like, place a slice of toasted French bread into each serving bowl.

Top with shredded mozzarella or grated Parmesan cheese.

Let the cheese melt before serving.

What You Need

3 yellow onions

2 tablespoons butter or margarine

2 (10½-ounce) cans condensed beef broth (do not dilute)

½ cup water

1 teaspoon Worcestershire sauce

Dash pepper

What You Do

1. Remove and discard the outer skin of the onions. Cut the onions into thin slices. Melt the butter (or margarine) in a large frying pan over low heat. Stir in the onions. Cook for about 20 minutes, until tender. Scoop the onions and butter into a slow cooker or Dutch oven.

2. Stir in the beef broth, water, Worcestershire sauce, and pepper. Cover. In a slow cooker, cook on low for 4 to 6 hours (or 2 to 3 hours on high). In a Dutch oven, cook over low heat for 30 minutes until heated through.

How Do I Prevent Tears When I Chop an Onion?

Some people are quite sensitive to the tear-producing quality in onions. If your eyes water when you slice or chop onions, refrigerate them first. To cut down on onion odors in the kitchen, store leftover cut onions in a sealed container and refrigerate immediately. And, immediately discard unused pieces of onion in your outside garbage. To remove odor, wash your hands with soap after handling.

LEVEL **E**

SERVINGS **6**

Peachy Beef-Zucchini Stew

This hearty stew brings a splash of orange color to your dinner table.

Serve with Cheese Biscuits (page 236) or Easy Dinner Rolls (page 259).

If your meat market doesn't offer cubed stewing beef, use round steak cut into 1" cubes.

What You Need

1 pound beef stew meat

1 (8-ounce) can tomato sauce

1 cup water

1 teaspoon salt

3 carrots

2 medium-size potatoes

1 zucchini

1 small white or yellow onion

1 (15-ounce) can sliced peaches, with liquid

What You Do

1. Place the meat, tomato sauce, water, and salt in a Dutch oven. Stir. Bring to a boil over medium-high heat. Cover and reduce heat to low. Simmer for 1½ hours, stirring occasionally.

2. While the meat mixture is cooking, rinse the carrots, potatoes, and zucchini under cold, running water. Peel and cut into bite-size pieces. Slice the zucchini about ½" thick. Chop the onion. Place all the vegetables in a small mixing bowl. Cover and refrigerate until the meat is done.

3. Add the vegetables to the Dutch oven; stir. Cover and continue to simmer for 30 minutes. Add the peaches. Cook for 10 minutes more.

Miners' Stew

You can serve this dish by itself. Or, place a piece of toast on the serving plate.

Place a slice of American cheese on top, and spoon Miners' Stew over it.

What You Need

½ small onion

1 pound ground beef

1 (15-ounce) can pork and beans

¼ cup ketchup

What You Do

1. Chop the onion. Add to the ground beef in a frying pan. Brown over medium-high heat. Drain.

3. Return beef and onion to the frying pan. Reduce heat to low.

2. Stir in pork and beans, onions, and ketchup. Warm, stirring occasionally, until heated through.

Here's another easy soup using different vegetables and full-of-fiber beans.

Serve with saltine crackers.

Fiesta Bean Soup v

What You Need

¼ red bell pepper

½ cup canned red kidney beans

½ cup canned chickpeas (also called garbanzo beans)

½ (8-ounce) can cut green beans (or ½ cup frozen cut green beans)

½ cup frozen chopped broccoli

½ cup frozen cut carrots

1 (14½-ounce) can stewed tomatoes, with juice

2 vegetable bouillon cubes (or substitute chicken bouillon cubes for non-vegetarian)

¼ teaspoon celery salt

¼ teaspoon garlic salt

2 teaspoons dried parsley flakes

¼ teaspoon salt

⅛ teaspoon pepper

Water, as needed (about 1 quart)

What You Do

1. Chop the red bell pepper. Place in a slow cooker, Dutch oven, or stew pot. Drain the kidney beans, chickpeas, and green beans. Add to the pot, along with the broccoli, carrots, and tomatoes.

2. Unwrap the bouillon cubes and add to the pot. Sprinkle with celery salt, garlic salt, parsley flakes, salt, and pepper. Add water to the Dutch oven to just cover all the ingredients; stir. In a slow cooker, cover and cook on low for 10 to 12 hours or on high for 5 to 6 hours. In a Dutch oven or stew pot, cover and simmer over low heat for 1 to 2 hours.

Gazpacho

When it's hot outside, you can still enjoy this nutritious soup served cold.

Gazpacho is most often served as an appetizer in place of salad.

What You Need

½ cucumber

¼ green bell pepper

1 fresh tomato

¼ small white or yellow onion

¼ cup beef broth

¼ cup tomato juice

1 tablespoon vegetable oil

2 tablespoons red wine vinegar

½ teaspoon salt

Hot pepper sauce, to taste

Worcestershire sauce, to taste

What You Do

1. Rinse the cucumber, bell pepper, and tomato in cold, running water. Peel the cucumber. Remove the seeds from the bell pepper. Chop the cucumber, green pepper, tomato, and onion, and place in large mixing bowl.

2. Gently stir in the beef broth, tomato juice, vegetable oil, wine vinegar, and salt. Add the hot pepper sauce and Worcestershire sauce a few drops at a time, to taste. Cover and chill for at least 1 hour in the refrigerator before serving.

Spices and pepper blend with the mild flavor of avocado to add some zip to this soup, which you can serve by itself or as an appetizer.

Garnish with fresh chopped parsley and a lemon slice or sour cream with crumbled bacon.

A ripe avocado is soft to the touch regardless of color. The Hass variety turns black when ripe, but most varieties remain green.

Cold Avocado Soup

What You Need

1 ripe avocado

2 (10½-ounce) cans chicken broth

1 cup heavy cream

½ teaspoon salt

½ teaspoon pepper

¼ to ½ teaspoon curry powder (to taste)

Hot pepper sauce, to taste

What You Do

1. Peel the avocado and remove the seed. Cut into fourths and place in an electric blender. Add the chicken broth, cream, salt, pepper, curry powder, and hot pepper sauce. Blend until smooth. Cover and refrigerate for several hours (overnight is okay).

2. When ready to serve, blend again. Serve cold.

How Do I Remove Avocado Seeds?

Here's an easy way to remove the seed from an avocado: slice through the avocado lengthwise, deep enough to touch the seed. Cut all the way around the fruit. With one hand on each half, gently twist to separate. Plunge the knife into the seed with a quick thrust. Twist the seed, and lift out.

Veggie Lovers' Chili v

Each serving of this tasty vegetarian chili provides approximately 19 grams of protein and 18 grams of fiber.

Serve with saltine crackers.

What You Need

½ large white or yellow onion

2 tablespoons vegetable oil

1 (15-ounce) can red kidney beans

1 (8½-ounce) can corn

1 medium-size zucchini (about 8" long)

1 (14½-ounce) can stewed tomatoes, with juice

¼ teaspoon dried minced garlic

1 tablespoon chili powder

2 teaspoons oregano

What You Do

1. Chop the onion. In a frying pan, cook the onion in the vegetable oil over medium-high heat, stirring constantly until tender. Transfer the onion and oil to a Dutch oven, stew pot, or 2-quart slow cooker.

2. Drain the beans and corn. Add to the pot.

3. Rinse the zucchini under cold, running water. Chop the zucchini and add to the pot.

4. Stir in the tomatoes, with the juice. Add the garlic, chili powder, and oregano. In a Dutch oven or stew pot, cover and bring to a boil over medium-high heat. Reduce heat to low. Cook for about 15 minutes, until the zucchini is tender. Uncover for the last 5 minutes. In a slow cooker, cover and cook for 1 hour on high. Reduce heat to low until ready to serve. Uncover for the last 5 minutes.

Curried Vegetable Stew v

You don't have to be a vegetarian to enjoy this spicy and colorful stew.

Serve with saltine crackers or easy Dinner Rolls (see page 259).

You can use the other half of the sweet potato for another meal in Stir-Fry Parsnip Medley (page 222).

You can substitute 1¼ cups canned lima beans, drained.

You can substitute 1 cup canned green beans, drained.

Wrap the unused ½ of the potato and store in the refrigerator for another use.

What You Need

1 (10-ounce) package frozen lima beans

1 cup frozen cut green beans

½ fresh sweet potato

3 zucchini (6"–8" long)

1 large white or yellow onion

1 red bell pepper

2 tablespoons olive oil

1 teaspoon curry powder

Salt and pepper, to taste

2 cups water, or enough to cover ingredients

What You Do

1. Thaw the lima beans and the green beans and place in a Dutch oven, stew pot, or 2-quart slow cooker.

2. Cut the sweet potato in half lengthwise and peel. Cut in half lengthwise again. Slice crosswise. Place in a large mixing bowl. Cut the zucchini in half lengthwise; then slice crosswise. Chop the onion and red bell pepper. Add to the mixing bowl.

3. Heat the olive oil in a frying pan over medium-high heat. Fry the sweet potato, zucchini, onion, and red bell pepper, stirring until tender but still firm. Sprinkle with curry powder, salt, and pepper. Add the mixture to the slow cooker or other pot. Add the water.

4. In a slow cooker, cover and cook on high for 1 hour. Reduce heat to low and cook until the potatoes are tender. In a Dutch oven or stew pot, cover and bring to a boil. Reduce heat to low. Keep covered. Simmer for 30 minutes. Keep warm until ready to serve.

Beef Barley Soup

What You Need

1 small white or yellow onion

2 tablespoons vegetable oil

1 pound ground beef

2 raw carrots

2 stalks celery

1 (8-ounce) can tomatoes, with juice

⅓ cup barley

1 tablespoon dried parsley flakes

2 beef bouillon cubes

½ to 1 teaspoon salt (to taste)

¼ teaspoon pepper

¼ teaspoon basil

2½ cups water

What You Do

1. Thinly slice the onion. Pour the vegetable oil into a large frying pan over medium-high heat. Stir in the onion. Crumble the ground beef into the pan. Stir often until the beef browns. Drain off the fat. Transfer the mixture to a slow cooker or Dutch oven.

2. Rinse the carrots and celery under cold, running water. Peel the carrots. Thinly slice the carrots and celery crosswise. Add to the pot. Stir in the tomatoes, barley, parsley, bouillon cubes, salt, pepper, basil, and water. Cover. In a slow cooker, cook on high for 5 to 6 hours (or on low for 10 to 12 hours). In a Dutch oven, bring the mixture to a boil over medium-high heat. Reduce heat to low. Cook, covered, for 1 hour, stirring occasionally.

Chicken Veggie Stew

This stew is quick, easy, and nutritious.

Okra is known for thickening and flavoring soups and stews. It is highly perishable, so buy only what you need.

Instead of fresh, you can use frozen or canned chopped okra in this recipe.

What You Need

1½ cups precooked chicken (see "How Should I Save Cooked Chicken for Other Recipes?" on page 153)

1 large potato

½ cup fresh or frozen cut okra

½ cup frozen lima beans

½ cup frozen corn

2 cups chicken broth

1 (8-ounce) can crushed tomatoes, with juice

1½ teaspoons white granulated sugar

½ teaspoon salt

¼ teaspoon rosemary

⅛ teaspoon pepper

Dash ground cloves

1 bay leaf

What You Do

1. Cut the chicken into bite-size cubes. Place in a slow cooker or Dutch oven. Rinse the potato under cold water. Peel and cut into ½" cubes. Add to the pot.

2. Rinse the fresh okra under cold, running water. Slice crosswise into circles. (If using canned okra, drain.) Add the okra to the pot, along with the lima beans and corn. Stir in the chicken broth, tomatoes, sugar, salt, rosemary, pepper, cloves, and bay leaf. Cover.

3. In a slow cooker, cook on high for 4 to 5 hours. In a Dutch oven, bring to a boil over high heat. Reduce heat to low. Cook for 1 hour. Remove the bay leaf before serving.

Rich and creamy, this potato soup is a winter favorite.

To prevent scorching, be sure to add the milk just before serving.

Potato Soup   v

What You Need

3 medium potatoes

½ small white or yellow onion

2 tablespoons butter

1 teaspoon salt

⅛ teaspoon pepper

1 teaspoon caraway seed

3–4 cups water

2 cups milk

What You Do

1. Peel and chop the potatoes. Chop the onion. Add the potatoes and onion to a Dutch oven or soup kettle. Add the butter, salt, pepper, and caraway seed. Cover with water. Stir. Cook over medium-high heat for about 10 minutes, until the potatoes are tender.

2. Reduce heat to low. Stir in the milk. Cook until heated through. (Do not boil.)

LEVEL **M**

SERVINGS **4**

Here's a new way to enjoy a Mexican food favorite.

Serve with tortilla chips and shredded cheese.

If you have leftover cooked chicken, you can substitute it for the beef.

Taco Soup

What You Need

1 small white or yellow onion

1 clove garlic (or ⅛ teaspoon dried minced garlic)

1 pound ground beef

1 (4-ounce) can diced green chilies

1 (16-ounce) can Mexican-flavored stewed tomatoes, with liquid

1 (15-ounce) can tomato sauce

2 cups water

1 cup bottled or fresh salsa

1 (15-ounce) can pinto beans, with liquid

1 (15-ounce) can kidney beans, with liquid

1 (2¼-ounce) envelope taco seasoning or 2 tablespoons chili powder

What You Do

1. Chop the onion and garlic. Place the ground beef in a large frying pan. Add the onion and garlic. Brown the beef (see "How Do I Brown Ground Beef?" on page 111). Drain off the fat. Place the beef mixture in a Dutch oven or stew pot.

2. Drain the chilies. Add to the pot. Stir in the stewed tomatoes, tomato sauce, water, salsa, pinto beans, kidney beans, and taco seasoning (or chili powder). Bring to a boil over medium-high heat, stirring occasionally. Reduce heat to low. Cover and cook for 30 minutes.

Pepperoni with Bean Soup

For ease of preparation, use a slow cooker for this spicy soup Or, if you prefer, you can cook it in a Dutch oven or stew pot. Bring to a boil, then reduce heat to low and cook for 1 hour, stirring occasionally.

What You Need

½ green bell pepper

½ medium onion

1 clove garlic (or ⅛ teaspoon dried minced garlic)

1 (4-ounce) package sliced pepperoni

2 (15-8/10-ounce) cans great northern beans, with liquid

1 (14½-ounce) can crushed tomatoes, with liquid

½ teaspoon salt

2 cups water

What You Do

1. Rinse the green pepper under cold, running water. Slice in half lengthwise. Remove and discard the seeds and inner ribs. Cover half and refrigerate for another use. Chop the remaining half. Chop the onion. Chop the garlic into very small pieces. Place the green bell pepper, onion, and garlic in a slow cooker. Cut the pepperoni slices into fourths. Add to the pot.

2. Stir in the great northern beans, tomatoes, salt, and water. Cover. Cook for 3 to 4 hours on high or for 1 hour on high plus 5 to 6 hours on low.

Black Bean Soup   v

What You Need

2 cups dried black beans

6 cups, plus 2 quarts water

½ small white or yellow onion

2 stalks celery

2 teaspoons salt

⅛ teaspoon pepper

1 tablespoon butter

2 tablespoons all-purpose flour

1 lemon

2 hard-boiled eggs (see Boiled Egg on page 8)

What You Do

1. Place the beans and the 6 cups water in a Dutch oven or soup kettle. Bring to a boil over high heat. Cover and reduce heat to low. Simmer for 1½ hours. Remove from heat and let cool. Refrigerate overnight.

2. Drain beans in a colander. Rinse in cold, running water. Drain. Return to the Dutch oven. Chop the onion and celery. Add to the pot. Stir in the 2 quarts water, salt, and pepper. Cook over low heat for 3 to 4 hours.

4. In a saucepan, melt the butter over low heat. Stir in the flour until well blended. Gradually add in a few tablespoons of the soup liquid from the Dutch oven, stirring until thickened. Pour the thickened liquid back into the Dutch oven with the beans.

5. Rinse the lemon in cold running water and thinly slice (do not peel). Remove the shell from the hard-boiled eggs and slice. When ready to serve, place egg and lemon slices on top of each serving.

Veggie Beef Soup

This aromatic blend of spices makes a delicious homemade soup to warm a cold winter night.

Serve with Hot Cheese Toast (page 42) or dinner rolls with Honey Butter (page 12).

This soup is easy to make in a slow cooker.

What You Need

1 pound cubed beef for stew (or ask your butcher to cube round steak for you)

½ (10-ounce) package frozen mixed vegetables (carrots, peas, potatoes, and green beans)

1 (14½-ounce) can crushed or stewed tomatoes, with juice

1 baking potato (or 2–3 russet potatoes smaller than baseballs)

1½ large stalks celery

½ small white or yellow onion (or substitute 1 tablespoon dried minced onion)

½ teaspoon salt

⅛ teaspoon pepper

1 bay leaf

⅛ teaspoon garlic powder

⅛ teaspoon basil

⅛ teaspoon rosemary

Pinch of thyme

¼ teaspoon dried parsley flakes

2 beef bouillon cubes

Water, as needed (about 1 quart)

What You Do

1. Place the beef, mixed vegetables, and tomatoes with juice in a Dutch oven, stew pot, or slow cooker. Rinse the potato and celery under cold, running water. Peel the potato. Cut in half lengthwise; then cut crosswise to make 1½" cubes. Add to the pot.

Veggie Beef Soup—continued

2. Chop the celery and onion. Add to the pot. Sprinkle with salt, pepper, bay leaf, garlic powder, basil, rosemary, thyme, and parsley. Unwrap the bouillon cubes and add to the pot.

3. Add enough water to cover all the ingredients; stir. In a slow cooker, cover and cook on low for 10 to 12 hours or on high for 5 to 6 hours. In a stew pot, cover and simmer over low heat for 3 or 4 hours, until the meat is tender and cooked through. Remove the bay leaf before serving.

LEVEL **H**
SERVINGS **4**

Variation: Vegan Veggie Soup v

For a vegetarian variation, substitute 1 eggplant for the beef. Rinse the eggplant under cold, running water. Peel and remove the seeds. Cut the eggplant into ½" cubes. Substitute vegetable bouillon cubes or granules for the beef bouillon.

?

What Do I Do with the Remaining Frozen Vegetables?

When a recipe calls for a portion of a 10-ounce package of frozen vegetables (which come in a frozen block), just place the package on a cutting board and cut it crosswise with a sharp knife. Wrap the part you won't use in aluminum foil and replace in the freezer for later use. Or, purchase the vegetables in a 16-ounce bag and simply pour out the amount you need.

Chili Blue

Here's an old favorite from Girl Scout camp.

The chili has a sweet flavor that tastes almost as good cooked indoors as it does over an open fire in the woods.

You'll find chili sauce in the ketchup aisle.

Serve with French bread (see "How Do I Prepare French Bread," page 114) or Mexican Corn Bread (page 248).

What You Need

3 slices bacon

1 pound ground beef

¾ cup bottled chili sauce

¼ cup brown sugar

2 teaspoons prepared mustard

2 (15-ounce) cans pork and beans

What You Do

1. Preheat oven to 350°F. Fry the bacon (see Makin' Bacon on page 5) until crisp. Remove the bacon from the pan and set it aside on paper towels to absorb excess fat. Brown the ground beef in the bacon drippings (see "How Do I Brown Ground Beef?" on page 111). Use a slotted spoon to remove the meat from the frying pan and place into an ungreased 9" × 13" ovenproof baking pan.

2. Stir in the chili sauce, brown sugar, mustard, and pork and beans until well mixed. Cover with aluminum foil and bake for 30 to 45 minutes, until thoroughly heated. Or, place all the ingredients in a slow cooker. Cover and cook on high for 1 to 3 hours or on low for 2 to 6 hours until heated through.

Black-Eyed Peas

Eating black-eyed peas on New Year's Day is thought to bring good luck in the coming year.

Serve with corn muffins made from a mix.

To prepare in a slow cooker, perform step 1 the day before.

If you like, you can substitute cut-up turkey ham for the ham hocks.

Remove the bay leaves before serving.

What You Need

4–6 cups water

1¼ cups dry black-eyed peas

½ medium-size white or yellow onion

1½ stalks celery

1½ pounds smoked ham hocks

2 bay leaves

⅛ teaspoon cayenne pepper

Method 1: On a Stovetop

1. In a covered Dutch oven, bring 4 cups water and the peas to a boil. Boil for 2 minutes. Keeping the cover in place, remove from heat. Let sit for 1 hour.

2. Chop the onion and celery. Add to the pot along with the ham hocks, bay leaves, and cayenne pepper. Stir. Bring to a boil. Cover and reduce heat to low. Simmer for 1 hour, stirring occasionally.

3. Uncover and cook for 1 more hour. Remove ham hocks and cut the meat from the bone. Discard the bones, and add the meat to the pot and stir.

Method 2: In a Slow Cooker

1. In a Dutch oven, bring 6 cups water and the peas to a boil. Cover. Reduce heat to low. Cook for 1½ hours. Remove from heat. Uncover and cool at room temperature. Cover and refrigerate overnight. (The peas will absorb most of the water.)

2. In the morning, chop the onion and celery. Add to slow cooker along with the peas, ham hocks, bay leaves, and cayenne pepper. Stir until well mixed. Cover, and cook on low for 10 to 12 hours or on high for 5 to 6 hours. Stir occasionally.

Italian Sausage Soup

A taste of Italy in a bowl. The aroma of this soup cooking will make you imagine yourself in a villa in Venice.

What You Need

¾ pound Italian sausage

½ medium-size white or yellow onion

3 stalks celery

1 clove garlic

2 tablespoons olive oil

1 (8-ounce) can tomatoes, with liquid

½ cup tomato purée

2 (10½-ounce) cans chicken broth

¼ cup water

¼ teaspoon oregano

¼ teaspoon basil

¼ teaspoon thyme

1 tablespoon dried parsley flakes

½–¾ cup uncooked macaroni noodles

Grated Parmesan cheese, as needed

What You Do

1. Remove the sausage casing with a sharp knife and place the meat in a skillet. Use a wooden spoon to break up the meat. Brown the sausage as you would ground beef (see "How Do I Brown Ground Beef?" on page 111). Drain off the fat.

2. Chop onion and celery. Mince garlic. Pour oil into a Dutch oven over medium-high heat. Stir in onion and celery; cook, stirring constantly until tender. Stir in sausage, tomatoes, tomato purée, chicken broth, water, oregano, basil, thyme, and parsley. Reduce heat to low. Cover. Cook for 1 hour, stirring occasionally.

3. Add macaroni noodles. Cook for 30 minutes, stirring occasionally. To serve, top bowls with cheese.

LEVEL **H**

SERVINGS **6**

Curry gives this heavily spiced, flavorful soup an East Indian flavor.

You can cook this soup on a stovetop or in a slow cooker.

If using a slow cooker, melt the butter in a small frying pan and cook the onion, stirring constantly until tender. Then add it to the slow cooker along with the remaining ingredients.

Mulligatawny Soup

What You Need

1 each: carrot, stalk celery, green bell pepper, apple

1 medium-size white or yellow onion

¼ cup butter

1 cup precooked chicken (see "How Should I Save Cooked Chicken for Other Recipes?" on page 153)

2 (10½-ounce) cans chicken broth

⅓ cup all-purpose flour

1 teaspoon curry powder

1 teaspoon lemon juice

½ teaspoon white granulated sugar

2 whole cloves

1 teaspoon dried parsley flakes

1 (8-ounce) can crushed tomatoes

Salt and pepper, to taste

What You Do

1. Rinse the carrot, celery, green pepper, and apple. Peel carrot. Chop carrot, celery, and green bell pepper. Peel and core apple. Slice vertically. Slice onion.

2. Melt the butter in the bottom of a Dutch oven over medium heat. Add the onion, stirring constantly until tender. Reduce heat to low. Stir in carrot, celery, green bell pepper, apple, chicken, and chicken broth.

3. Transfer some of the liquid to a mixing bowl and stir in flour a little at a time until blended. Return to the pot. Stir in curry powder, lemon juice, sugar, cloves, parsley, tomatoes, salt, and pepper. Cover and cook for 30 minutes. (In a slow cooker, cook on low for 8 to 10 hours.) Remove the cloves before serving.

LEVEL 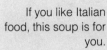 **H**

SERVINGS **4**

If you like Italian food, this soup is for you.

If you don't have time to cook the dried beans, you can substitute one 15½-ounce can of beans (drained) and reduce the cooking time to 45 minutes total.

Minestrone

What You Need

½ cup dried kidney beans or great northern beans

1 cup beef stock

3 cups water

1 carrot

1 stalk celery

1 medium-size potato

½ large white or yellow onion

1 tablespoon olive oil

⅛ teaspoon dried minced garlic

¼ cup uncooked macaroni noodles

½ (8-ounce) can crushed tomatoes

1½ teaspoons salt

⅛ teaspoon pepper

What You Do

1. In a Dutch oven, bring the beans, beef stock, and water to a boil. Cover and reduce heat to low. Cook for 3 to 4 hours. Stir once or twice per hour.

2. During the last half-hour of cooking time, prepare the vegetables. Rinse the carrot, celery, and potato under cold, running water. Peel the carrot and potato. Chop the carrot, celery, potato, and onion. Place the olive oil in a large skillet over medium-high heat. Cook the chopped vegetables in the olive oil, stirring constantly until tender but still firm.

3. Stir the vegetables and garlic into the beans. Cover and continue cooking for 30 minutes. Stir often.

4. Stir in the macaroni noodles, tomatoes, salt, and pepper. Cook for 15 minutes.

Spicy meat and dried oregano say, "That's Italian!" Top with grated Parmesan cheese.

You'll find the sausage in the refrigerated meat section near bacon, hot dogs, or lunchmeat.

Italian Sausage & Noodles Stew

What You Need

1 (8-ounce) package precooked Italian sausage

¾ cup water

1 (8-ounce) can red kidney beans

1 (14½-ounce) can Italian-style diced tomatoes, with juice

1 (14½-ounce) can beef broth

¼ teaspoon oregano

½ (12-ounce) package uncooked wide egg noodles

½ (16-ounce) package frozen Italian blend vegetables

What You Do

1. Slice sausage crosswise into circles about ½" thick. Place in a Dutch oven or stewpot with ¼ cup of the water. Cover and cook over medium heat until warmed through. Drain. Set aside.

2. Drain kidney beans in a colander. Rinse under cold running water. Add to the Dutch oven. Stir in tomatoes, beef broth, oregano, and the remaining ½ cup water. Bring to a boil.

3. Stir in noodles. Bring to a boil. Reduce heat to low and cook 20 minutes, stirring occasionally.

4. Stir in frozen vegetables. Cook 5 to 10 minutes, stirring occasionally until vegetables are tender.

This creamy, flavorful soup is Popeye's favorite! And it's easy and quick to prepare.

Spinach Soup v

What You Need

2 (10-ounce) bags of fresh spinach

4 cups milk, divided

1 small onion

2 tablespoons butter

2 tablespoons flour

Salt, pepper, and nutmeg, to taste

What You Do

1. Put the spinach in a colander and rinse under cold, running water. Drain, but do not pat dry. Break off the stems and discard. Stuff the spinach into a soup pot and cover. (No need to add water; use only the moisture that clings to the leaves.) Cook over medium heat 5 to 15 minutes (or longer) until leaves wilt and shrink.

2. Transfer the spinach to a blender. Add 2 cups milk. Blend until smooth. Set aside.

3. Peel and chop the onion into small pieces. Melt the butter in the soup pot over medium heat. Stir in the onion. Cook about 5 minutes until tender. Reduce heat to low. Stir in the flour until well blended.

4. Add the remaining 2 cups of milk. Cook, stirring often, until the mixture thickens.

5. Stir in the spinach mixture. Cook until soup is warm. (Do not boil.) Sprinkle with salt, pepper, and nutmeg.

Chapter 4

Salads

Easy

Orange-Banana Salad 80
Fruit & Coconut Salad 80
Nutty Banana-Strawberries 81
Grape Salad 82
Quick Cottage Cheese Salad 83
Avocado & Shrimp Salad 84
Variation: Sliced Avocado Salad 84
Cucumber Salad 85
Broccoli-Cauliflower Salad 86
Cold Mixed Veggies Salad 87
Mustard Vinaigrette 88
Creamy Caesar Salad Dressing 89
Garlic Salad Dressing 90
Mandarin Orange Salad 91
Cold Ham & Lima Bean Salad 92
Orange & Banana Salad 93
Variation: White Grape Salad 93
Four-Bean Salad 94

Medium

Waldorf Salad 95
Caesar Salad 96
Chilled Pea Salad 97
Three-Color Pasta Salad 98
Old-Fashioned Coleslaw 99
Exotic Couscous Salad 100
Tabbouleh Salad 101
Artichoke-Lettuce Salad 102
Warm Bacon-Avocado Salad 103

Hard

Potato Salad 104
Hot German Potato Salad 105

Orange-Banana Salad v

LEVEL E

SERVINGS 4

Fresh bananas and sweet mandarin oranges blend for a mellow flavor you can use as a snack, salad, or light dessert.

Bananas are tropical fruits, so do not refrigerate until after they are cut.

You can substitute chopped walnuts for the chopped pecans.

What You Need

2 bananas

Lemon juice, as needed (a few drops)

1 (8-ounce) can mandarin orange slices

¼ cup chopped pecans

What You Do

1. Peel the bananas. Slice crosswise into circles about ¼" thick and place in a medium-size mixing bowl.

2. Sprinkle bananas with a few drops of lemon juice to help prevent browning. Drain off the liquid from the oranges and add the orange slices to the bowl.

3. Add the pecans, stirring gently until well mixed. Chill in the refrigerator until ready to serve.

Fruit & Coconut Salad v

LEVEL E

SERVINGS 4

You can eat this salad right away if you like, but if you make it the day before and chill it in the refrigerator overnight, the flavors will blend for an even more delicious result.

What You Need

1 cup mandarin orange slices

1 cup pineapple tidbits

1 cup flaked coconut

1 cup sour cream

What You Do

1. Pre-chill the mandarin oranges and pineapple tidbits in the cans. Drain. Place in a mixing bowl.

2. Add coconut and sour cream. Gently stir together until ingredients are coated with sour cream. Cover and refrigerate for at least 1 hour before serving.

Nutty Banana-Strawberries v

You can substitute sliced almonds for the chopped pecans.

You can substitute mandarin oranges (drained) for the strawberries.

For a lower-calorie, vegan variation, substitute frozen nondairy whipped topping for the whipped cream.

What You Need

½ cup strawberries

½ teaspoon white granulated sugar

1 banana

A few drops of lemon juice

¼ cup chopped pecans

Pressurized, canned whipped cream, as needed

What You Do

Clean and slice the strawberries (see "How Should I Clean Strawberries?" on page 274). Sprinkle with sugar. Peel and slice the banana. Sprinkle the slices with a few drops of lemon juice to help prevent browning. Gently stir together the banana, strawberries, and pecans. Place in serving dishes. Top each serving with whipped cream.

Grape Salad v

If you'd like to add color and flavor, use ½ bunch of each color of seedless grapes for this cool fruit salad.

For a vegan variation, substitute tofu sour cream (see "How Do I Make Tofu Sour Cream?" on page 201).

What You Need

½ cup slivered almonds

1½ pounds red and/or green seedless grapes

½ cup sour cream

1 teaspoon brown sugar

What You Do

1. Preheat oven to 400°F. Place the almonds on a baking sheet that has been sprayed with nonstick cooking spray. Bake for about 4 to 5 minutes until brown. (Watch carefully so they don't burn!) Remove from oven. Set aside.

2. Rinse the grapes under cold, running water. Drain. Remove from stem.

3. In a large mixing bowl, stir together the sour cream and brown sugar. Add the grapes and stir until coated. When ready to serve, spoon into serving dishes and top with toasted almonds.

Quick Cottage Cheese Salad v

Low in fat and chock-full of vegetables, this satisfying salad is a great midday pick-me-up.

Keep covered in the refrigerator until ready to eat.

What You Need

2 green onions

1 green bell pepper

2 carrots

½ bunch radishes

1 (24-ounce) carton small-curd cottage cheese

What You Do

1. Rinse the green onions, green bell pepper, carrots, and radishes under cold, running water. Chop the green onions (including the dark green tops) and the green bell pepper. Place in a medium-size mixing bowl. Use a potato peeler to remove the outer skin of the carrots. Use the large holes on the grater to grate the carrots into the bowl with the onions and green pepper. Slice the radishes and add to the bowl.

2. Gently stir in the cottage cheese until all the ingredients are well mixed. Cover and chill in the refrigerator for at least 1 hour before serving.

LEVEL **E**

SERVINGS **2**

Avocado & Shrimp Salad

The avocado peel creates a decorative serving bowl for this salad.

To eat, spoon the avocado and shrimp from the peeling.

The shrimp in this recipe is also called baby shrimp or cocktail shrimp.

You can serve this dish for lunch or as an appetizer.

What You Need

1 ripe avocado

¾ cup frozen salad shrimp

2 teaspoons minced red onion

½ cup sour cream

⅛ teaspoon garlic powder

¼ teaspoon pepper

¼ teaspoon celery salt

Lemon juice, as needed (a few drops)

What You Do

1. Pre-chill the avocado. Set out the shrimp to thaw. Mince the onion (chop into very small pieces) and place in a medium-size mixing bowl. Add the sour cream, shrimp, garlic powder, pepper, and celery salt. Stir together until well blended. Cover and chill in refrigerator.

2. Cut the avocado in half lengthwise and remove the seed. Place halves on serving plates. Sprinkle lemon juice on the avocado to help prevent browning. Spoon chilled shrimp mixture on top of the avocado halves.

LEVEL **E**

SERVINGS **2**

Variation: Sliced Avocado Salad

Prepare Avocado and Shrimp Salad as directed, except peel and slice the avocado. Sprinkle with a few drops of lemon juice to help prevent browning. Arrange the slices on top of a bed of salad greens. Top with the shrimp mixture.

This cool, crisp salad makes a refreshing contrast to main courses with heavy sauce.

If the dressing is too tart for your taste, add sugar.

If it's too sweet, add a little vinegar.

Cucumber Salad v

What You Need

2 cucumbers

2 green onions

Water, as needed (about 1 quart)

1 teaspoon salt

¼ cup white vinegar

5 teaspoons white granulated sugar

⅛ teaspoon pepper

What You Do

1. Rinse the cucumbers under cold, running water. Peel and thinly slice the cucumbers crosswise. Place in a medium-size mixing bowl. Slice the green onions, including the dark green tops. Add to the cucumbers. Add enough water to the bowl to cover the cucumbers and onions. Stir in the salt until it dissolves. Soak in the refrigerator for 2 to 3 hours. The cucumber slices will soften.

2. In a small mixing bowl, stir together the vinegar and sugar until the sugar dissolves. Set aside.

3. Drain the cucumbers and green onions. Gently squeeze the cucumbers with your hands to remove excess salt water (do not rinse). Place in a serving bowl and sprinkle with pepper. Stir in the vinegar and sugar mixture. (There will be extra liquid in the serving bowl.) Serve with a slotted spoon.

Broccoli-Cauliflower Salad v

Black olives accent the bright red, deep green, and white vegetables that make this salad colorful as well as delicious.

A clear glass serving bowl makes an attractive presentation.

You can substitute grape tomatoes for the cherry tomatoes.

What You Need

1 pint cherry tomatoes

½ head cauliflower

½ bunch broccoli

1 (8-ounce) can pitted black olives

Bottled Italian salad dressing

What You Do

1. Rinse the cherry tomatoes, cauliflower, and broccoli in cold, running water. Drain.

2. Remove the stems from the cauliflower and broccoli, and cut the crowns into bite-size pieces.

3. In a serving bowl, gently stir together the cherry tomatoes, cauliflower, and broccoli. Drain the olives and add to the serving bowl. Gently stir to mix the ingredients. Cover with plastic wrap and chill in the refrigerator.

4. When ready to serve, sprinkle with Italian salad dressing. Gently stir until all the ingredients are lightly coated.

How Can I Use Broccoli Stems?

After cutting broccoli florets (the "treetops") from a bunch of broccoli, save the stems. Cover and store in the refrigerator for another use. You can eat them raw with veggie dip, or cut them into bite-size pieces and add to soup or tossed salad. You can also steam them for a side dish. Or, place them on a piece of toast and cover with melted cheese for an easy hot lunch.

Cold Mixed Veggies Salad v

This crisp, cold salad is a nice accompaniment to creamy casserole dishes.

Try it with Mac 'n' Cheese (page 189).

What You Need

1 green bell pepper

1 carrot

2 stalks celery

1 cucumber

1 medium-size red onion

1 teaspoon lemon juice

3 tablespoons vegetable oil

½ teaspoon water

¼ teaspoon basil

¼ teaspoon salt

What You Do

1. Rinse the green bell pepper, carrot, celery, and cucumber in cold, running water. Peel the carrot and cucumber. Chop all the vegetables and place in a large mixing bowl. Chop the onion and add it to the bowl.

2. In a small mixing bowl, stir together the lemon juice, vegetable oil, water, basil, and salt until well mixed. Pour the mixture over the chopped vegetables. Stir until the vegetables are well coated. Cover and refrigerate at least 1 hour until ready to serve.

Mustard Vinaigrette v

You can make this salad dressing in a cruet or jar with a lid.

Place all the ingredients in it.

Cover and shake well.

What You Need

3 tablespoons olive oil or vegetable oil

2 tablespoons vinegar

⅛ teaspoon dried minced garlic

1 teaspoon Dijon mustard

¾ teaspoon dried tarragon

⅛ teaspoon pepper

1 teaspoon salt

What You Do

Stir together all ingredients until well blended.

?

How Do I Know What Type of Vinegar to Choose?

Vinegar is an acidic liquid with a sharp, tangy taste that enhances the flavor of salad dressings, soups, and other foods. It has also been used as a beverage, food preservative, solvent, home-cleaning product, and cure for wounds. Vinegar was first discovered about 10,000 years ago as a good wine gone bad—wine that had fermented beyond the alcohol stage. In fact, the word derives from the French *vinaigre*, for "sour wine." Vinegar can be distilled from almost any food that contains sugar. Popular vinegars include cider vinegar, which comes from apples; white vinegar, from grains; red wine vinegar, from (duh!) red wine; and rice vinegar from (duh again!) rice. In addition, gourmet vinegars are flavored with such herbs as garlic, basil, and tarragon, as well as fruits or fruit juices. Unless you're adventurous (and willing to risk disaster), it's best not to substitute one type of vinegar for another in a recipe.

Creamy Caesar Salad Dressing ∨

Dressing makes the salad, and that's especially true with the popular Caesar Salad (see page 96).

You can use bottled dressing, but it's so easy to make your own. Give it a try!

What You Need

2 large cloves garlic

1 cup extra-virgin olive oil

½ teaspoon Worcestershire sauce

1½ teaspoons lemon juice

1 tablespoon red wine vinegar

⅓ cup heavy cream

¼ teaspoon salt

¼ teaspoon pepper

What You Do

1. Mince the garlic by chopping it into very small pieces. Place in a small mixing bowl.

2. Stir in the olive oil, Worcestershire sauce, lemon juice, vinegar, cream, salt, and pepper until well blended. When ready to serve, spoon 1 or 2 tablespoons at a time onto the salad. Toss until lightly coated.

How Do I Know What Type of Olive Oil to Choose?

If you've tried to buy olive oil, you've likely stared at the labels wondering which type to choose. The three main types are pure, virgin, and extra-virgin. These labels pertain to the olive oil's grade, which is determined by the amount of oleic acid. The less acid, the better. So extra-virgin, which has the least acid—as well as the strongest smell and flavor—is the best quality. If you see "light" olive oil, don't think it's a diet food. The term applies to the pale color and bland flavor, not the calorie count.

Fresh garlic is a must for this one.

This dressing separates easily, so stir well just before serving.

Garlic Salad Dressing v

What You Need

½ clove fresh garlic

¼ cup olive oil

¼ cup vegetable oil

2 tablespoons vinegar

2 tablespoons lemon juice

½ teaspoon salt

¼ teaspoon dry mustard

¼ teaspoon paprika

⅛ teaspoon black pepper

What You Do

1. Mince the garlic by chopping it into very small pieces. Place in a small mixing bowl.

2. Stir in the olive oil, vegetable oil, vinegar, lemon juice, salt, dry mustard, and paprika. Chill for 1 hour. Stir well before serving.

How Do I Prepare a Head of Lettuce for a Salad?

To prepare head lettuce for salad, find the bottom of the core (a round, white circle about 1-inch in diameter). Face the core toward your (clean) counter. Hold the head of lettuce like a basketball and whack it on the counter. Turn over the head and use your fingers to twist out the core; discard it. Hold the lettuce upside-down under cold running water, letting it run into the hole where the core was. Turn the lettuce right-side up and let water drain. Repeat several times under the water. Place hole-side-down in a colander set in the sink. Drain. Pat dry with paper towels. Tear off a section of lettuce leaves about the size of your palm and about ¼" thick. Tear the leaves into bite-size pieces and place them in a salad bowl.

This salad with an Asian flair is a nice break from "everyday" tossed salads.

Mandarin Orange Salad v

What You Need

2 cups romaine lettuce

2 green onions

½ (4-ounce) can mandarin oranges

½ cup slivered almonds

Bottled poppy seed salad dressing

2 tablespoons grated Parmesan cheese

What You Do

1. Rinse romaine, drain, and blot dry with paper towel. Tear into bite-size pieces and place in a large mixing bowl. Cover and refrigerate at least 1 hour.

2. Preheat oven to 400°. Place almonds on an ungreased cookie sheet or pie plate. Roast until golden brown (about 6 minutes). Set aside until ready to serve.

3. When ready to serve, chop green onions including about 2" of the dark green tops. Drain oranges. Add green onions, oranges, and almonds to the romaine.

4. Add dressing 1 tablespoon at a time. Toss lightly using salad utensils until ingredients are lightly coated. Place on serving plate. Sprinkle half of the grated Parmesan cheese on each salad.

Cold Ham & Lima Bean Salad

Curry powder wakes up the lima beans in this tasty salad you can make with leftovers.

Add tomato slices on the side.

What You Need

4 hard-boiled eggs

2 cups cooked ham

1 cup chopped celery

2 cups cooked lima beans (drained)

1 tablespoon minced onion

½ cup mayonnaise

½ teaspoon curry powder

Salt and pepper, to taste

What You Do

1. Peel and chop the hard-boiled eggs and place in a medium mixing bowl.

2. Cut the ham into ½" cubes. Add the ham and celery to the bowl.

3. Stir in the lima beans, onion, mayonnaise, curry powder, salt, and pepper until well mixed.

4. Refrigerate at least 1 hour before serving.

Serve this sweet, cold fruit salad for lunch, dinner, or even breakfast! For best results, use firm bananas, rather than soft, overripe ones.

Orange & Banana Salad v

What You Need

6 bananas

1 small can mandarin oranges

1 pint sour cream

1 cup brown sugar

1 teaspoon cinnamon

½ teaspoon nutmeg

What You Do

1. Slice the bananas crosswise into bite-size circles. Place in a serving bowl. Drain the mandarin oranges, and add to the bananas.

2. In a medium-size mixing bowl, stir together the sour cream, brown sugar, cinnamon, and nutmeg until well blended.

3. Pour over the bananas and oranges. Gently stir until the fruit is well coated. Refrigerate at least 1 hour before serving.

LEVEL **E**

SERVINGS **6**

Variation: White Grape Salad v

Prepare as above, but substitute 2 pounds white seedless grapes for the bananas and oranges. Wash the grapes and remove from stems before adding the dressing.

Four-Bean Salad   v

Here's a popular dish for potlucks and picnics.

Prepare it the night before. It needs several hours to chill.

Garbanzo beans are also known as chickpeas.

If you like, substitute lima beans for any of the other beans in this recipe.

What You Need

1 medium onion

¾ cup sugar

½ teaspoon black pepper

⅓ cup corn oil

⅓ cup white vinegar

1 (15-ounce) can red kidney beans

1 (15-ounce) can garbanzo beans

1 (15-ounce) can cut green beans

1 (15-ounce) can yellow wax beans

What You Do

1. Peel and chop the onion into small pieces. Place in a large mixing bowl. Stir in the sugar, black pepper, corn oil, and vinegar until well blended.

2. Place a colander in the sink. Open the red kidney beans, garbanzo beans, green beans, and yellow wax beans and pour into the colander. Stir a few times to let the liquid drain.

3. Add the drained beans to the bowl. Stir until the beans are well coated with the dressing. Cover and refrigerate at least 3 hours. Stir before serving.

Waldorf Salad v

This cold salad has been a favorite for generations.

The lemon juice helps keep the apples from turning brown.

Serve in a bowl or on a lettuce leaf on a salad plate.

You can substitute canned whipping cream for the frozen nondairy whipped topping.

What You Need

3 medium-size apples (about ¾ pound total)

4 stalks celery

½ cup chopped walnuts

¼ cup mayonnaise

1 tablespoon white granulated sugar

½ teaspoon lemon juice

⅛ teaspoon salt

½ cup frozen nondairy whipped topping

What You Do

1. Rinse the apples and celery under cold, running water. (Do not peel the apples.) Remove the core with a knife or apple corer. Cut the apples into 1" cubes. Chop the celery. Place in a medium-size mixing bowl. Stir in the walnuts.

2. In a large mixing bowl, stir together the mayonnaise, sugar, lemon juice, and salt until well blended. Stir in the frozen nondairy whipped topping or whipped cream.

3. Add about ⅓ of the apple mixture to the mayonnaise mixture and stir to coat the fruit. Continue adding about ⅓ of the mixture at a time until the ingredients are well coated.

How Do I Store Celery?

Save the sleeve packaging and use it to cover celery when you store it in the refrigerator. If left uncovered, it will become dehydrated. If that happens, don't throw it out. Place it in a large container of ice water. The celery will absorb the moisture. Celery is a good source of vitamin C, and 2 stalks contain only 25 calories.

Caesar Salad   v

A popular favorite, this salad calls for a special type of dark lettuce called romaine.

The original recipe called for anchovies, a small saltwater fish. However, many people don't care for them, so they are seldom used today.

Use purchased croutons, or make your own (see below).

What You Need

2–3 cups romaine lettuce

2–3 tablespoons bottled or homemade Creamy Caesar Salad Dressing (see page 89)

¼ cup croutons

Freshly grated Parmesan cheese, to taste

What You Do

1. Tear off any limp or discolored leaves from the head of romaine lettuce. Pull off 4 to 6 leaves. Place in a colander and rinse under cold, running water. Turn the leaves to rinse both sides. Drain. Pat dry with paper towels, so the dressing will stick to the leaves. Wrap the lettuce in dry paper towels and chill in the refrigerator for at least 30 minutes.

2. Tear the lettuce into bite-size pieces. Place in a salad bowl or large mixing bowl. Add the salad dressing 1 tablespoon at a time. Toss with salad utensils or 2 large spoons. Continue adding dressing and tossing salad until the lettuce is lightly coated.

3. Add the croutons. Sprinkle with Parmesan cheese. Toss again until well mixed. Serve immediately.

How Do I Make My Own Croutons?

Preheat the oven to 375°. In a clean paper or plastic bag (or a plastic container with a lid), mix together 1 teaspoon salt, 1 teaspoon paprika, and 3 tablespoons grated Parmesan cheese. Set aside. Remove the crust from a slice of bread. Lightly butter both sides. Cut to make ½" cubes. Place the cubes on an ungreased baking sheet. Bake for 10 minutes or until golden brown. Remove the cubes from the oven and immediately put into the bag with the seasonings. Shake until well coated. Spread on a plate to cool. Makes enough for 2 salads.

Bright green and red ingredients give this salad a festive look.

You can use canned peas (drained), but frozen peas look and taste much better.

For a vegan variation, omit the egg and substitute your choice of nondairy bottled salad dressing for the mayonnaise.

?

Chilled Pea Salad v

What You Need

1 egg

1 cup frozen peas

1 tomato

½ stalk celery

2 tablespoons mayonnaise

What You Do

1. Hard-boil the egg (see Boiled Egg on page 8).

2. Rinse the peas in cold water, drain, and let thaw.

3. Chop the tomato, celery, and egg, and place in a bowl.

4. Gently stir in the peas. Stir in the mayonnaise until all the ingredients are lightly coated. Chill in the refrigerator for at least 1 hour before serving.

How Can I Use Peas in Recipes?

Peas are eaten raw, added to salads, steamed, and stir-fried, as well as used in soups and stews. A half-cup serving provides 30 percent of the Recommended Daily Allowance of vitamin C. Peas originated in Middle Asia as long as 5,000 years ago. Ancient Greeks and Romans cultivated them for their dried seeds. In Athens, Greek street vendors commonly sold hot pea soup. And in ancient Rome, fried peas were a common snack at the theater—much the way popcorn is in America today. The first mention of green peas occurred after the Norman Conquest of England in 1066. By the seventeenth century in France, green peas were used raw or cooked in the pod and considered quite a delicacy.

Three-Color Pasta Salad v

For best results, you'll need to start early (or the day before) to give the flavors a chance to mingle in this popular cold salad.

What You Need

½ bunch raw broccoli

½ head raw cauliflower

2 raw carrots

2 scallions or green onions

¼ cup sliced black olives

8 ounces uncooked tri-color spiral pasta

1 to 1½ cups Italian salad dressing

½ cup cubed Cheddar cheese

⅓ cup shredded Gouda

⅓ cup grated Parmesan cheese

Salt and pepper, to taste

What You Do

1. Rinse the broccoli, cauliflower, and carrots under cold, running water. Peel the carrots. Chop and place together in a medium-size mixing bowl. Remove outer skin of scallions and slice them crosswise into circles. Add to the bowl. Drain the black olives. Add to the bowl. Stir in ½ cup of the salad dressing until the veggies are well coated. Set aside for 30 minutes at room temperature, stirring occasionally.

2. Cook the pasta. Drain. Transfer to a mixing bowl and add ¼ cup of the salad dressing. Cool to room temperature, stirring occasionally. Cover both bowls and refrigerate for at least 6 hours (or overnight).

3. When almost ready to serve, cut the Cheddar into cubes. Shred the Gouda using the large holes on a cheese grater. Grate the Parmesan using the small holes on the grater. Add the vegetables to the bowl of pasta. Toss. Sprinkle with salt and pepper.

Coleslaw is a favorite summer-time side dish.

You can also spoon it onto a sandwich to add flavor and crunch.

Use it on a Grilled Rachel Sandwich (page 43) or on a turkey or bologna and cheese sandwich.

Old-Fashioned Coleslaw v

What You Need

½ head cabbage

4 carrots

3 tablespoons vinegar

½ teaspoon salt

¼ teaspoon paprika

3 tablespoons white granulated sugar

½ cup sour cream

What You Do

1. Remove the outer leaves of the cabbage. Cut in half lengthwise. Store ½ in the refrigerator for another use. Cut the remaining half crosswise into 2 pieces. Use the large holes on a grater to grate the cabbage into a colander. (Grate only the amount you need. Do not store grated or shredded cabbage for future use.)

2. Peel the carrots and rinse under cold, running water. Grate the carrots, using the large holes on the grater, into the bowl with the shredded cabbage. Use two forks to toss together. Cover and refrigerate for at least 2 hours.

3. In a small mixing bowl, stir together the vinegar, salt, paprika, sugar, and sour cream until well blended.

4. Remove the cabbage mixture from the refrigerator. Add the slaw dressing 1 tablespoon at a time, using two table forks to toss until the cabbage and carrots are lightly coated. Chill and serve.

Exotic Couscous Salad v

If you'd like to try something a bit different, consider this flavorful cold salad.

Couscous is a North African dish made from a rice-like steamed, crushed grain.

You'll find instant couscous in the rice aisle of your supermarket.

What You Need

1 (10-ounce) box instant couscous

1 cucumber

3 fresh tomatoes

2 green onions

3 roasted red bell peppers (from a jar)

1 (4¼-ounce) can chopped black olives

2 cloves fresh garlic (or ¼ teaspoon dried minced garlic)

¼ cup olive oil

¼ cup lemon juice

1 teaspoon ground cumin

¼ teaspoon salt

⅛ teaspoon black pepper

⅛ teaspoon cayenne pepper (optional)

What You Do

1. Cook the couscous according to package directions.

2. Peel and chop the cucumber. Chop the tomatoes, green onions, and roasted red bell peppers. Stir together in a medium-size mixing bowl. When the couscous is done, fluff with a fork. Stir in the cucumber, green onion, tomatoes, and peppers. Drain the chopped olives. Add to the salad and stir. Set aside.

3. Finely chop the garlic and place in a small mixing bowl. Stir in the olive oil, lemon juice, cumin, salt, black pepper, and cayenne pepper. Pour over the salad. Toss with two forks until well mixed. Chill for about 1 hour, until cool.

Tabbouleh Salad v

What You Need

1 small cucumber

2 medium-size tomatoes

Fresh chives (enough to yield 2 tablespoons chopped)

1 cup fresh parsley

3 scallions

1 cup uncooked cracked instant bulgur wheat (or instant couscous)

½ cup olive oil

½ cup lemon juice

Salt and pepper, to taste

What You Do

1. Rinse the cucumber, tomatoes, chives, and parsley under cold, running water. Drain. Chop and place in a large mixing bowl. Remove the outer layer of the scallions. Chop and add to the bowl.

2. Cook the wheat or couscous according to package directions. While it's cooking, stir together the olive oil, lemon juice, salt, and pepper until well mixed. When the wheat is done, add it to the vegetables in the large mixing bowl.

3. Pour the dressing over the ingredients in the mixing bowl. Gently toss until well coated. Cover and refrigerate for 2 to 3 hours to allow the flavors to mingle.

Make this salad a day early to give the flavors time to blend.

Artichoke-Lettuce Salad v

What You Need

½ (14-ounce) can artichoke hearts

1 (15-ounce) can sliced carrots

1 (3-8/10-ounce) can sliced black olives

6 tablespoons Italian dressing

4 cups lettuce chunks

¼ pound fresh spinach

Blue cheese crumbles, as needed

Croutons, as needed

What You Do

1. Drain the artichoke hearts. Slice into halves. Place in a small mixing bowl. Drain the carrots and olives. Add to the bowl. Stir in the Italian dressing. Cover and marinate in the refrigerator overnight (or for at least 3 hours).

2. Prepare the lettuce as for tossed salad (see "How Do I Prepare a Head of Lettuce for a Salad?" on page 90) and place in a large salad bowl. Tear the spinach into bite-size pieces. Add the marinated artichoke hearts, carrots, and olives. Gently toss using salad utensils. Sprinkle with blue cheese crumbles and croutons.

Don't let the long list of ingredients scare you away from this easy-to-prepare salad.

You can substitute juice of ½ lime for the lemon juice.

Warm Bacon-Avocado Salad

What You Need

2 slices bacon

½ orange bell pepper

1 green onion

¼ cup butter

3 tablespoons sugar

3 tablespoons ketchup

3 tablespoons red wine vinegar

1 tablespoon soy sauce

1 small head Bibb lettuce

4 avocados

Lemon juice, as needed (about 1 teaspoon)

What You Do

1. Fry bacon. Drain on paper towels. When cool, crumble. Set aside.

2. Chop orange bell pepper and entire green onion, including the dark green top.

3. In a saucepan over low heat, stir together the green onion, orange bell pepper, butter, sugar, ketchup, vinegar, and soy sauce until sugar dissolves. Keep warm.

4. Cut lettuce head in fourths. Rinse in running water. Drain. Pat dry with paper towels. Separate leaves to make a bed of lettuce on each serving plate.

5. Peel and slice avocados. Arrange on top of the bed of lettuce. Sprinkle a few drops of lemon juice over avocado slices to prevent browning. Top with warm dressing and crumbled bacon. Serve immediately.

Potato Salad v

There's no single "right" way to make potato salad. It's likely that almost every family in America has its own recipe. Here's a basic recipe to get you started.

You can substitute 2 to 3 small red russet potatoes (about 1 handful total) for each baking potato.

What You Need

4 medium-size white potatoes

2 eggs

¼ medium white onion

1 stalk celery

¾ cup mayonnaise or mayonnaise-like salad dressing

1 teaspoon prepared mustard

½ teaspoon celery seed

½ teaspoon salt

½ teaspoon pepper

1 teaspoon white granulated sugar (optional)

What You Do

1. Rinse potatoes under cool, running water and place in a Dutch oven. Cover with water. Boil for 30 to 35 minutes, until tender when pierced with a fork. Drain and let cool. Peel and cut into ¾" cubes. Place in a large mixing bowl.

2. While the potatoes are cooking, hard-boil the eggs (see Boiled Egg on page 8). Peel and chop the eggs. Add to the potatoes. Chop the onion and celery. Add to the potatoes.

3. In a separate small mixing bowl, stir together the mayonnaise, mustard, celery seed, salt, and pepper until well blended. (Taste the mixture. Add 1 teaspoon sugar if you like.) Pour over the potato mixture. Gently stir until the potatoes are well coated. Refrigerate for at least 1 hour before serving.

Hot German Potato Salad

This potato salad is traditionally served warm.

If the dressing is too tangy for your taste, use 1 additional teaspoon of sugar.

What You Need

4 medium-size potatoes

6 slices bacon

½ small white onion

2 tablespoons all-purpose flour

4 teaspoons white granulated sugar

1½ teaspoons salt

½ teaspoon celery seed

⅛ teaspoon pepper

⅔ cup water

6 tablespoons vinegar

What You Do

1. Place rinsed potatoes in a 2-quart saucepan. Cover with water. Bring to a boil. Boil for 8 to 10 minutes, until the potatoes are soft when pierced with a fork. Drain and let cool. Peel and slice crosswise ¼" thick.

2. Fry the bacon (see Makin' Bacon on page 5) in a large frying pan. Leave the fat in the pan. Drain the bacon on paper towels. When the bacon is cool, break it into crumbles. Set aside.

3. Chop the onion. Heat the bacon fat over medium-high heat. Cook the onion until tender. Reduce heat to low. Stir in the flour, sugar, salt, celery seed, and pepper until well blended and the mixture bubbles. Remove the frying pan from the heat.

4. Stir in the water and vinegar. Return the frying pan to the stovetop. Stir constantly until the mixture boils. Continue boiling for 1 minute. Remove from heat. Gently stir in the potatoes and bacon until coated. Cover to keep warm until ready to serve.

Chapter 5

Main Dishes—Beef

Easy

Beef Roast. 108
Tacos. 110
Baked Spaghetti. 112
Variation: Vegetarian Spaghetti. 112
Slow-Cooked Swiss Steak. 113
Variation: Creamy Swiss Steak 113
Hamburger Pizza Casserole 114
Tomato Rice & Beef Casserole 115
Beef & Coleslaw Stir Fry 116

Medium

Spaghetti & Meatballs 117
Easiest Lasagna in the World. 118
Boiled Corned Beef & Cabbage 119
Cowboy Hash. 120
Beef & Noodles 121
Pot Roast. 122
They'll Think You're a Genius Beef Brisket. 124
Hot Tamale Casserole. 125

Hard

Enchiladas 126
Stuffed Green Bell Peppers. 127
Meat Loaf 128
Beef Stroganoff 129
Shepherd's Pie 130

Chapter 5

Main Dishes—Pork

Easy
Pork Roast 132
Easy Pork Tenderloin. 133
Pork Chops in Cherry Sauce. 134
Polish Sausage & Kraut. 135
Ham Fettuccine Casserole 136
Ham & Asparagus Roll-Ups 137
Ham Slice with Pineapple 138

Medium
Pork Chops with Rice 139
Pork in Mushroom Sauce 140
Red Beans & Rice. 141
Pineapple Pork Chop Bake 142

Hard
Pork Chops with Sweet Potatoes 143
Spaghetti with Ham Sauce. 144

*This recipe makes 2 servings per pound.

When people talk about "meat and potatoes," they're talking about beef. Because roast beef is simple and unadorned, when it is served as an entrée, it opens up a wide variety of interesting salads and side dishes with or without sauces.

Serve with Garlic Mashed Potatoes (page 210), Green Bean Casserole (page 211), or Broccoli-Cauliflower Salad (page 86).

Beef Roast

What You Need

Rump or round roast (any size cut)

Garlic salt, to taste

Salt and pepper, to taste

What You Do

1. Preheat oven to 325°F. Be sure to set the dial to "bake" before cooking food. Rinse the meat under cold, running water. Place fat-side-up in a roasting pan or ovenproof baking pan. Insert a meat thermometer into the thickest part of the meat (optional). Sprinkle with garlic salt, salt, and pepper.

2. For rare meat, roast for 22 to 26 minutes per pound, or until the meat thermometer reads 140°F. For medium, roast for 26 to 30 minutes per pound, or until the meat thermometer reads 160°F. For well done, roast for 33 to 35 minutes per pound, or until the meat thermometer reads 170°F.

3. Remove from oven. Slice as needed. (As the roast sits outside the oven, it will continue to cook. So if you like rare or medium-rare meat, cook it for the shorter amount of time listed.) Note: For best results, you should always let roasts sit for about 5 minutes before slicing to give juices time to settle. Serve warm.

?

What Are the Cooking Times for Bone-In Roasts?

If you had two roasts that weighed the same, but one had a bone and the other didn't, you'd have to cook the one without the bone a bit longer. Leaving the bone in the meat helps it cook faster, because the bone conducts heat and helps cook the meat.

Beef Roast—continued

How Do I Bake a Potato?

One of America's favorite side dishes is a simple baked potato, served with a variety of toppings: butter, sour cream, chopped chives, or cottage cheese. Or, try sour cream mixed with ranch or French onion flavored dried soup or dip mix.

To bake a potato, rinse the potato under cold, running water. Cut two slits in an "X" shape on the top of the potato to let heat escape during baking. Place directly on baking rack in oven. Or, for a softer potato skin and mushy flesh, rub butter or margarine on the skin and wrap the potato in aluminum foil before placing in oven. Bake at 350°F for 1 hour. Test for doneness by piercing with a fork or gently squeezing potato (while holding a potholder). When done, potato will feel soft.

Tacos

Here's an easy favorite you're probably used to buying at fast-food drive-up windows. Instead, make your own.

You can substitute reheated precooked chicken (see "How Should I Save Cooked Chicken for Other Recipes?" on page 153) or pork (see Pork Roast on page 132), cut into bite-size pieces, for the beef.

What You Need

1 pound ground beef

2 tablespoons chili powder or 1 (1¼-ounce) packet dry taco seasoning mix

1 tablespoon dried minced onion (optional)

¼ head iceberg lettuce

1 large tomato

6–8 prepared taco shells OR 6" flour tortillas (for soft tacos)

1 cup shredded Cheddar cheese

½ cup salsa or picante sauce

2 tablespoons sour cream

What You Do

1. In a frying pan, brown the ground beef (see "How Do I Brown Ground Beef?" on page 111) along with chili powder (or taco seasoning mix) and the onion. Drain off the fat. Cover to keep warm.

2. While the meat is browning, shred the lettuce using the large holes on a grater. (Or slice into narrow strips with a knife.) Place in a serving bowl. Chop the tomato and place in a small serving bowl.

3. Heat the taco shells according to package directions. (If you're using flour tortillas for soft tacos, omit this step. Instead, wrap the tortillas together in aluminum foil.)

Tacos—*continued*

4. Set the oven to the lowest temperature, and place the tortillas in the oven before you begin browning the meat. Remove the tortillas from the oven when you are ready to serve. Or, you can wrap the tortillas individually in damp paper towels and heat them for 40 seconds on high in the microwave. Heated flour tortillas taste better, and they are easier to roll up.

5. To serve, spoon about ¼ cup of the beef mixture into each taco shell. Top each with some lettuce, tomato, cheese, salsa, and sour cream.

How Do I Brown Ground Beef?

Ground beef is a versatile meat for casseroles and other dishes. Use your hands to crumble the meat into a frying pan over medium-high heat. Stir occasionally as meat cooks. Heat until juices run clear and there is no tinge of pink in the meat. Drain. You can brown ground pork sausage using the same method. (Note: Do not pour fat down kitchen sink. Discard by pouring into an empty coffee can with a plastic lid. Cover and store in refrigerator until fat turns solid. Throw away. You can add used fat from other sources to the can until it is full, and then throw away.)

Baked Spaghetti

This mild but hearty casserole makes a fine Italian-style main course for a crowd, without the need for last-minute preparation. You won't have to rattle around in the kitchen boiling noodles after your guests arrive.

Prepare ahead and store in the refrigerator until ready to bake.

Serve with grated Parmesan cheese, a mixed greens salad, and French bread (see "How Do I Prepare French Bread?" on page 114).

Cover and store leftovers in the refrigerator for up to 3 to 4 days.

What You Need

1 (10-ounce) package thin spaghetti

1 pound ground beef

¼ cup milk

1 egg

1 (28-ounce) jar spaghetti sauce (any kind)

2 cups shredded mozzarella cheese

What You Do

1. Break the uncooked spaghetti into thirds and cook according to package directions (boil for 8 minutes, until the noodles are tender but still firm).

2. While the noodles are cooking, brown the ground beef (see "How Do I Brown Ground Beef?" on page 111) in a large frying pan. Drain off the fat.

3. Preheat the oven to 350°F. Spray a 9" × 13" ovenproof baking pan with nonstick cooking spray. When the noodles are done, drain. Pour noodles into pan.

4. In a mixing bowl, stir together the milk and egg with a fork until well blended. Pour the mixture onto the noodles and stir until the noodles are well coated.

5. Stir the beef into the noodles. Add the spaghetti sauce and stir until blended. Cover the surface with mozzarella. Bake uncovered for 30 minutes.

Variation: **Vegetarian Spaghetti** v

Omit the beef. For more substance, use a jar of spaghetti sauce with vegetable chunks. Or, substitute 1 diced eggplant for the meat.

Slow-Cooked Swiss Steak

Round steak is the tastiest choice for this recipe. However, because this dish cooks slowly, you can use arm steak or chuck roast, which are less expensive cuts.

Serve with baked potatoes (see "How Do I Bake a Potato?" on page 109) and a green vegetable.

What You Need

1 pound round steak, about 1" thick

½ medium white or yellow onion

1 (28-ounce) can stewed tomatoes, with juice

¼ teaspoon garlic salt

Salt and pepper, to taste

What You Do

1. Rinse the meat under cold, running water. Cut into serving-size pieces. Place into a slow cooker or a 9" × 13" ovenproof baking pan that has been sprayed with nonstick cooking spray.

2. Slice the onion and place on top of the meat. Pour the tomatoes and juice over the top. Sprinkle with garlic salt, salt, and pepper.

3. Cover the slow cooker or baking pan. In a slow cooker, cook on high for 1 hour. Reduce heat to low and cook for another 8 or 9 hours until the meat is tender. In the oven, bake at 350°F for 1½ to 2 hours, until the meat is tender. To serve, place the meat on a serving plate. Spoon onions, tomatoes, and drippings over the meat.

Variation: Creamy Swiss Steak

Substitute 1 (10½-ounce) can condensed mushroom soup for the tomatoes. When meat is done, use the drippings as gravy.

Hamburger Pizza Casserole

What You Need

2 pounds ground beef

1 (7-ounce) can mushroom stems and pieces (optional)

1 (15-ounce) can pizza sauce

1 (7½-ounce) can refrigerator biscuits

1 cup grated Parmesan cheese

What You Do

1. Brown the ground beef in a frying pan (see "How Do I Brown Ground Beef?" on page 111). Drain off the fat. Reduce heat to low. Drain the mushrooms, and add to the beef along with the pizza sauce. Stir.

2. Lay the uncooked biscuits on top of the meat. Sprinkle with cheese. Cover and simmer for 20 to 25 minutes, until the biscuits are cooked.

How Do I Prepare French Bread?

Purchase an unsliced loaf of French bread. Preheat the oven to 400°F. Slice 1" thick pieces. Leave standing in a loaf shape. Take a heelpiece and spread butter or margarine on the interior side. Replace the heel on the end of the loaf. One by one take out a slice, spread butter on both sides. Replace it in the loaf. When finished, wrap entire loaf in aluminum foil. Bake for 10 minutes. Plan for 2 to 3 slices per person. If you don't need an entire loaf, cut the amount you need from the whole loaf. Tightly wrap the portion you won't use in aluminum foil and freeze for another meal or for Hot Cheese Toast (see page 42).

Tomato Rice & Beef Casserole

This casserole is a meaty variation of a Mexican side dish.

You can substitute cooked pork from a leftover roast or pork chops for the beef.

You also can substitute 2 servings of instant rice.

What You Need

2 cups water

1 cup uncooked rice

1 teaspoon salt

1 pound ground beef

1 medium onion

1 (14½-ounce) can stewed tomatoes, with juice

Salt and pepper, to taste

What You Do

1. In a saucepan over high heat, bring the water, rice, and salt to a boil. Reduce heat to low and cover. Simmer for about 15 minutes until all the water is absorbed.

2. While the rice is cooking, crumble the ground beef into the frying pan. Chop the onion and add it to the frying pan. Brown the beef and onion (see "How Do I Brown Ground Beef?" on page 111). Drain off the fat.

3. Stir in the stewed tomatoes with juice until well blended. Sprinkle with salt and pepper. Stir in the rice. Cook uncovered for 5 to 10 minutes, until heated through.

LEVEL **E**

SERVINGS **2**

Beef & Coleslaw Stir Fry

Warm and light for a summer supper, this easy and elegant dish with an Asian look is nothing more than good old American coleslaw and roast beef with stir-fry sauce.

You'll find the coleslaw mix in the produce section.

What You Need

4 ounces thinly sliced deli roast beef

1 tomato

1 tablespoon vegetable oil

3 cups packaged broccoli, red cabbage, carrot coleslaw mix

¼ cup bottled stir-fry sauce

What You Do

1. Slice the roast beef into strips about 1½" long and ¼" wide. Set aside.

2. Rinse the tomato under cold, running water. Cut into 8 wedges. Set aside.

3. Preheat the vegetable oil in a nonstick frying pan over medium-high heat. Add the coleslaw mix and cook for 2 minutes, stirring constantly.

4. Gently stir in the beef strips, stir-fry sauce, and tomato wedges. Cook another 2 to 3 minutes, gently stirring constantly until the coleslaw mix is heated through but still crisp.

Spaghetti & Meatballs

Tired of spaghetti sauce that comes in a jar? Make your own and add tasty meatballs for an authentic Italian dinner.

Serve over spaghetti cooked according to the directions on a 10-ounce package.

What You Need: For the meatballs

1 pound ground beef

2 eggs

⅛ teaspoon dried minced garlic

¼ cup grated Parmesan cheese

1 teaspoon salt

3 tablespoons vegetable oil

What You Need: For the sauce

1½ cups water

2 (6-ounce) cans tomato paste

1 teaspoon dried sweet basil

1 teaspoon salt

⅛ teaspoon pepper

½ teaspoon white granulated sugar

What You Do

1. Crumble the ground beef into a mixing bowl. In a separate mixing bowl or cup, beat the eggs with a table fork until well blended. Add to the beef, along with the garlic, cheese, and salt. Use your hands to squish the ingredients together until well blended. Pour the vegetable oil into a large frying pan over medium heat. With wet hands, form the beef mixture into about 16 meatballs. Fry in the oil until well browned. Drain off the fat. Reduce the heat to low.

2. Heat the water in a saucepan until small bubbles form. Pour into a bowl. Stir in the tomato paste, basil, salt, pepper, and sugar until well blended. Pour the sauce over the meatballs. Cover and cook for at least 1 hour, stirring occasionally.

Easiest Lasagna in the World

This popular layered pasta dish is a favorite at potluck dinners.

You can use cottage cheese in place of the ricotta.

What You Need

1 pound ground beef

1 (32-ounce) jar spaghetti sauce

1 egg

12 ounces ricotta cheese[i]

1 cup shredded mozzarella cheese

1 teaspoon dried basil

1 teaspoon dried oregano

Salt and pepper, to taste

Dash chili powder (optional)

9 uncooked lasagna noodles

¼ cup grated Parmesan cheese

What You Do

1. Brown the ground beef (see "How Do I Brown Ground Beef?" on page 111). Drain off the fat. Stir in the spaghetti sauce.

2. In a mixing bowl, beat the egg with a fork until well blended. Stir in the ricotta and mozzarella, along with basil, oregano, salt, pepper, and chili powder.

3. Preheat oven to 350°F. Use enough of the sauce mixture to cover the bottom of an ovenproof 7" × 11" × 3" baking dish. Place 3 of the uncooked noodles on top of the sauce in a row to form a bottom layer. Spread about ⅓ of the cheese mixture on the noodles; then spread about ⅓ of the sauce mixture on top of the cheese. Repeat the process twice: 3 noodles, cheese mixture, sauce mixture; 3 noodles, cheese mixture, sauce mixture. Sprinkle with Parmesan cheese. Cover with aluminum foil. Bake for 1 hour. Uncover and bake 15 minutes more, until the noodles are soft. Let stand 10 to 15 minutes before cutting.

Boiled Corned Beef & Cabbage

Nothing is more traditional for St. Patrick's Day than boiled corned beef and cabbage.

Use leftover corned beef for Grilled Reuben Sandwiches (page 43).

What You Need

3 to 4 pounds packaged corned beef brisket with spice packet

Water, as needed (about 1 quart)

2 small heads green cabbage

What You Do

1. Unwrap the meat and rinse under cold, running water. Place in a Dutch oven. Cover with water. Stir in the contents of the spice packet. On the stovetop, cover and bring to a boil over medium-high heat. Reduce heat to low. Simmer for 2½ hours or until the meat is tender when pierced with a fork.

2. Remove and discard the outer leaves from the cabbages. Rinse the cabbage under cold, running water. Cut in half from top to bottom. Cut each half from top to bottom in half again to make wedges. Place the cabbage in the pot surrounding the meat. Cover and cook another 30 minutes. (In a slow cooker, place the cabbage in the pot first. Place the meat on top of the cabbage. Cover with water. Cook on low for 8 to 10 hours.)

How Do I Choose and Store Cabbage?

Cabbage is high in vitamin C and very low in sodium. When purchasing, avoid heads with outer leaves that have separated from the stem. Do not rinse cabbage before storing. (Moisture favors decay.) If shredding, do it only when ready to use. Do not store shredded cabbage for future use.

Cowboy Hash

LEVEL **M**

SERVINGS **4**

How easy is this? It makes you feel right at home on the range.

Serve with Hot Cheese Toast (page 42) and ketchup, barbecue sauce, or chunky salsa.

What You Need

4 small white or red russet potatoes

1 small white or yellow onion

1 green bell pepper (optional)

¼ cup vegetable oil

1 pound ground beef

1 teaspoon chili powder

1 teaspoon salt

¼ teaspoon pepper

What You Do

1. Peel and slice the potatoes. Set aside. Chop the onion and green bell pepper. Pour the vegetable oil into a large frying pan over medium-high heat. Add the onions and green bell pepper. Cook until tender but still firm, stirring frequently.

2. Crumble the ground beef into the pan and brown it (see "How Do I Brown Ground Beef?" on page 111). Gently stir in the potatoes. Add the chili powder, salt, and pepper; mix well. Continue frying for about 30 minutes, stirring often. Cook until the potatoes are tender and golden brown. Drain off excess fat before serving.

Beef & Noodles

In the grocery store, look for stew beef that has already been cut into approximately 1½" cubes. Or, ask the meat cutter to cube round steak for you.

Plan ahead to use the leftover onion soup mix, mushroom soup, and canned mushrooms for Cranberry Chicken (page 147) and Green Bean Casserole (page 211) in the next day or so.

What You Need

1 pound cubed stew beef

½ (1¼-ounce) envelope dry onion soup mix

½ (10¾-ounce) can condensed cream of mushroom soup

½ (7-ounce) can sliced mushrooms

½ (12-ounce) package uncooked wide egg noodles

What You Do

1. Place the beef into an ovenproof baking pan that has been sprayed with nonstick cooking spray.

2. In a small mixing bowl, stir together the onion soup mix and undiluted mushroom soup until well blended. Gently stir in the mushrooms. Pour over the meat. Cover and bake at 300°F for 3 hours. You don't have to preheat if cooking time exceeds 1 hour.

3. During the last 15 minutes of cooking time, cook the egg noodles according to package directions. Drain. Place the noodles on serving plates. Spoon the beef mixture on top. Serve immediately.

Pot Roast

This is best when prepared with rump or eye of round roast. But because this cooks slowly, you can cook it with a less expensive cut of beef, such as chuck roast or arm roast.

Serve with Garlic Mashed Potatoes (page 210).

What You Need

4 carrots

3 stalks celery

1 medium-size white or yellow onion

2 tablespoons vegetable oil

2-pound beef round, chuck, or arm roast

Salt and pepper, to taste

½ cup water

Optional gravy

3 tablespoons all-purpose flour

⅓ cup cold water

What You Do

1. Rinse the carrots and celery under cold running water. Peel the carrots. Cut the carrots and celery diagonally into 1"- to 1½"-long sections. Chop the onion. Place the carrots, celery, and onion in a slow cooker.

2. Heat the vegetable oil over medium-high heat. Place the roast in the hot oil and brown on one side. Turn the roast. Generously sprinkle salt and pepper over the browned side. When the second side is browned, sprinkle with salt and pepper. Place in a slow cooker.

3. Pour ½ cup water over the beef. Cover. Cook on low for 8 to 10 hours (or on high for 4 to 5 hours).

Pot Roast—*continued*

4. To make the gravy: At the end of the cooking time, pour the cooking liquid from the slow cooker into a saucepan over medium-high heat. (Leave the beef and vegetables in the cooker to keep warm.) In a small mixing bowl, stir together the flour and ⅓ cup water until well blended. Pour into the cooking liquid. Stir constantly until the mixture bubbles and thickens.

5. When ready to serve, place the meat on a serving dish. Use a slotted spoon to remove the vegetables. Spoon around the beef to form a border along the edge of the serving dish. Serve the gravy on the side.

How Do I Roast Meat and Poultry?

Roasting is the easiest way to prepare meat. All you do is rinse it under cold running water, place in a roasting pan, sprinkle with seasonings, and put it in the oven. All you need to know is the time and temperature for each type of meat. A meat thermometer inserted into the meat takes the guesswork out of roasting, but you can roast meat without one. If you use a meat thermometer, be sure the tip does not touch bone. If it does, it will give an inaccurate reading. To serve, slice across the grain.

They'll Think You're a Genius Beef Brisket

*This recipe makes 2 servings per pound.

This dish is so tasty that they'll think you're a genius! Prepare this recipe the day before you plan to serve it.

What You Need

3- to 6-pound beef brisket

½ (3½-ounce) bottle liquid smoke

1 cup lemon juice

1 tablespoon celery seed

½ teaspoon garlic salt

¼ teaspoon pepper

½ cup water

About ¾ cup bottled barbecue sauce

What You Do

1. Rinse the brisket in cold, running water. Place in a shallow roasting pan, fat-side-up. Pour the liquid smoke and lemon juice over the top. Sprinkle with celery seed, garlic salt, and pepper. Bake uncovered at 275°F for 1½ hours.

2. Remove from oven. Pour water into the side of the roasting pan (not on top of the meat). Tightly cover with aluminum foil. Return to the oven. Cook for another 2½ hours.

3. Uncover. Pour the barbecue sauce over the top. Reseal the foil. Cook for another 30 minutes. Remove from oven. Remove the foil until the meat has cooled. Cover and refrigerate in the juices overnight. (Don't cut the meat before it's chilled!)

4. Preheat oven to 350°F. Remove brisket from the juices and place on cutting board. (Discard juices.) Thinly slice the cold brisket crosswise. Place in an ovenproof baking pan that has been sprayed with nonstick cooking spray. Cover and heat in the oven for 20 to 30 minutes, until warmed through.

Hot Tamale Casserole

If you like hot tamales, this one-dish meal is for you.

You can omit the onion if you prefer.

What You Need

1 (15-ounce) can chili (with or without beans)

¼ medium white or yellow onion (about 2½" in diameter)

1 (15-ounce) can of tamales (with liquid)

1 (8-ounce) package shredded Cheddar cheese

What You Do

1. Preheat oven to 350°F. Spray a 9" × 12" ovenproof baking pan with nonstick cooking spray. Pour chili into the pan.

2. Chop the onion. Stir into the chili. Stir in the liquid from the tamale can until well mixed.

2. Remove any paper from the tamales. Arrange tamales in a row on top of the chili. Top with Cheddar cheese. Bake uncovered for 30 minutes until cheese melts and tamales and chili are heated through. Or, cover and zap in the microwave for about 5 minutes on high until cheese melts and ingredients are heated through.

Enchiladas

Don a sombrero and invite some friends over for a fiesta!

What You Need

1¼ cups canned red enchilada sauce

1 (10½-ounce) can condensed cream of mushroom soup

1 (10¾-ounce) can condensed tomato soup

1 small white or yellow onion

2 pounds ground beef

1½ cups shredded Cheddar cheese

10 (6") flour tortillas

What You Do

1. Spray a 9" × 13" ovenproof baking pan with nonstick cooking spray. Set aside. In a saucepan, stir together the enchilada sauce, undiluted mushroom soup, and undiluted tomato soup. Cook over medium heat until well blended. Remove from heat.

2. Chop the onion. Place in a frying pan. Crumble the ground beef into the pan. Brown the beef and onion together (see "How Do I Brown Ground Beef?" on page 111). Drain off fat. Stir in ½ cup of the enchilada sauce mixture and ½ cup of the shredded cheese.

3. Preheat oven to 350°F. Scoop ⅓ cup to ½ cup of the beef mixture and spoon it in a 2"-wide line down the middle of a flour tortilla. Fold the bottom ¼ of the tortilla over the beef mixture. Wrap the right side of the tortilla halfway over the beef mixture (and the already folded bottom section). Wrap the left side of the tortilla over the right side. Carefully turn over the enchilada and place seam side down in the baking pan. Repeat until all the enchiladas are prepared and placed in the pan. Pour the remaining sauce mixture over the enchiladas. Top with the remaining cheese. Bake uncovered for 30 minutes.

The green peppers in this recipe double as serving bowls.

You can use instant rice to make ½ cup cooked rice if you like.

Stuffed Green Bell Peppers

What You Need

¼ cup uncooked rice

2 large green bell peppers

Water, as needed (about 2 quarts)

½ small white or yellow onion

¾ pound lean ground beef

1 (8-ounce) can tomato sauce

Salt and pepper, to taste

2 slices American cheese

What You Do

1. Cook rice according to package directions. Set aside.

2. Rinse the green bell peppers under cold, running water. Cut off the tops, remove the seeds, and carefully cut out the ribs from the inside of the pepper. Fill a 2-quart saucepan with water. Bring to a boil. Place the green peppers in the boiling water. Cover and cook for 5 minutes to soften. Drain.

3. While peppers are cooking, chop onion. Brown ground beef along with onion (see "How Do I Brown Ground Beef?" on page 111) in frying pan. Drain off fat. Stir in tomato sauce, cooked rice, salt, and pepper.

4. Preheat oven to 325°F. Place the green peppers open-side up in a 1-quart ovenproof baking pan that has been sprayed with nonstick cooking spray. Spoon ¼ of the beef mixture into each pepper. Top with one slice of cheese. Use a knife or your fingers to tear off any cheese that hangs over the edge of the pepper.

5. Add ¼ cup water to the bottom of the baking pan. Bake uncovered for 1 hour, or until the peppers are tender.

Meat Loaf

What You Need

¾ pound ground beef

3 slices white bread

2 tablespoons dried minced onion

½ teaspoon salt

⅛ teaspoon pepper

⅛ teaspoon dry mustard

⅛ teaspoon celery salt

⅛ teaspoon garlic salt

1½ teaspoons Worcestershire sauce

½ cup milk

1 egg

½ cup bottled barbecue sauce

What You Do

1. Preheat oven to 350°F. Use your hands to crumble ground beef into a mixing bowl. Tear bread and crusts into pieces about ½" to 1". Add to beef in the bowl. Sprinkle with onion, salt, pepper, dry mustard, celery salt, garlic salt, and Worcestershire sauce.

2. In a small mixing bowl, beat together the milk and egg until well blended. Pour over the beef mixture.

3. With your hands, squish together all ingredients until well blended. Form into a loaf shape. (Always wash your hands with soap and water after handling raw meat, especially raw ground meat.) Place in a shallow roasting pan that has been sprayed with nonstick cooking spray. Pour the barbecue sauce over the loaf. Bake for 1 hour. To serve, cut crosswise into slices about 1" thick.

Sour cream makes this creamy dish fit for a king—or a Russian baron.

Serve over fluffy cooked rice or egg noodles.

You can substitute ground beef for the round steak if you like.

Beef Stroganoff

What You Need

1 pound round steak or cubed stew beef

¼ medium-size white or yellow onion

¼ cup butter or margarine

⅛ teaspoon dried minced garlic

2 tablespoons all-purpose flour

¼–½ teaspoon salt, or to taste

¼ teaspoon pepper

1 pound fresh sliced mushrooms

1 (10½-ounce) can condensed cream of chicken soup

1 cup sour cream

1 tablespoon parsley flakes

What You Do

1. Cut the beef into 1" to 2" cubes. Set aside. Chop the onion. Melt the butter (or margarine) over medium heat. Stir in the onion. Cook until tender. Stir in the beef and garlic. Cook until the meat is browned, stirring often.

2. Stir in the flour, salt, and pepper until thickened. Reduce heat to low. Add the mushrooms and soup. Cook for 15 minutes, stirring often.

3. Stir in the sour cream. Remove from heat. Sprinkle with parsley flakes. Serve hot.

Shepherd's Pie

Although this recipe calls for beef, traditional Shepherd's Pie is made with lamb.

You can substitute cooked chopped lamb if you prefer.

Serve with Cold Mixed Veggies Salad (page 87) or cold sliced peaches.

What You Need

2½ pounds baking potatoes

Water, as needed

4 tablespoons butter, divided

1 cup milk

Salt and pepper, to taste

1 medium-size white or yellow onion

2 cloves fresh garlic (or ¼ teaspoon dried minced garlic)

1 tablespoon vegetable oil

1½ pounds ground beef

1 tablespoon all-purpose flour

½ cup beef broth

1 teaspoon dried thyme

1 teaspoon dried rosemary

Dash of nutmeg

What You Do

1. Boil and mash potatoes (see Mashed Potatoes on page 210) with 2 tablespoons of the butter, the milk, and salt and pepper. Set aside.

2. Chop the onion and mince the garlic. Pour the vegetable oil into a large frying pan over medium heat. Stir in the onion and garlic. Crumble the ground beef into the pan. Brown the meat (see "How Do I Brown Ground Beef?" on page 111). Drain off the fat.

Shepherd's Pie—*continued*

3. Stir in the flour. Continue stirring for 2 to 3 minutes to thicken. Stir in the beef broth, thyme, rosemary, and nutmeg. Season with salt and pepper, to taste. Reduce heat to low. Cook, uncovered, 15 minutes, stirring occasionally. Remove from heat.

4. Pour the mixture into a deep-dish pie pan or oven-proof baking dish that has been sprayed with non-stick cooking spray. Spread the mashed potatoes in an even layer over the mixture, covering it completely (as though you are frosting a cake). Cut the remaining 2 tablespoons butter into small pieces and place a few inches apart on top of the mashed potatoes. Bake for 35 minutes, until the mashed potatoes are lightly browned.

How Do I Choose Ground Beef?

Types of ground beef depend on the cut of meat ground. The more expensive the cut, the higher the price (unless it's on sale). For the best value, choose ground beef or ground chuck. Ground round and ground sirloin taste great, but may not be worth the extra expense. Still, lower-fat ground beef choices have greater value because less fat cooks out, leaving more meat. To kill bacteria that can cause illness, always cook ground meat until there is no tinge of pink inside. And wash your hands with soap and warm water after handling raw ground beef.

Pork Roast

*This recipe makes 2 servings per pound.

Applesauce is a traditional side dish with pork.

For different apple flavors, serve with Baked Apples (page 275) or Waldorf Salad (page 95).

What You Need

1 pork roast

Salt and pepper, to taste

Garlic salt, to taste (or seasoned salt)

What You Do

1. Preheat oven to 350°F. Rinse the meat under cold, running water. Place fat-side up in a roasting pan or ovenproof baking pan. (Always wash your hands with soap after handling raw meat.) Insert a meat thermometer into the thickest portion of the meat (optional). Sprinkle with salt, pepper, and garlic salt.

2. Roast according to the following times: loin or center cut roast, 35 to 40 minutes per pound; leg roast, 25 to 40 minutes per pound; shoulder roast, 35 to 40 minutes per pound; butt roast, 45 to 50 minutes per pound.

3. Check for doneness. The meat thermometer should read 185°F. If you don't use a meat thermometer, cut into the center of the roast and check color. Pork is done when there is no tinge of pink.

?

Which Cut of Pork Should I Roast?

You can roast loin end, center cut, leg, butt, and shoulder cuts of pork. However, center cut roasts have a bone running through the middle, which makes serving difficult. Boneless pork roasts are more expensive, but you'll have no waste. Roast all cuts at 350°F until a meat thermometer reads 185°F. Time varies according to cut. To kill any harmful bacteria, all cuts should be cooked until well done.

Sweet and tender, pork tenderloin makes a romantic entrée for your dinner date.

Serve with peas and applesauce.

Do not substitute white vinegar in this recipe.

Easy Pork Tenderloin

What You Need

2 tablespoons cider vinegar

¼ cup honey

2 tablespoons brown sugar

1 tablespoon prepared spicy whole-grain mustard

1-pound pork tenderloin

What You Do

1. Preheat oven to 425°F. In a large mixing bowl, stir together the vinegar, honey, brown sugar, and mustard until well blended.

2. Rinse the pork under cold, running water and place in a roasting pan. Pat dry with a paper towel. (Always wash your hands with soap after handling raw meat.) Pour the honey mixture over the pork. Roast for 25 minutes or until the juices run clear and the pork has no tinge of pink. If using a meat thermometer, it should read 185°F.

Pork Chops in Cherry Sauce

For easy preparation, make this dish in a slow cooker.

Because you are using a slow cooking method, you can substitute a less expensive cut of pork, like shoulder steak, with equally delicious results.

To serve, pour the remaining sauce into a serving bowl. Spoon the sauce over the meat.

What You Need

1 tablespoon vegetable oil

4 pork chops

Salt and pepper, to taste

⅔ cup canned cherry pie filling

1¼ teaspoons lemon juice

¼ teaspoon instant chicken bouillon granules

1/16 teaspoon ground mace

1 teaspoon dried parsley flakes

What You Do

1. Place the vegetable oil in a large frying pan over medium-high heat. Brown the pork chops on each side, but don't cook through. Remove from heat. Sprinkle with salt and pepper.

2. Place the cherry pie filling in a slow cooker. Stir in the lemon juice, bouillon granules, and mace until well mixed. Place the browned pork chops on top of the sauce. Cover and cook on low for 4 to 5 hours. To serve, place the pork chops on a serving plate. Spoon the sauce over. Sprinkle with parsley.

Polish Sausage & Kraut

What You Need

1 pound Polish sausage

1 (14-ounce) can sauerkraut, with liquid

¼ teaspoon caraway seed

1½ tablespoons white granulated sugar

1 tablespoon dried minced onion (or ¼ cup chopped fresh onion)

2 cups water

What You Do

1. Slice each sausage into 4 pieces of equal length. Place in a slow cooker or a large saucepan.

2. In a medium-size mixing bowl, stir together the sauerkraut, caraway seed, sugar, and onion. Place on top of the sausage. Add the water and cover.

3. In a slow cooker, cook on low for 3 to 4 hours. On the stovetop, cook over low heat for 1 hour.

Ham Fettuccine Casserole

What You Need

1 (12-ounce) package uncooked fettuccine

½ pound ham

3 tablespoons butter or margarine

2 tablespoons olive oil

¼ teaspoon dried minced garlic

1½ cups frozen broccoli florets

1 (14-ounce) can diced tomatoes, with juice

¼ teaspoon black pepper

Salt, to taste

¼ cup grated Romano cheese

What You Do

1. Cook fettuccine according to package instructions.

2. While the noodles are cooking, slice the ham into 2"- to 3"-long flat strips about the width of cooked fettuccine noodles.

3. Place the butter and olive oil in a large frying pan and heat over medium-high heat until the butter melts. Add the ham, garlic, and broccoli; sauté, stirring constantly, for about 5 minutes. Stir in the tomatoes and juice. Season with salt and pepper. Cook until the broccoli is tender but still firm.

4. Drain noodles when done. Add to the frying pan. Gently stir until all the ingredients are well mixed and heated through. Sprinkle with grated Romano cheese.

This makes a nice lunch or a light supper.

Serve with Fruit & Coconut Salad (page 80) or sliced tomatoes.

Ham & Asparagus Roll-Ups

What You Need

1 (15-ounce) can whole asparagus spears

4 slices packaged ham lunchmeat

½ (10¾-ounce) can condensed Cheddar cheese soup

2 tablespoons milk

1 teaspoon prepared mustard

⅛ teaspoon paprika

What You Do

1. Preheat oven to 350°F. Drain the asparagus. Divide the asparagus spears evenly among the ham slices. Place 3 or 4 spears near one edge on top of each slice of ham. Roll the ham over the asparagus. Place seam side down in an ovenproof baking pan that has been sprayed with nonstick cooking spray.

2. In a medium-size mixing bowl, stir together the soup, milk, and mustard. Pour the mixture over the ham. Sprinkle with paprika. Bake uncovered for 30 minutes, until heated through.

Ham Slice with Pineapple

LEVEL E

SERVINGS 2

If you have leftover cooked ham, you can use it in this recipe by reducing the cooking time to 30 minutes.

You can substitute 2 peeled and sliced tart apples (McIntosh, Granny Smith, or Jonathan varieties) and ¼ cup water or apple juice for the pineapple and juice in this recipe.

What You Need

1-pound uncooked ham slice

4 cloves

½ cup canned crushed pineapple, with juice

3 tablespoons brown sugar

What You Do

1. Place the ham in an ovenproof baking pan that has been sprayed with nonstick cooking spray. Stick the cloves into the ham several inches apart.

2. Spoon the pineapple and juice over the ham. Sprinkle with brown sugar.

3. Cover with aluminum foil (or a baking dish lid). Bake at 325°F for 1 hour and 15 minutes. Uncover and bake for 15 minutes more.

What Does Horseradish Go With?

Horseradish has a pungent flavor that can rival hot chili peppers in its ability to make your eyes water! So, you will use only a small amount at a time. Horseradish is often used as a condiment with ham, roast beef, and steak, as well as in Cocktail Sauce (see "How Can I Make My Own Easy Cocktail Sauce?" on page 169). Horseradish is the grated or shredded root of a plant that originated in Europe and western Asia. It is sold in a jar in the grocery store's refrigerated section.

Pork Chops with Rice

To serve, carefully remove the chops from the pan, maintaining the layered ingredients for a nice visual effect.

Top each pork chop with a sprig of parsley.

What You Need

4 pork chops

Salt and pepper, to taste

1 tablespoon vegetable oil

4 thin (about ⅛" thick) slices white or yellow onion

4 thin (about ⅛" thick) slices green bell pepper

¼ cup uncooked rice

1 (28-ounce) can whole peeled tomatoes

4 sprigs fresh parsley (a sprig is a little "branch")

What You Do

1. Sprinkle the pork chops with salt and pepper. In a frying pan, brown both sides in the vegetable oil over medium-high heat. Spray a 9" × 13" ovenproof baking pan or a roasting pan (large enough for all the pork chops to lie flat) with nonstick cooking spray. Place the pork chops in the bottom of the pan.

2. Place one slice of onion and one slice of green pepper on top of each pork chop. Spoon 1 tablespoon uncooked rice inside of each pepper ring, and place 1 whole tomato on top of the rice. Pour the juice from the tomatoes, along with any leftover tomatoes, around the sides of the pork chops.

3. Cover with baking pan lid or aluminum foil. Bake at 350°F for 1½ hours, until the meat is tender and has no tinge of pink.

Pork in Mushroom Sauce

Cook this dish in a slow cooker.

Serve with rice or Mashed Potatoes (page 210), a steamed green vegetable (see Appendix C), and Baked Apples (page 275).

To serve, remove the pork chops from the cooker.

Stir together the remaining liquid and use as gravy.

What You Need

4 pork chops or 2 pounds pork shoulder

1 medium-size white or yellow onion

½ cup canned sliced mushrooms (or stems and pieces)

1 can cream of mushroom soup

½ cup milk

Salt and pepper, to taste

What You Do

1. Place the pork chops in a slow cooker.

2. Slice the onion. Separate the rings. Add to the pot.

3. In a small mixing bowl, stir together the mushrooms, soup, and milk. Pour over the onions. Season with salt and pepper. Cover and cook for 4 to 5 hours on high or for 1 hour on high plus 6 to 8 hours on low.

 ## How Can I Make an Easy Gravy?

Our grandmothers learned to make gravy from their mothers. With years of practice, they made pretty good gravy. But, believe me, gravy is really difficult to make. It turns out too runny or too lumpy. It's easy to burn. And, it's not worth the trouble. So, take my advice. Buy jars of prepared gravy. Place in saucepan over medium heat until warm. Hide the empty jars.

Red Beans & Rice

You'll have to start the night before serving for this traditional dish from the Big Easy.

Choose your favorite sausage.

Serve with cooked rice, either on the side or mixed together with the beans.

You can substitute 2 (16-ounce) cans of red beans (drained), omit the overnight soaking, and reduce the cooking time until the onion and green bell pepper are just tender.

What You Need

1 (16-ounce) package dried small red beans

Water, as needed

1 medium-size white or yellow onion

½ green bell pepper

2 cloves garlic

½ pound sausage

Cayenne pepper, to taste

Salt and pepper, to taste

What You Do

1. Place the dried beans in a colander and rinse with cool, running water. Place the beans in a large mixing bowl or Dutch oven. Fill with enough cold water to cover the beans. Set aside for 8 hours or overnight (but not longer than 24 hours).

2. Drain the beans and rinse with cold water. Drain again. Place the beans in a Dutch oven or large pot.

3. Chop the onion, green bell pepper, and garlic. Add to the beans. Slice the sausage and add it to the beans. (If using ground sausage, crumble into the beans.) Cover the ingredients with water. Season with cayenne, salt, and pepper. Cover and cook over medium heat, stirring occasionally, until the beans are tender, about 1 to 1½ hours. During the cooking, add water as needed to keep all the ingredients simmering in thick gravy.

Pineapple Pork Chop Bake

Preparation for this delicious dish takes only minutes. The pork bakes slowly, simmering in apple and pineapple flavors. The result is tender, sweet meat you'll want to make again and again.

What You Need

2 tablespoons vegetable oil

4 pork chops

2 tablespoons all-purpose flour

1 apple

1 small onion

1 (8-ounce) can pineapple slices in juice

¾ cup water

1 chicken bouillon cube

Salt and pepper, to taste

What You Do

1. Heat the vegetable oil in a large frying pan over medium-high heat. Dust the pork chops with the flour. Cook in the hot oil for 3 minutes per side. Place the pork chops in an ovenproof baking pan that has been sprayed with nonstick cooking spray. Set aside.

2. Preheat oven to 350°F. Peel, core, and chop the apple. Chop the onion. Spoon the apple and onion over the pork chops. Arrange the pineapple slices in a layer on top. Reserve the pineapple juice.

3. In a small saucepan, stir together the juice from the canned pineapple, the water, and the bouillon cube. Heat on low until the cube dissolves. Pour over the pork chops. Sprinkle with salt and pepper. Cover with aluminum foil or baking dish lid. Bake for 45 minutes.

Pork Chops with Sweet Potatoes

This unusual dinner-in-a-dish with blended flavors goes well with simple sides like a tossed green salad or steamed green beans.

You can use either dark brown or light brown sugar in this recipe.

What You Need

1 pound fresh sweet potatoes

½ teaspoon salt

6 slices bacon

12 slices canned pineapple, divided

6 pork chops

6 tablespoons brown sugar, divided

What You Do

1. Rinse sweet potatoes in cold running water. Place whole in a sauce pan. Add the salt. Cover with water. Boil over high heat for 10 minutes.

2. Cut the bacon slices in half horizontally. Set aside.

3. Arrange 6 slices of pineapple in the bottom of a 9" × 13" × 2" ovenproof baking pan that has been sprayed with nonfat cooking spray. Place 1 pork chop on top of each slice. Top each pork chop with another pineapple slice.

4. Drain the sweet potatoes. Cool until comfortable to touch. Slice potatoes crosswise into circles about ¼" thick. Place one slice on top of each pineapple-pork chop-pineapple stack.

5. Sprinkle each stack with 1 tablespoon brown sugar.

6. Make an "X" on top of each stack with 2 halves of the bacon strips.

7. Bake 1 hour at 375° until pork shows no sign of pink and juices run clear.

Spaghetti with Ham Sauce

It might not be Italian, but for a new flavor, use ham instead of beef in your spaghetti sauce.

Serve with additional grated Parmesan cheese.

Remove the bay leaves before serving.

What You Need

4 cups precooked ham

2 medium white or yellow onions

½ cup parsley

1 stalk celery

¾ cup olive oil

4 cups canned tomato sauce

2 tablespoons grated Parmesan cheese

5 large bay leaves

4 cloves fresh garlic

½ (10-ounce) package uncooked thin spaghetti noodles

Water, as needed to boil spaghetti

What You Do

1. Cut the ham into ½" cubes. Chop the onions, parsley, and celery. Keep separate. Set aside.

3. Preheat the olive oil in a large cooking pot over medium heat for 3 minutes. Add the onions, stir about 2 minutes. Add the celery and parsley, stirring constantly for 8 to 10 minutes until the celery and onions are tender.

4. Add the ham and tomato sauce. Blend well. Cook for 10 minutes, stirring occasionally. Add the Parmesan cheese and bay leaves.

5. Finely chop the garlic. Add to the sauce. Reduce heat and simmer 45 minutes, stirring every 3 minutes. Remove from heat. Let stand while pasta cooks.

6. Fill a pot with water and bring to a boil. Add spaghetti noodles. Cook 8 minutes, until just tender. Drain. Place noodles on serving plates. Top with the sauce.

Chapter 6
Main Dishes—Poultry

Easy

Roast Chicken 146
Cranberry Chicken 147
Roast Turkey 148
Baked Lemon Chicken 149
Salsa Chicken 150
Chicken Breasts & Broccoli 151
Chicken & Stuffing Casserole 152
Chicken & Rice Casserole. 153
Marinated Grilled Chicken. 154
Baked Chicken Provolone. 155

Medium

Italian-Style Chicken Spaghetti. 156
Asian Fried Rice. 157
Bayou Chicken. 158
Six-Layer Casserole. 159
Spinach Chicken Lasagna. 160
Chicken and Ham Casserole 161
Slow-Cooked Garlic Chicken 162
Bow-Tie Chicken & Pasta 163

Hard

Mediterranean Chicken 164

Roast Chicken

Whole fryers often cost less than packaged chicken parts.

Cut leftovers into bite-size pieces and refrigerate or freeze for later use in salads or casseroles.

What You Need

1 whole fryer chicken

Salt, as needed (about ½ teaspoon)

Vegetable oil or solid vegetable shortening, as needed (about 1 teaspoon)

What You Do

1. Rinse the chicken under cold, running water. Pat dry with a paper towel. Use your fingers to rub salt on the inside of the neck and body cavities. Place in roasting pan or ovenproof baking pan, breast-side up. Fold the wings back and under the chicken for support.

2. With your fingers, a paper towel, or cooking brush, spread vegetable oil over the entire chicken. Insert a meat thermometer, if desired. (To prevent illness, always wash hands with soap and water after handling raw chicken. Also wash any utensils and surfaces that came in contact with raw chicken.) Roast the chicken in the oven at 375°F. For a 4-pound chicken, roast for about 1½ hours. Reduce or increase cooking time according to weight.

3. Test for doneness. When done, the juices should run clear and the drumstick should easily move in the joint. Protect your fingers with a paper towel or cloth and gently squeeze the large end of the drumstick. The meat should feel very soft. If using a meat thermometer, it should read 190°F.

Here's your chance to use that potato masher in your kitchen drawer. If you don't have a potato masher, use a table fork.

Cranberry Chicken

What You Need

1 prepackaged cut-up fryer chicken

1 (8-ounce) can whole-berry cranberry sauce

1 (1¼-ounce) package dry onion soup mix

What You Do

1. Rinse the chicken in cold, running water. Pat dry with a paper towel. Place the chicken in a roasting pan or a 9" × 13" ovenproof baking pan that has been sprayed with nonstick cooking spray. (Always wash hands with soap after handling raw chicken.)

2. In a small mixing bowl, mash the cranberry sauce. Stir in the onion soup and mix until well blended. Spoon over the chicken pieces. Cover with aluminum foil and bake at 350°F for 2 hours.

?

Why Should I Preheat the Oven?

For cooking times less than 1 hour, preheat the oven to ensure even heating. Turn the oven dial to preheat, and turn the temperature selector to the desired temperature. Electric ovens use both the top coil (the one used for broiling) and the bottom coil when set to preheat. Be sure to change the dial to bake before placing food in the oven. If you forget, the top of the food will heat too much. Some foods will be crusty, dry, or burned on top.

Roast Turkey

If you buy a frozen
turkey, thaw it in the
refrigerator for 24 to
48 hours. (Thawing
at room tempera-
ture encourages
growth of harmful
bacteria.) Rinse
under cold, running
water. Remove the
neck and package
of turkey innards
from both cavities.
You can discard
them or place them
in a saucepan and
simmer until tender
and cooked through.
Some people like to
chop them and add
them to stuffing mix
or gravy. Others feed
them to their pets.

Don't worry about
stuffing the turkey.
Instead, use stuffing
mix, cooked on a
stovetop according to
package directions.

Serve with Mashed
Potatoes (page 210),
canned gravy, and
cranberry sauce.

Use leftover turkey
as a substitute for
cooked chicken in
casserole recipes.

What You Need

1 turkey (any size)

1 tablespoon vegetable oil

1 teaspoon salt

What You Do

1. Pat the turkey dry with a paper towel. Place breast-side up in a large roasting pan (you can buy a disposable foil pan if you don't have a pan big enough). If you have a meat thermometer, insert it into the center of a thigh or breast. Be sure it doesn't touch bone, or it will register an inaccurate temperature.

2. Use your hands to spread vegetable oil all over the outside of the turkey. Sprinkle salt on your hand and rub it inside the neck and body cavities. Bend the wings up and under the turkey for support.

3. Roast the turkey at 325°F, checking it after 2 hours or so and every 30 minutes after that. Approximate turkey roasting times vary according to weight. Here are roasting times at 325°F:

8 to 12 pounds	4 to 4½ hours
12 to 16 pounds	4½ to 5½ hours
16 to 20 pounds	5½ to 7 hours
20 to 24 pounds	7 to 8½ hours

4. When the turkey is as brown as you like, make a tent with aluminum foil and place it loosely on top of the turkey so it won't brown further. The turkey is done when the meat thermometer reads 190°F, or when the drumstick easily twists out of the joint. If you buy a turkey with a built-in timer, roast until the timer pops up. Let the cooked turkey sit about 20 minutes before carving.

Citrus brings out the flavor of this baked chicken dish that's easy and delicious.

Serve with warm rice, if you like.

Baked Lemon Chicken

What You Need

4 boneless, skinless chicken breast halves

½ cup butter or margarine

¼ cup, plus 2 tablespoons lemon juice

1 teaspoon garlic powder

1 teaspoon poultry seasoning

½ teaspoon salt

½ teaspoon pepper

What You Do

1. Rinse the chicken in cold, running water. Place in an ovenproof baking pan that has been lightly greased with solid shortening or sprayed with non-stick cooking spray.

2. Preheat oven to 350°F. Melt the butter (or margarine) in a small saucepan or frying pan. Pour into a medium-size mixing bowl. Stir in the lemon juice, garlic powder, poultry seasoning, salt, and pepper until well blended. Pour over the chicken. Cover the pan with aluminum foil or a baking pan lid. Bake for 1 hour. While the chicken is cooking, frequently spoon sauce from the bottom of the pan over the chicken.

?

How Do I Prevent Salmonella Poisoning?

To avoid salmonella poisoning, always wash your hands with soap and warm water after handling raw chicken and turkey. Also wash all dishes, utensils, and surfaces that touched the raw poultry. Take along sanitary hand wipes to picnics or tailgate parties. Use before and after touching the chicken.

LEVEL **E**

SERVINGS **2**

Olé! Here's an easy, spicy chicken dish.

Parmesan cheese adds extra zing, even though it's usually used in Italian-style dishes.

Salsa Chicken

What You Need

2 skinless, boneless chicken breasts

1 cup salsa

¼ cup grated Parmesan cheese

What You Do

1. Preheat oven to 350°F. Spray a 2-quart ovenproof baking pan with nonstick cooking spray. Cut the chicken breasts in half lengthwise. Place side-by-side in the baking pan.

2. Pour the salsa over the chicken. Top with Parmesan cheese.

3. Cover and bake for 30 minutes. Uncover and bake for another 10 minutes.

?

How Can I Save Money When I Buy Chicken?

You can purchase packaged chicken according to your preferred pieces. Or, you can purchase a whole fryer and cut it yourself at a lower price per pound. Cut into 2 wings, 2 breasts, 2 thighs, and 2 drumsticks or leave wings attached to breasts and legs attached to thighs, depending on your preferences and cooking method. Use kitchen scissors and cut pieces apart at the joints. Wash hands, surfaces, and scissors with soap and warm water after handling raw chicken.

Chicken Breasts & Broccoli

This makes an elegant entrée when prepared with whole chicken breasts and whole broccoli spears.

You can also make this as a casserole with frozen chopped broccoli and cooked chicken or turkey cut into bite-size pieces.

Serve with chilled canned whole spiced peaches placed on a piece of leaf lettuce.

What You Need

1 (16-ounce) package frozen broccoli spears

4 skinless chicken breasts

2 (10½-ounce) cans condensed cream of chicken soup

½ teaspoon curry powder

¼ teaspoon paprika

What You Do

1. Spray a 10" × 13" ovenproof baking pan with non-stick cooking spray. Boil the broccoli for 5 minutes only. Drain.

2. Line the bottom of the prepared pan with the broccoli spears, alternating floret-side up and stem-side up, so the broccoli fits closely together. Arrange the chicken breasts on top of the broccoli.

3. Preheat oven to 350°F. In a small mixing bowl, stir together undiluted soup and curry powder. Pour over the chicken and broccoli. Lightly sprinkle with paprika. Bake uncovered for 40 to 45 minutes. Or, microwave on high for about 6 to 8 minutes until the chicken is tender and the juices run clear.

Chicken & Stuffing Casserole

This meal-in-a-dish provides meat, bread, and dairy products.

All you need is a green vegetable or chilled canned fruit to complete the meal.

What You Need

4 boneless, skinless chicken breast halves

4 slices Swiss cheese

1⅓ cups herb-seasoned stuffing mix

1 (10½-ounce) can cream of chicken soup

1 soup can water

What You Do

1. Preheat oven to 350°F. Rinse the chicken under cold, running water. Pat dry with a paper towel. Place in an ovenproof baking pan that has been sprayed with nonstick cooking spray. (Always wash your hands with soap after handling raw chicken.)

2. Place a slice of cheese on each piece of chicken. Sprinkle the dry stuffing mix on top of the cheese.

3. In a small mixing bowl, stir together the soup and water until well blended. Pour over the stuffing mix. Bake uncovered for 45 to 50 minutes.

Chicken & Rice Casserole

Serve with chilled canned spiced peaches and frozen peas cooked according to package directions.

If you have leftover mushrooms from another recipe, toss them in before heating.

What You Need

2 cups uncooked rice

2 cups cooked chicken (see below)

1 stalk celery

1 (10½-ounce) can cream of mushroom soup

½ soup can milk

What You Do

1. Cook the rice according to package directions. While the rice is cooking, chop the celery and cut the cooked chicken into bite-size pieces.

2. Preheat oven to 350°F. Place the rice, chicken, and celery in a 2-quart ovenproof or microwave-safe baking pan. Stir in the mushroom soup and milk. Cover and bake for 30 minutes, or cover and microwave on high for 5 minutes, until heated through.

?

How Should I Save Cooked Chicken for Other Recipes?

To cook chicken to use later in casseroles or salads, rinse the chicken under cold, running water. Place in an ovenproof baking pan that has been sprayed with nonstick cooking spray. Sprinkle with salt and pepper. Put a pat of butter or margarine on each piece of chicken. Cover with baking pan lid or aluminum foil. Bake at 350°F for 1 hour or until the chicken is tender and the juices run clear. Remove from the oven and let cool. Remove skin. Cut away the meat from the bones into bite-size pieces. Separate into 1- or 2-cup servings. Cover and refrigerate or freeze until needed. (Always wash your hands with soap after handling raw chicken.) About 3 pounds of chicken breasts or thighs yields 4 to 5 cups).

Marinated Grilled Chicken

You can marinate the raw chicken while you're waiting for the charcoal fire.

Or, you can marinate as long as overnight before cooking.

You can use the leftover marinade during cooking, but to kill bacteria associated with raw chicken, boil the marinade after removing the chicken.

What You Need

¼ cup bottled Italian salad dressing

¼ cup olive oil

2 teaspoons lemon juice

4 skinless, boneless chicken breasts

What You Do

1. In a small mixing bowl, stir together the salad dressing, olive oil, and lemon juice. Pour into a shallow baking pan large enough to hold the chicken.

2. Rinse chicken in cold, running water. Place chicken in the marinade. Cover and refrigerate for at least 30 minutes (turn once after about 15 minutes). Remove chicken from marinade and place on a plate until ready to grill.

3. Bring the remaining marinade to a boil in a saucepan over medium-high heat to kill bacteria from the raw chicken. Wash hands with soap and water.

? What Is a Meat Marinade?

Marinating is soaking meat, fish, poultry, or vegetables in a marinade, a mixture of vinegar or lemon juice, oil, herbs, and other ingredients. A marinade adds flavor before grilling, but contrary to widely held belief, it does nothing to tenderize meat. Be sure to marinate foods in the refrigerator to keep bacteria from forming. Also, if you marinate raw chicken or fish, be sure to bring the marinade to a boil before you reuse or serve it. You can marinate either by letting food sit in the marinade mixture for one-half the allotted time, then turning to the other side, or by pouring the marinade over the food to coat it, then letting it sit. Marinate foods—except for all kinds of fish—for anywhere from 30 minutes to all day, or even overnight. Limit marinating fish, including shellfish, to 1 hour, because acid (such as that in lemon juice) begins to "cook" the fish after that time.

Baked Chicken Provolone

This chicken has an Italian accent, so serve it with Italian Zucchini (see page 212) and a tossed salad with Italian vinaigrette dressing.

You'll need two pie pans to prepare this recipe.

What You Need

1–2 tablespoons olive oil

1 cup Italian flavored bread crumbs

4 to 6 skinless, boneless chicken breasts

4 to 6 slices Provolone cheese (1 for each breast)

1 jar spaghetti sauce, warmed

What You Do

1. Preheat oven to 375°F. Spray a 9" × 12" baking pan with nonstick cooking spray.

2. Pour the olive oil into one pie pan. Place the bread crumbs in another. Dip each chicken breast in the oil and then in the crumbs. Arrange in the bottom of the baking pan.

3. Bake for 40 to 45 minutes or until the chicken is tender. Remove from oven, and place one slice of Provolone on each chicken breast. Return to the oven and bake 5 minutes more until cheese melts.

4. While the cheese is melting, pour the spaghetti sauce into a medium saucepan over medium heat. Stir occasionally until warmed through. To serve, spoon warm sauce over the chicken breasts.

Italian-Style Chicken Spaghetti

This is not your mama's Italian spaghetti, but it's sure to become a new favorite.

For quicker preparation, use precooked chicken (see "How Should I Save Cooked Chicken for Other Recipes?" on page 153).

To prevent illness, always wash your hands with soap after handling raw chicken. Also wash all utensils and surfaces that touched the raw chicken.

What You Need

¾ pound uncooked chicken

¾ cup bottled Italian salad dressing, divided

½ cup fresh or frozen cauliflower florets

½ cup fresh or frozen cut carrots

½ cup fresh or frozen cut asparagus (not whole spears)

Water, as needed (about 2 quarts)

½ (10-ounce) package thin spaghetti or angel hair pasta

What You Do

1. Cut the chicken into thin strips about ½" wide and 2" long. Place in a large frying pan with ¼ cup of the salad dressing. Cook over medium-high heat, stirring constantly until the chicken slightly browns.

2. Reduce heat to low. Stir in the cauliflower, carrots, and asparagus. Pour in the remaining ½ cup salad dressing. Cover and cook over low heat for 7 to 9 minutes. Stir often until the vegetables are tender but still firm.

3. While the vegetables are cooking, bring 2 quarts water to a boil in a Dutch oven or stew pot. Break pasta into thirds and cook according to package directions (about 10 minutes) until tender but still firm. Drain. Stir into chicken and vegetable mixture.

?

How Should I Thaw Frozen Meat and Poultry?

Thaw frozen meat and poultry in the refrigerator to avoid bacteria growth. You can also thaw meat in the microwave on the "defrost" setting. Underestimate defrosting time so the meat doesn't start to cook. You can always zap it again if not completely thawed. Once you have defrosted meat, never refreeze it.

Asian Fried Rice

What You Need

1½ cups uncooked rice

½ pound raw chicken, pork, or beef

1 large white or yellow onion

¼ cup vegetable oil

½ teaspoon dried minced garlic

1 tablespoon soy sauce

1 teaspoon salt

½ teaspoon pepper

1 teaspoon white granulated sugar

1 cup frozen or leftover vegetables (type of your choice)

2 eggs

What You Do

1. Cook rice according to package directions. Set aside.

2. Cut the meat into 1" cubes. Chop the onion.

3. Heat the oil in large frying pan over medium heat. Add the meat, onion, minced garlic, soy sauce, salt, pepper, and sugar. Cook, stirring frequently, until the meat is done.

4. Reduce heat to low. Stir in the rice and vegetables. Heat until warm. Just before serving, beat eggs in a small mixing bowl. Stir into the mixture until the eggs are cooked.

Traditional Cajun spices perk up ordinary chicken and transport you to the French Quarter in New Orleans.

Serve for Mardi Gras, or anytime.

Bayou Chicken

What You Need

2 teaspoons paprika

2 teaspoons cayenne pepper or chili powder

1 teaspoon onion powder

¾ teaspoon garlic powder

¼ teaspoon ground cumin

Salt and pepper, to taste

½ cup milk

3 tablespoons butter

3 skinless, boneless chicken breasts

What You Do

1. In a medium-size mixing bowl, stir together the paprika, cayenne pepper (or chili powder), onion powder, garlic powder, cumin, salt, and pepper.

2. Pour the milk into a small mixing bowl.

3. Melt the butter in a large frying pan over medium heat. Rinse the chicken under cold, running water. Dip the chicken into the milk to coat. Place in the melted butter. Sprinkle the chicken with ½ of the spice mixture.

4. Place chicken in frying pan. Cover and cook for 10 minutes. Uncover and sprinkle with the remaining spice mixture. Cook uncovered for 20 to 25 minutes more, until the juices run clear.

Six-Layer Casserole

Use ground beef or ground turkey in this delicious dinner in a dish that also has yellow vegetables.

Serve with something dark green: broccoli, asparagus, or spinach.

What You Need

1½ pounds ground beef or turkey

Salt and pepper, to taste

2 medium potatoes

2 medium onions

½ cup uncooked rice

2 stalks celery

3 medium carrots

2 cups chicken broth

What You Do

1. Brown the ground beef or turkey in a frying pan until beef is medium-rare. Drain excess fat. Set aside.

2. Preheat the oven to 350°. Rinse the potatoes. Peel and slice them and arrange them in the bottom of an ovenproof baking pan that has been sprayed with nonstick cooking oil. Lightly sprinkle with salt and pepper.

3. Peel and slice the onions. Layer the onion on top of the potatoes. Lightly sprinkle with salt and pepper.

4. Pour the beef or turkey on top of the onions. Sprinkle the uncooked rice over the meat. Lightly sprinkle with salt and pepper.

5. Rinse the carrots and celery under cold, running water. Peel and slice crosswise. Spread on top of the rice.

6. Pour the broth over the entire casserole. Cover and bake for 40 to 45 minutes or until rice is cooked and the potatoes and onions are tender. Remove from oven, and let stand 10 minutes before serving.

Spinach Chicken Lasagna

Easy, creamy, and yummy, this makes a good potluck dish or an entrée for company.

What You Need

1 (10-ounce) package frozen chopped spinach

2 (10¾-ounce) cans cream of chicken soup

1 (9-ounce) package diced cooked chicken (or 3 breasts, cut up)

1 cup low-fat milk

1 (8-ounce) carton sour cream

½ cup grated Parmesan

⅓ cup chopped onion

½ teaspoon salt

¼ teaspoon pepper

⅛ teaspoon nutmeg

9 uncooked lasagna noodles

1 cup shredded mozzarella

What You Do

1. Line a colander with a paper towel. Place the frozen spinach on the towel to thaw. When thawed, place another paper towel on top and press excess liquid out of the spinach. Place the spinach in a large mixing bowl.

2. Add the cream of chicken soup, cooked chicken, milk, sour cream, Parmesan, onion, salt, pepper, and nutmeg.

3. Spray slow cooker with cooking spray. Place 3 lasagna noodles in the bottom of the cooker. Spoon ⅓ of the chicken mixture on top. Sprinkle with ⅓ of the mozzarella. Repeat layers.

4. Cook on high for 1 hour. Reduce heat to low for 5 hours more.

This is a delicious use of leftover chicken and ham. You can use ham steak, ham lunchmeat slices, or turkey ham, which is less expensive than "real" ham. Serve with chilled canned spiced peaches and dinner rolls.

Chicken and Ham Casserole

What You Need

1 cup cooked chicken

1 cup cooked ham

1 (10½-ounce) can condensed cream of chicken soup

½ cup milk

4 slices Swiss cheese

2 teaspoons dried parsley flakes

What You Do

1. Preheat oven to 350°F. Spray a 2-quart ovenproof baking pan with nonstick cooking spray. Cut chicken and ham into bite-size pieces and place in the pan.

2. In a small mixing bowl, stir together soup and milk until well blended. Pour over chicken and ham. Top with Swiss cheese. Sprinkle parsley flakes over the cheese.

3. Bake for 30 minutes until cheese melts. Or, microwave for 3 to 5 minutes on high until cheese melts.

Slow-Cooked Garlic Chicken

What You Need

1 large onion

3 pounds chicken pieces

1 teaspoon salt

1 teaspoon paprika

½ teaspoon pepper

1 teaspoon olive oil

1 medium whole bulb garlic

What You Do

1. Slice the onion and place in a slow cooker lightly coated with cooking spray.

2. Rinse chicken pieces in cold, running water. Place on top of the onion.

3. In a small mixing bowl, blend the salt, paprika, pepper, and olive oil. The mixture will be thick. Spread onto the chicken pieces.

4. Separate the garlic into cloves. Leave on the peel. Add to the cooker under and on top of the chicken. Cover and cook 7 hours on low or 3½ hours on high until juices run clear.

Bow-Tie Chicken & Pasta

All dressed up in formalwear, this casserole is good enough for company.

For an everyday dinner, you can substitute shells or macaroni elbows for the bow-tie pasta.

What You Need

1 pound skinless, boneless chicken

1 tablespoon vegetable oil

1 onion

1½ cups fresh mushrooms

1 (19-ounce) can stewed tomatoes, with liquid

1 cup water

1 teaspoon dried basil

2 cups uncooked bow-tie pasta

Salt and pepper, to taste

What You Do

1. Cut the chicken into ½" cubes. Heat the oil in a large frying pan over medium-high heat. Add the chicken and cook, stirring constantly until juices run clear (about 5 to 7 minutes). Use a slotted spoon to transfer the chicken to a plate or bowl. Set aside.

2. Chop the onion. Slice the mushrooms. Add both to the hot oil in the pan. Reduce the heat to medium. Cook the vegetables, gently stirring, for about 4 to 5 minutes until tender.

3. Add the tomatoes, water, basil, and bow-tie pasta, and mix well. Cover. Reduce heat to low. Cook 8 to 10 minutes, stirring occasionally, until pasta is done.

4. Add the chicken. Sprinkle with salt and pepper. Stir ingredients to mix well. Cook uncovered another 5 minutes or until ingredients are heated through. While the chicken is cooking, wash hands and any utensils that touched raw chicken with warm, soapy water.

You can substitute 4 lamb chops for the chicken in this recipe.

Mediterranean Chicken

What You Need

1 small white or yellow onion

1 red bell pepper

2 skinless, boneless chicken breasts

1 tablespoon olive oil

1 (14½-ounce) can whole peeled tomatoes

⅛ teaspoon dried minced garlic

3 tablespoons fresh chopped basil

2 tablespoons chopped black olives

What You Do

1. Thinly slice the onion and red bell pepper. Set aside.

2. In a large frying pan, cook the chicken in olive oil over medium-high heat until golden brown on each side. Reduce heat to low.

3. Add the onion and pepper. Cook for about 3 minutes, until tender. Add the tomatoes, garlic, and basil. Cook uncovered for 20 minutes until the chicken is tender and the juices run clear. Stir in the olives and serve.

Chapter 7

Main Dishes—Seafood

Easy

Tuna Noodle Casserole 166
Breaded Oven-Baked Fish. 167
Orange Roughy Picante. 168
Hot Boiled Shrimp. 169
Broiled Salmon 170
Baked Cod 171

Medium

Shrimp Pesto Pasta 172
Baked Tuna Loaf 173
Crabmeat Casserole 174
Haddock with Rice Casserole. 175
Garlicky Pasta with Shrimp 176
Crab Tetrazzini 178
Tuna Chow Mein 179
Hot & Spicy Salsa Shrimp 180
Tuna Tomato Pasta 181
Linguine & Clam Sauce 182
Tuna Burgers 183

Hard

Broiled Orange Roughy. 184
Salmon Patties. 185
Jambalaya. 186

Quick, cheap, easy—and good. What more can you ask for? Serve with cooked frozen peas and Fruit & Coconut Salad (page 80).

Tuna Noodle Casserole

What You Need

2 eggs

1 stalk celery

2 cups egg noodles

1 (6-ounce) can tuna

1 (10½-ounce) can condensed cream of mushroom soup

½ soup can milk

4 slices American or Cheddar cheese

What You Do

1. Hard-boil the eggs (see Boiled Egg on page 8). Let cool. Peel and chop. Rinse the celery under cold, running water. Chop. Set aside.

2. Cook the noodles according to package directions. Drain. Place in a 2-quart ovenproof or microwave-safe baking pan that has been sprayed with non-stick cooking spray. Preheat oven to 350°F. Drain the tuna. Flake with a fork and add to the noodles. Gently stir in the mushroom soup and milk until well blended. Stir in the celery and eggs. Top with the cheese. Cover and bake for 30 minutes. Or, cover and microwave on high for 5 minutes.

You can use your favorite fish. Sole, catfish, and halibut work well in this recipe.

Breaded Oven-Baked Fish

What You Need

2 cups milk

1 tablespoon, plus 1 teaspoon salt

1½ pounds fish fillets (sole, catfish, halibut, or other)

1 cup bread crumbs or cornmeal

½ cup butter (1 stick)

1 tablespoon lemon juice

What You Do

1. In a large mixing bowl, stir together the milk and 1 tablespoon salt. Soak the fish in the salted milk for 10 minutes.

2. Preheat oven to 350°F. Place the bread crumbs (or cornmeal) in a medium-size mixing bowl. Drag both sides of the milk-soaked fillets through the bread crumbs so they stick to the fillet. Place the fish in a greased 9" × 13" baking pan.

3. Melt the butter and use a spoon to drizzle a few drops at a time over the fish. Sprinkle with lemon juice and about 1 teaspoon salt. Bake uncovered for 20 minutes or until the fish flakes easily with a fork.

Orange Roughy Picante

This tasty fish with a Southwestern flair makes an attractive, easy-to-prepare main course.

You can substitute any other white fish fillet.

You can substitute bottled salsa for the picante sauce.

For a nice color contrast, serve with steamed green beans or steamed broccoli (see Appendix C).

What You Need

2 orange roughy fillets (about ½ pound each)

½ cup bottled picante sauce

1 cup shredded Cheddar cheese

What You Do

1. Preheat oven to 350°F. Spray an ovenproof baking pan with nonstick cooking spray. Place the fillets on the bottom of the pan. Cover each fillet with ½ of the picante sauce. Top with shredded cheese.

2. Bake uncovered for 20 minutes or microwave on high for 3 to 4 minutes until the cheese melts and the fish flakes easily.

Shrimp is expensive, but it's quick and easy to fix.

Serve with baked potatoes (see "How Do I Bake a Potato?" on page 109), a salad, French bread (see "How Do I Prepare French Bread," page 114), and bottled cocktail sauce (or homemade—see below).

Cut a whole fresh lemon into wedges and place on serving plates.

?

Hot Boiled Shrimp

What You Need

1 quart water

½ (3-ounce) package shrimp and crab boil spices (1 bag)

1 tablespoon salt

¼ cup lemon juice

2 pounds uncooked shrimp in the shell

What You Do

1. Pour the water into a Dutch oven. Add the boil spices, salt, and lemon juice. Bring to a boil over high heat.

2. Place the shrimp in a colander and rinse under cold, running water. Add to the boiling water. Bring back to a boil. Cook for 3 to 5 minutes. Test 1 shrimp for tenderness after the first 3 minutes. Continue to test 1 shrimp every minute until pink and tender. Drain. Serve hot in the shell, or let cool and chill in the refrigerator for about 1 hour to serve cold.

How Can I Make My Own Easy Cocktail Sauce?

If bottled cocktail sauce is too spicy or too mild, make your own. Pour contents of 1 bottle chili sauce into a small mixing bowl. Stir in 1 teaspoon lemon juice. Stir in horseradish (from a jar) ½ teaspoon at a time, to taste. Look for horseradish in a refrigerated section of the store. Chill at least 1 hour to let flavors blend. This sauce goes well with crab, shrimp, and fish. Store leftover sauce in the chili sauce bottle in the refrigerator.

Broiled Salmon

Fresh herbs give salmon a delicate flavor. For a different taste, substitute fresh thyme for the dill weed.

Choose salmon steaks or ½ of a whole salmon.

Garnish with sliced fresh lemon.

If you use olive oil, you don't have to heat it first.

Serve with Cheesy Asparagus (page 213) and a baked potato (see "How Do I Bake a Potato?" on page 109).

?

What You Need

¼ cup butter or olive oil

2 pounds salmon fillets

Salt and pepper, to taste

1 tablespoon lemon juice

½ (¾-ounce) package fresh prewashed dill weed (or dried dill weed, as needed)

What You Do

1. Melt the butter in a saucepan over low heat.

2. Preheat the broiler. Place the salmon skin-side down on the rack of a shallow broiling pan that has been sprayed with nonstick cooking spray. Drizzle the butter over the salmon. Sprinkle with lemon juice, salt, and pepper.

3. Lay sprigs of fresh dill weed diagonal to the length of the fish, evenly spaced about 1½" apart. (Or, lightly sprinkle with dried dill.)

4. Broil for 6 to 10 minutes. Test for doneness. The salmon should be opaque and flake easily with a fork.

Why Serve Lemon with Fish?

Many people like to squeeze fresh lemon juice from a lemon wedge (about ¼ of a lemon, cut lengthwise) to add flavor according to their own taste as they dine. So, if you're serving seafood, make lemon wedges available. However, flavor is only one reason to use lemon juice with fish. It also helps remove the fishy smell from your hands after preparing or eating "hands-on" dishes like shrimp and crab legs.

Baked Cod

Here's a quick-fix recipe you can serve in minutes.

If you can't find cod, you can substitute any white fish in this recipe.

What You Need

4 cod fillets

1 large white or yellow onion

2 tablespoons butter or margarine

2 tomatoes

What You Do

1. Preheat oven to 400°F. Place the fillets in an oven-proof baking pan that has been sprayed with non-stick cooking spray.

2. Slice the onion. Layer the slices over the fish. Melt the butter (or margarine) in a saucepan or small frying pan over low heat. Pour over the fish and onion. Bake uncovered for 20 minutes.

3. While the fish is cooking, rinse the tomatoes in cold, running water. Slice the tomatoes. When the fish is done, remove from oven. Layer the tomato slices on top.

4. Return to the oven and bake for 10 minutes more.

Shrimp Pesto Pasta

Even though shrimp can be expensive, this recipe calls for a small enough amount to be affordable and still contribute its seafood flavor.

Look for basil pesto sauce in the dairy section of the grocery store, or make your own (see Pesto on page 217).

What You Need

½ pound raw tiger shrimp

8 ounces uncooked bow-tie pasta

2 tablespoons olive oil

½ (7-ounce) package basil pesto sauce or ¼ cup homemade pesto (see page 217)

Grated Parmesan cheese, as needed

What You Do

1. Rinse the shrimp in cold, running water. Peel off the shells. Remove the veins from the outer edge of the shrimp backs.

2. Cook the pasta according to package directions (boil for about 11 minutes).

3. While the pasta is cooking, cook the shrimp in the olive oil in a frying pan over medium-high heat, stirring constantly to keep them from sticking. Cook for 5 to 8 minutes, until the shrimp just turns pink. (Be careful not to overcook the shrimp, or it will become rubbery.)

4. Drain the pasta and return it to the pot. Stir in the pesto sauce. Spoon the pasta onto serving plates. Top with shrimp. Sprinkle with grated Parmesan cheese. Serve immediately.

Baked Tuna Loaf

Take a break from tuna salad with a tuna dish served warm.

Serve with Chilled Pea Salad (page 97) or sliced fresh tomatoes and a steamed green vegetable (see Appendix C).

What You Need

Shortening or vegetable oil, as needed

1 (12-ounce) can tuna

1 stalk celery

3 cups unseasoned bread crumbs

1 egg

1 tablespoon dried minced onion

1 teaspoon salt

¼ teaspoon pepper

½ (7-ounce) can mushroom stems and pieces

1 (10½-ounce) can condensed cream of chicken soup

What You Do

1. Preheat oven to 375°F. Use a paper towel and solid shortening (or vegetable oil) to grease a shallow ovenproof 9" × 13" baking pan. Set aside.

2. Drain the tuna. Use a fork to flake the tuna into a large mixing bowl.

3. Chop the celery. Add to the tuna along with the bread crumbs, egg, onion, salt, and pepper.

4. Use your hands to squish together all the ingredients, until well blended. Form into a loaf shape. Place in the prepared baking pan.

5. Drain the mushrooms and place in a small mixing bowl. Stir in the soup (do not dilute). Pour over the tuna loaf. Bake uncovered for 30 minutes.

Crabmeat Casserole

Here's an economical casserole that provides the flavor of crabmeat without the expense and without the effort of removing the shell.

Serve with Cucumber Salad (page 85), Cold Mixed Veggies Salad (page 87), or a steamed green vegetable (see Appendix C).

What You Need

½ cup milk

¾ cup bread crumbs, plus extra for sprinkling over the top

2 (4½-ounce) cans cooked crabmeat (or 8 ounces imitation crab)

3 hard-boiled eggs (see Boiled Egg on page 8)

¾ teaspoon salt

⅛ teaspoon dry mustard

Dash cayenne pepper

3 tablespoons butter

Shortening, vegetable oil, or nonstick cooking spray, as needed

What You Do

1. In a large mixing bowl, stir together the milk and bread crumbs. Drain the crabmeat (if using canned) or chop the imitation crab. Add to the bowl.

2. Peel the hard-boiled eggs. Cut the eggs in half lengthwise and separate the whites and yolks. Chop whites into small pieces. Add to bowl.

3. Preheat oven to 450°F. Place the egg yolks on a saucer or in a separate small bowl. Mash with a fork. Add to the crab mixture along with salt, dry mustard, and cayenne pepper.

4. Melt the butter. Drizzle the butter over the ingredients in the bowl. Gently stir the ingredients together until well mixed.

5. Pour mixture into a greased baking dish. Top with bread crumbs. Bake uncovered for 15 minutes, until heated through.

LEVEL **M**

SERVINGS **4**

Haddock with Rice Casserole

The smoked flavor of this dish makes it a favorite example of Scottish cuisine.

Serve with sliced tomatoes and a steamed green vegetable (see Appendix C).

What You Need

½ pound smoked haddock fillets

1 cup uncooked rice

1 hard-boiled egg (see Boiled Egg on page 8)

2 tablespoons butter or margarine

2 tablespoons lemon juice

2 teaspoons dried parsley flakes

Salt and pepper, to taste

What You Do

1. Preheat oven to 400°F. Place the fillets in an oven-proof baking pan that has been sprayed with non-stick cooking spray. Bake uncovered for 25 minutes. Remove from oven.

2. While the fish is cooking, prepare the rice by cooking it according to package directions.

3. When the fish is done, flake it with a fork. (Remove the skin if present.) Peel and crumble the hard-boiled egg. In a large frying pan, melt the butter (or margarine) over low heat. Add the fish. Cook for 3 minutes, stirring to reheat the fish evenly. Stir in the cooked rice, egg, lemon juice, parsley flakes, salt, and pepper. Serve immediately.

Garlicky Pasta with Shrimp

This simple and delicious pasta has tons of variations. Use your imagination (or whatever leftovers you have in your fridge) to make this quick pasta dish.

You can use fresh or frozen cooked or raw shrimp in this recipe. If precooked, thaw first. If raw, thaw and cook in 1 tablespoon of olive oil over medium-high heat just until almost tender. (It will cook more when combined with the other ingredients.)

Cremini or button mushrooms are both good choices to use in this recipe.

What You Need

16 large precooked shrimp (thaw if frozen)

2 fresh plum or Roma tomatoes

1 red bell pepper

½ cup fresh spinach or frozen chopped spinach (thawed)

½ medium-size white or yellow onion

2 cloves fresh garlic (or ¼ teaspoon dried minced garlic)

2 tablespoons olive oil

½ (8-ounce) package fresh sliced mushrooms

8 ounces uncooked penne rigate pasta

1 tablespoon lemon juice

Salt and pepper, to taste

1 to 2 tablespoons grated Parmesan or Romano cheese

What You Do

1. Remove the shells, tails, and veins from the shrimp, if necessary. Rinse the tomatoes and pepper under cold water. Remove the seeds and inner ribs from the pepper. Chop the tomatoes, bell pepper, and spinach. Set aside. Chop the onion and mince the garlic by chopping the cloves into very small pieces.

Garlicky Pasta with Shrimp—*continued*

If you're using dried minced garlic, add it later with the rest of the vegetables instead.

2. Pour the olive oil into a large frying pan over medium-high heat. Stir in the onion and fresh garlic and cook for 1 minute, stirring constantly. (If you're using dried minced garlic, add it later with the rest of the vegetables instead.) Reduce heat to medium. Add the tomatoes, bell pepper, and mushrooms. Cook the vegetables, stirring constantly, until they are tender but still firm.

3. Cook the pasta according to package directions until tender but still firm. Drain and rinse immediately with cold water. Stir into the vegetable mixture along with the shrimp and spinach. Use two table forks to toss until well mixed.

4. Add the lemon juice, salt, and pepper. Stir until heated through. Sprinkle with cheese.

Crab Tetrazzini

There's nothing like the sweet taste of crabmeat to turn everyone into a seafood lover.

Serve with cold spiced peaches and steamed green beans (see Appendix C).

Add ½ cup water or milk to the leftover tomato soup and serve for lunch.

What You Need

½ (10-ounce) package spaghetti noodles

Shortening, vegetable oil, or nonstick cooking spray, as needed

½ small white or yellow onion

1 tablespoon butter or margarine

¼ pound fresh sliced mushrooms

½ (10¾-ounce) can condensed tomato soup

¾ cup crabmeat or imitation crab

1 cup tomato juice

Salt and pepper, to taste

1 cup shredded sharp Cheddar cheese

What You Do

1. Break the spaghetti into thirds and cook according to package directions. Drain. Preheat oven to 350°F. Grease an ovenproof baking pan with shortening or vegetable oil, or spray with nonstick cooking spray.

2. While the noodles are cooking, chop the onion. Melt the butter (or margarine) over medium heat in a small saucepan. Stir in the onion and mushrooms; cook until tender. Transfer the mixture to the prepared baking pan.

3. Stir in the soup, crabmeat, tomato juice, salt, pepper, and ½ of the cheese. When the noodles are done, drain. Gently stir into the crab mixture. Top with the remaining cheese. Bake for 35 to 40 minutes.

Tuna Chow Mein

With crispy noodles and crunchy cashews, this dish presents tuna as you may never have tasted it before.

Serve with sliced fresh tomatoes.

What You Need

1 (6-ounce) can tuna

1 cup celery

½ cup salted cashew pieces

¼ cup dried minced onion

¼ cup water

¼ teaspoon pepper

1 (5-ounce) can chow mein noodles

1 (10-½-ounce) can condensed cream of mushroom soup (undiluted)

What You Do

1. Drain and flake tuna with a fork. Place in a 2-quart saucepan that has been sprayed with nonstick cooking spray.

2. Chop celery. Add to saucepan. Stir in the cashews, onion, water, pepper, and mushroom soup. Add ½ of the noodles. Heat over medium heat until heated through. (Or, zap in the microwave for 3 minutes or so.)

3. Top with the rest of the noodles and serve.

Hot & Spicy Salsa Shrimp

You can squeeze fresh lime juice or use juice made from concentrate in this recipe.

Serve piping hot over rice cooked according to package directions.

What You Need

1½ pounds medium size raw shrimp

1 tablespoon olive oil

1½ teaspoons chili powder

1 teaspoon garlic salt

1 teaspoon cumin

2 tablespoons lime juice, divided

1½ cups whole kernel corn

¾ cup bottled salsa

1 tablespoon dried parsley flakes

2 cups canned black beans

What You Do

1. Peel the shrimp and remove the vein running across the back.

2. Heat the olive oil in a large frying pan over medium-high heat. In a small mixing bowl, stir together the chili powder, garlic salt, and cumin. Place the shrimp in the frying pan. Sprinkle with the spices and 1 tablespoon of the lime juice. Cook 3 to 5 minutes, stirring constantly until shrimp is tender. Transfer the shrimp to a mixing bowl. Set aside.

3. Drain the black beans in a colander. Rinse with cool, running water. Set aside.

4. Drain the corn. Add the corn to the frying pan stirring constantly until corn is lightly coated with oil. Stir in the salsa, parsley, and black beans. Cook 30 seconds. Add the remaining 1 tablespoon lime juice. Cook until warmed through. Pour the sauce over the shrimp. Serve over rice.

Tuna Tomato Pasta

Here's a tuna dish with a touch of Italy.

Serve with garlic bread and a tossed salad or chilled fruit.

What You Need

2 tablespoons olive oil

3 cloves garlic

1 (6½-ounce) can tuna

1 (28-ounce) can crushed tomatoes, with liquid

½ teaspoon dried oregano

½ teaspoon red pepper flakes

½ teaspoon salt

4 servings fusilli or other small pasta

Grated Parmesan cheese, as needed

What You Do

1. Heat the oil in a large frying pan over medium-high heat. Mash the garlic and add to the skillet. Cook, stirring constantly, until garlic softens (2 minutes).

2. Drain tuna. Add tuna, tomatoes, oregano, and red pepper flakes to frying pan. Stir to mix until boiling. Reduce heat to low. Cook 15 minutes, stirring occasionally.

3. While the sauce is cooking, bring a large saucepan full of water to a boil. Add the pasta. Cook according to package instructions until tender. Drain the pasta and transfer to serving plates. Top with the sauce. Sprinkle with Parmesan cheese.

? How Should I Test Pasta for Doneness?

Test noodles when you have 1 minute left in the amount of time called for in package directions. Use a slotted spoon to withdraw noodles from the pot. Place in a colander and let cool for 15 seconds. Bite into the noodle. It should be tender, but still a bit firm. For spaghetti use a slotted spoon to remove 1 noodle from the pot. When cool enough to touch, throw it onto the refrigerator door. If it sticks, it's done.

Linguine & Clam Sauce

For seafood lovers only, this creamy, filling dish is a good choice for a cold winter evening.

Serve with steamed broccoli.

What You Need

3 small cans minced clams (about ½ cup), with liquid

4 cups water

1 (16-ounce) package uncooked linguine

1 cup heavy cream

8 tablespoons butter, divided

1 tablespoon minced garlic

4 tablespoons chopped parsley

3 tablespoons chopped basil

1 teaspoon thyme

Salt and pepper, to taste

½ cup grated Parmesan cheese

What You Do

1. Drain the clams over a large cooking pot. Set clams aside. Add the water to the clam liquid. Bring to a boil. Cook linguine according to package instructions.

2. While noodles are cooking, pour the cream into a small saucepan. Heat over medium heat just to boiling. In a separate, medium saucepan, melt half of the butter over low heat. Add the clams, garlic, parsley, basil, thyme, and pepper. Stir in the cream.

3. Drain linguine. Return to the cooking pot, away from heat. Pour the clam sauce over the noodles and toss all the ingredients together. Add remaining butter and toss again. Sprinkle with the Parmesan cheese. Sprinkle with salt and pepper to taste.

Tuna Burgers

Grill these patties on a preheated grill or fry them indoors in a frying pan.

Serve on buns with sliced tomatoes, lettuce, mayonnaise, and prepared mustard.

Or, make the patties much smaller and serve as appetizers with your favorite tartar or mustard sauce.

What You Need

1 (6-ounce) can tuna

1 medium carrot

1 small onion

1 raw egg

2 tablespoons mayonnaise

½ cup breadcrumbs

1 teaspoon vegetable oil, plus 1 tablespoon for frying

Salt and pepper, to taste.

4 slices American cheese (optional)

4 hamburger buns

What You Do

1. Chop the carrot and onion into tiny pieces. Drain the tuna.

2. Place the carrot, onion, and tuna in a mixing bowl. Use a fork to flake the tuna and mix together.

3. Add the egg, mayonnaise, breadcrumbs, and 1 teaspoon of the vegetable oil. Use a potato masher to blend all the ingredients. Use your hands to form ¼ of the mixture into a patty shape. Repeat for the rest of the mixture.

4. Grill outside, or use a skillet with 1 tablespoon vegetable oil to fry. Cook for 10 minutes per side until golden brown. (Optional) If you like, add a slice of cheese while the burgers are cooking on the second side.

5. Serve on hamburger buns.

Broiled Orange Roughy

You'll often find orange roughy fillets in the frozen foods section of your supermarket.

Thaw before cooking.

What You Need

1 pound orange roughy fillets

½ cup mayonnaise

½ cup grated Parmesan cheese

1 tablespoon lemon juice

Garlic salt, to taste

Dash paprika

1 medium-size white or yellow onion

¼ cup parsley flakes

What You Do

1. Spray a broiler rack with nonstick cooking spray. Place the fillets on the rack.

2. In a small mixing bowl, stir together the mayonnaise, cheese, lemon juice, garlic salt, and paprika. Spread the mixture onto the fillets.

3. Preheat the broiler. Thinly slice the onion. Arrange the slices on top of the fillets. Sprinkle with parsley. Cover the pan with aluminum foil. Broil for 7 minutes. Remove from oven. Uncover and broil for 5 to 6 minutes more, until golden brown. (No need to turn the fillets.)

These tasty patties are a fish alternative to hamburgers.

Serve with fresh lemon wedges and Cheesy Asparagus (page 213) or Rice Casserole (page 225).

You can buy "plain" or "seasoned" packaged bread crumbs.

Seasoned bread crumbs are preferred in this recipe.

Salmon Patties

What You Need

1 (14¾-ounce) can salmon

2 green onions

1 egg

½ cup seasoned bread crumbs

Vegetable oil, as needed

What You Do

1. Drain the salmon. Use a table fork to flake the salmon into a large mixing bowl. Slice the green onions, including the dark green tops. Add to the bowl. Stir with the fork.

2. In a small mixing bowl, use the fork to beat the egg enough to break the yolk and slightly mix it with the white. Stir in 2 tablespoons of the bread crumbs. Add mixture to the salmon and green onions. Place the remaining bread crumbs on a saucer. Set aside.

3. Use your hands to form the mixture into 6 patties, as you would make hamburger patties.

4. Pour the vegetable oil to about ¼" deep in a large frying pan over medium heat. Dip both sides of each patty into the bread crumbs on the saucer. Place the patties in the frying pan. Cook for 4 minutes, until the bottom is crisp and golden brown. Use a pancake turner to flip to the other side. Cook for another 4 minutes.

Jambalaya

You can use any type of poultry, sausage, fish, or seafood in this Cajun favorite. For the best results, use a combination of 2 or 3 of these ingredients.

For traditional flavor, choose from andouille sausage, chicken, shrimp, oysters, crayfish, or alligator, but any fish or sausage will work, particularly the spicy and flavorful chorizo sausage popular in Mexico. Common combinations include chicken/sausage and shrimp/oysters.

What You Need

3 cups cooked poultry, sausage, fish, or seafood

1 medium-size white or yellow onion

1 green bell pepper

2 stalks celery

2 tablespoons vegetable oil

¼ teaspoon dried minced garlic

1 teaspoon cayenne pepper

Salt and pepper, to taste

1 (14½-ounce) can chicken or vegetable broth

¼ cup water

1 cup uncooked rice

What You Do

1. Cut the meat and/or fish into bite-size pieces. Set aside. Chop the onion, green bell pepper, and celery. Keep chopped ingredients separate.

2. Pour the vegetable oil into a large frying pan. Cook the meat/fish, onion, and garlic in the oil over medium-high heat for 5 minutes, stirring often. Stir in the green bell pepper and celery; cook 3 minutes more. Sprinkle with cayenne pepper, salt, and pepper.

3. Stir in the broth and water. Bring to a boil. Add the rice. Cover and cook for about 20 minutes, until the rice is tender. Stir occasionally.

Chapter 8

Main Dishes—
Vegetarian and Vegan

Easy

Ramen Noodles Extreme 188
Mac 'n' Cheese. 189
Variation: Nutty Mac 'n' Cheese 189
Parmesan Noodles 190

Medium

Eggplant Surprise 191
Broiled Portabella Caps. 192
Stir-Fry Veggie Combo. 193
Pesto Rigatoni 194
Linguine with Basil 195
Spinach & Feta Quesadillas 196
Yugoslavian Spinach Bread 197
Couscous with Tomato Sauce 198
Four-Bean Stew 199

Hard

Vegan Enchiladas 200
Spinach & Eggplant Casserole. 202
Eggplant Parmigiana. 203
Black Bean Burritos. 204
Mushroom Stir-Fry 206
Open-Face Veggie Melt 208

Turn Ramen noodles from a side dish into a vegetarian meal. It's inexpensive, tasty, and full of vitamin C and other nutrients.

Ramen Noodles Extreme v

What You Need

4 (3-ounce) packages Ramen noodles

1 cup frozen peas

1 (14½-ounce) can diced tomatoes

1 tablespoon butter or margarine

Grated Parmesan cheese, to taste

What You Do

1. Cook the noodles in a saucepan according to package directions. While cooking, stir in the frozen peas. Drain the noodles and return to the saucepan.

2. Reduce heat to low. Drain the tomatoes. Add the tomatoes and margarine to the noodles. Heat until butter (or margarine) has melted and the peas are tender. Spoon into serving bowls and sprinkle with Parmesan cheese.

How Can I Use a Frozen Bag of Veggies as First Aid?

You can use bags of frozen vegetables as first aid for headaches, bumps, and sprains. Just grab the bag from the freezer and use it as an ice pack. Don't place the frozen vegetable bag (or any ice pack) directly on the skin. Instead, use a kitchen towel between the injury and the ice. This tip is especially useful if you're babysitting someone's son or daughter. When you tell the parents about the big bump on their child's forehead, smile and say, "Don't worry, I put broccoli on it."

Mac 'n' Cheese v

What You Need

3 quarts water

2 cups uncooked macaroni noodles (about 8 ounces)

3 tablespoons butter or margarine

½ cup shredded Cheddar cheese

1 cup milk

Paprika, as needed

What You Do

1. Bring the water to a boil in a saucepan over high heat. Add the noodles. Cook according to package directions (about 8 minutes), until the noodles are tender but still firm. Drain. Return the noodles to the pan and reduce heat to low.

2. Stir in the butter and cheese until melted. Stir in the milk. Cook until heated through, stirring often. Sprinkle with paprika and serve.

Variation: Nutty Mac 'n' Cheese v

Pecans add a sweet flavor, and sour cream adds body for a main course or side dish. You'll never want plain macaroni and cheese again. In place of butter or margarine, add ½ cup sour cream and ½ cup chopped pecans.

Parmesan Noodles v

These cheesy noodles can serve as a tasty lunch, dinner entrée, or side dish. Although fresh ingredients taste better, you can use dried parsley flakes and canned grated Parmesan cheese.

What You Need

8 ounces medium egg noodles

¼ cup butter or margarine

¼ teaspoon garlic powder

2 tablespoons fresh parsley

2 tablespoons grated Parmesan cheese

What You Do

1. In a large saucepan, cook the noodles according to package directions. Drain and return to the pan.

2. While the noodles are cooking, melt the butter (or margarine) in a separate saucepan. Add the garlic powder. When the noodles are ready, pour the butter over them. Stir until the noodles are well coated.

3. Chop the parsley and sprinkle it over the noodles. Sprinkle with Parmesan cheese. Serve warm.

?

What Is the Quickest Way to Measure Butter?

The easiest way to measure butter or margarine in stick form is to look at the markings on the wrapper. Lines indicate 1 tablespoon increments. Here are commonly called for amounts:

4 tablespoons = ½ stick = ¼ cup

5⅓ tablespoons = ⅓ cup

8 tablespoons = 1 stick = ½ cup

No need for fancy dishes with this entrée. The eggplant shell placed on a dinner plate becomes your serving bowl.

For a vegan variation, omit the cheese.

Eggplant Surprise v

What You Need

1 whole fresh eggplant

1 Roma tomato (also known as plum tomato)

1 green onion

¼ cup sliced fresh mushrooms

¼ teaspoon minced garlic

⅛ teaspoon fresh ground black pepper

½ teaspoon dried basil

2 tablespoons olive oil

½ cup shredded mozzarella cheese

What You Do

1. Cut the eggplant in half lengthwise, remove the seeds, and scoop out the flesh. Leave ¼" to ½" of flesh attached to the interior of the shell for support. Set aside the shells.

2. Cut the eggplant flesh and tomato into bite-size pieces (about 1" cubes). Slice about 4" of the green onion, including about half of the dark green part.

3. In a frying pan over medium-high heat, cook the eggplant, tomato, onion, mushrooms, garlic, pepper, and basil in the olive oil, stirring constantly until tender but still firm. Remove from heat. Add the mozzarella cheese. Set aside until the cheese melts.

4. With a slotted spoon to drain off the oil, spoon half of the mixture into each eggplant shell half. Serve warm.

Broiled Portabella Caps v

This colorful, easy entrée looks and tastes like gourmet cooking, especially if you use fresh herbs.

You can make this recipe as an attractive side dish by using baby portabellas about 3" to 4" in diameter. Use 1 baby mushroom cap per serving.

What You Need

2 tablespoons butter or margarine

2 portabella mushroom caps (about 4" to 5" in diameter)

2 small tomatoes

2 tablespoons fresh basil (or ¼ to ½ teaspoon dried basil)

1 clove garlic (or ⅛ teaspoon dried minced garlic)

2 tablespoons olive oil

Freshly grated Parmesan cheese, as needed

What You Do

1. Melt the butter (or margarine) in a small frying pan over medium-high heat. Place the mushroom caps, rounded-side up, in the frying pan. Move the mushroom caps around during the cooking, until the mushrooms are tender. Remove from frying pan. Place, rounded-side down, in an ungreased pie tin (don't use glass).

2. Preheat broiler. Chop the tomatoes, basil, and garlic. Stir together in a small mixing bowl. Spoon the tomato mixture into the mushroom caps. Drizzle olive oil over the tomato mixture. Generously sprinkle with Parmesan cheese. Broil for 5 minutes, until the cheese bubbles. Serve warm.

LEVEL **M**

SERVINGS **4**

Chickpeas, also known as garbanzo beans, are high in protein, enabling this dish to be served over rice as a vegetarian main course. Or, you can serve this combo as a side dish for Pot Roast (page 122) or Roast Chicken (page 146).

Stir-Fry Veggie Combo v

What You Need

1 green bell pepper

1 stalk celery

¼ medium-size white or yellow onion

3 small zucchini (about 6" long)

1 medium tomato

2 tablespoons olive oil

½ cup chickpeas

What You Do

1. Cut the green pepper in half and remove the stem, seeds, and inner ribs. Chop the green pepper, celery, and onion. Place in a small mixing bowl. Set aside. Cut the zucchini in half lengthwise and then slice crosswise into ½"-thick pieces. Keep separate from the celery mixture. Cut the tomato into ½" cubes. Set aside.

2. Pour the olive oil into a frying pan over medium-high heat. Stirring constantly, cook the green pepper, celery, onion, and chickpeas in the olive oil for 6 minutes. Reduce heat to medium. Stir in the zucchini and cook for 5 more minutes. Stir in the tomatoes and continue cooking just until the tomato is tender.

Pesto Rigatoni   v

What could be more delicious than garlicky pesto flavor in a cheesy tomato pasta dish? Serve with a simple mixed greens salad and French bread (see "How Do I Prepare French Bread," page 114).

You can substitute linguine for the rigatoni. Just change the name to Pesto Linguine.

What You Need

3 pints cherry or grape tomatoes

1 whole head fresh garlic

½ cup fresh basil (or 2 tablespoons dried basil)

½ cup pine nuts

2 tablespoons olive oil

1 teaspoon salt

1 (16-ounce) package rigatoni

½ cup Parmesan cheese

What You Do

1. Rinse the tomatoes in cold, running water. Slice lengthwise into halves. Mince the garlic by cutting it into small pieces. Roughly chop the basil.

2. Place the pine nuts in a small, dry frying pan over medium heat. Stir until they turn brown. Remove from heat.

3. In a large saucepan, heat the olive oil on low. Add the tomatoes and salt. Cook for 3 minutes. Add the garlic and cook for 1 minute. Stir in the roasted pine nuts and the basil. Stir occasionally until the tomato mixture cooks down into a sauce.

4. Cook the pasta in a Dutch oven according to package directions. Drain. Return the pasta to the Dutch oven. Pour the sauce over the pasta. Stir until well mixed. Cook over low heat for about 2 minutes until heated through. Add the Parmesan and toss to mix.

This dish is best in summer made from homegrown, vine-ripened tomatoes and fresh basil.

Serve as a side dish or entrée immediately upon mixing the pasta and dressing.

You'll also enjoy leftovers served warm or cold the next day.

Linguine with Basil v

What You Need

4 tomatoes

1 pound Brie cheese

1 cup fresh basil

3 cloves fresh garlic

¾ cup extra-virgin olive oil

½ teaspoon salt

½ teaspoon seasoned salt

½ teaspoon pepper

1½ pounds uncooked linguine

1 cup grated Parmesan cheese

What You Do

1. Dice the tomatoes and place in a large glass serving bowl.

2. Remove the rind from the Brie and tear the cheese into irregular pieces. Chop the basil. Chop the garlic into very small pieces. Add the Brie, basil, and garlic to the tomatoes.

3. Stir in the olive oil, salt, seasoned salt, and pepper until well blended. Cover with a kitchen towel. Let sit at room temperature for 2 to 4 hours.

4. When ready to serve, fill a large pot with water. Cook the linguine according to package directions, but for only 10 minutes, so the noodles are tender but still firm.

5. Drain the pasta and add to the tomato dressing. Toss until noodles are well coated. Sprinkle with the Parmesan cheese.

Spinach & Feta Quesadillas   v

LEVEL **M**
SERVINGS **15**

Two delicious flavors combine for a festive entrée or appetizer.

Top with bottled or homemade salsa.

Be sure to wash your hands with soap and water after handling the chilies, or wear rubber gloves while handling the chilies, because the same substance that creates the hot flavor can also cause a burning sensation on the skin and in the eyes. Thoroughly wash cooking utensils with soap after use.

What You Need

4 serrano or jalapeño chilies

½ cup cooked spinach

2 tablespoons fresh cilantro

4 ounces feta cheese

¼ cup ricotta cheese

5 (8") flour tortillas

Water, as needed

Vegetable oil, as needed

What You Do

1. Remove stems and seeds from the chilies. Chop. Place in a mixing bowl. Drain and chop spinach. Add to bowl. Chop cilantro. Add to bowl. Stir in the feta and ricotta cheese until well blended.

2. Preheat a large frying pan. Place each tortilla on the skillet until soft. Remove from pan.

3. Place ⅕ of the filling on one-half of each tortilla. Moisten the tortilla edges with water and fold in half. Press together. Brush both sides of the tortillas with the vegetable oil. Brown one side of the quesadilla on a hot skillet. Flip and brown on the other side. Cut each tortilla into three triangles.

? How Can I Cut the Hotness of Chili Peppers?

If a chili pepper is too hot for your liking, combine with cheese, sour cream, or another dairy product. A protein in milk called casein neutralizes the burning substance of the pepper. During food preparation, you can reduce hotness by removing some or all of the ribs, inner membranes, and seeds, or by soaking for 30 minutes or less in cold water with a dash of salt or a little vinegar.

Serve this delicious bread as a side dish or vegetarian entrée.

Serve warm with whipped butter.

Yugoslavian Spinach Bread v

What You Need

1 (10-ounce) package frozen spinach, thawed

½ stick butter or margarine

2 eggs

1 cup flour

¾ teaspoon salt

1 teaspoon baking powder

1 cup milk

1 pound Monterey jack cheese, grated

What You Do

1. Place a paper towel in the bottom of a colander. Place the spinach on top to thaw. When thawed, cover with another paper towel. Press to drain the spinach well.

2. Melt the butter or margarine in a small saucepan. Pour into an 8" × 11" baking pan, tipping the pan until well coated. Return the melted butter or margarine to the saucepan. Preheat oven to 350°F.

3. In a large mixing bowl, beat the eggs. In a medium mixing bowl, stir together the flour, salt, and baking powder. Alternately add milk and the flour mixture to the eggs, stirring until well blended. Add the melted butter or margarine, drained spinach, and cheese. Mix well. Pour into the greased baking pan. Bake for 35 minutes.

4. Remove from oven. Cut into serving squares.

Couscous with Tomato Sauce   v

This main dish looks a bit like spaghetti, with couscous replacing the spaghetti noodles.

The beans, which are also known as chickpeas, provide a protein source.

Serve with a tossed salad.

What You Need

2 cups water

1⅓ cups uncooked couscous

1 (28-ounce) jar chunky vegetable spaghetti sauce

1 (15-ounce) can garbanzo beans

¼ teaspoon crushed red pepper flakes

2 tablespoons chopped fresh parsley

4 tablespoons grated Parmesan cheese

What You Do

1. Boil the water in a medium-size saucepan over high heat. Add the couscous and stir. Cover and remove from the burner. Let it steam for 5 minutes or until all the water is absorbed.

2. While the couscous is cooking, place the spaghetti sauce, garbanzo beans, and red pepper flakes in a separate saucepan. Stir well. Cook uncovered over medium heat until ingredients are heated through (about 5 to 7 minutes).

3. Use a fork to loosen the couscous. Spoon onto serving plates.

4. Spoon the sauce over each serving. Sprinkle 1 tablespoon of parsley flakes and 1 tablespoon of Parmesan cheese on each serving.

Four-Bean Stew v

Full of flavor and fiber, this stew will warm a cold winter night.

The fennel seed adds a hint of licorice.

If you're not a vegetarian, you can substitute pork and beans for the vegetarian version.

Serve with your favorite bread or rolls.

What You Need

1 (15½-ounce) can butter beans

1 (15½-ounce) can red kidney beans

1 (16-ounce) can vegetarian baked beans

1 (9-ounce) package frozen baby lima beans

3 carrots

1 small onion

1 (14½-ounce) can stewed tomatoes with Italian seasoning, with liquid

½ teaspoon garlic salt

⅛ teaspoon red cayenne pepper

⅛ teaspoon fennel seed

What You Do

1. Drain and rinse the butter beans and kidney beans. Place in a 4-quart slow cooker, along with the baked beans and lima beans.

2. Thinly slice the carrots. Chop the onion. Add to the pot.

3. Stir in the tomatoes. Use the side of a cooking spoon to break the tomatoes into small pieces, if necessary. Sprinkle mixture with garlic salt and cayenne pepper. Crush the fennel seed and add to the pot. Cover. Cook on low for 8 hours or high for 4 hours.

LEVEL **H**

SERVINGS **12**

Vegan Enchiladas v

If you don't eat meat, you can still enjoy the fiesta flavor of these enchiladas made with tofu instead of beef.

Top with tofu sour cream (see "How Do I Make Tofu Sour Cream?" on page 201).

Serve with shredded lettuce, black olives, or Easy Guacamole (page 240).

What You Need

2 baking potatoes

1 (28-ounce) can red enchilada sauce

1 (28-ounce) can water

9 ounces firm tofu

1 medium-size white or yellow onion

1 (15½-ounce) can chili beans

3 tablespoons chili powder

1 tablespoon cumin

2 tablespoons garlic powder

Salt and pepper, to taste

12 (8") flour tortillas

What You Do

1. Rinse the potatoes under cold, running water. Peel and cut into quarters. Boil for about 20 minutes, until tender. (Check by piercing with a fork.) Drain and let cool. Cut the potatoes into ½" cubes. Place in a large mixing bowl. Set aside.

2. Pour the enchilada sauce and water into a 1-quart saucepan over low heat. Stir often while preparing the rest of the tortilla filling.

3. Crumble the tofu or cut into ½" cubes. Chop the onion. Add to the potatoes in mixing bowl. Drain the beans. Add to the potatoes. Stir in the chili powder, cumin, garlic powder, salt, and pepper.

Vegan Enchiladas—*continued*

4. Preheat oven to 350°F. Spray a 9" × 13" ovenproof baking pan with nonstick cooking spray. Spoon in just enough enchilada sauce to cover the bottom of the pan.

5. Dip a tortilla into the remaining enchilada sauce in the saucepan and place in the baking pan. Spoon about ⅓ cup of the filling mixture across the tortilla. Fold the bottom ¼ of the tortilla over the filling mixture. Wrap the right side of the tortilla halfway over the filling (and the already folded bottom section). Wrap the left side of the tortilla over the right side. Carefully turn over the enchilada and place seam side down in the baking pan. Repeat with the remaining tortillas. Pour the remaining enchilada sauce over the enchiladas. Bake for 20 to 25 minutes.

❓ How Do I Make Tofu Sour Cream?

Use tofu sour cream to top your favorite dishes from Mexico and the American Southwest. In a small mixing bowl, use a wooden spoon or electric mixer to blend together 1 12-ounce package silken soft tofu, 2 tablespoons vegetable oil, 1 tablespoon lemon juice, 1½ teaspoons sugar (or honey), and ½ teaspoon salt. Makes about 1½ cups.

Eggplant takes on the flavors of surrounding ingredients and makes this casserole tasty and filling.

This is a great potluck dish.

Spinach & Eggplant Casserole v

What You Need

3 fresh tomatoes

2 cups fresh spinach

1 tablespoon parsley flakes

1 cup uncooked macaroni noodles

1¼ cups canned stewed tomatoes, with juice

1 eggplant

3 cloves garlic (or 3/8 teaspoon dried minced garlic)

⅓ cup olive oil

¾ teaspoon salt

¾ teaspoon pepper

What You Do

1. Rinse the tomatoes in cold water. Slice and place in a layer in the bottom of a greased ovenproof baking dish. Rinse the spinach in cold, running water. Drain and chop. Sprinkle the tomatoes with the spinach and parsley.

2. Place the noodles on a cutting board. Cover with waxed paper. Use a rolling pin to crush the macaroni. Sprinkle the crushed macaroni noodles in a layer over the sliced tomatoes. Pour the canned tomatoes and juice over the crushed noodles.

3. Preheat oven to 350°F. Rinse the eggplant in cold, running water. Slice in half lengthwise. Remove the seeds. Slice the eggplant crosswise. Place in a layer on top of the stewed tomatoes.

4. Mince the garlic by chopping it into very small pieces. Place in a small mixing bowl. Stir in the olive oil, salt, and pepper. Drizzle the mixture over the eggplant. Bake uncovered for 30 minutes.

Serve this delicious dish with tomato sauce on the side.

Eggplant Parmigiana v

What You Need

1 medium eggplant (about 1 pound)

Vegetable oil, for frying

3 eggs

½ cup milk

1 cup all-purpose flour

3 cups bread crumbs

1 (28-ounce) can tomato sauce

4 cups shredded mozzarella cheese

Fresh Italian parsley or whole fresh basil leaves

What You Do

1. Rinse eggplant in cold, running water. Remove stem. Cut in half lengthwise and remove the seeds. Thinly slice crosswise. Pour vegetable oil to about ½" deep in a frying pan. Heat on medium-high. Test for correct temperature by placing a piece of the eggplant in the oil. It will sizzle if the oil is ready.

2. In a small mixing bowl, beat together the eggs and milk. Place the flour on a dinner plate. Place the bread crumbs on another plate. Dip both sides of each eggplant slice first in the flour, then in the egg mixture. Place on the bread crumbs and press so the bread crumbs stick. Fry in the oil for about 3 minutes, until golden brown. Drain on paper towels.

3. Preheat oven to 350°F. Layer the eggplant slices in the bottom of an ovenproof baking dish that has been sprayed with nonstick cooking spray. Top each slice with 1 teaspoon of tomato sauce and a rounded spoonful of cheese. Bake for 15 minutes, until the cheese melts and the dish is brown and bubbling. Sprinkle with chopped parsley or whole basil.

Black Bean Burritos   v

Cilantro, also called Chinese or Mexican parsley, is an herb with a distinctive flavor similar to sage with citrus. Not everyone likes cilantro. If you've never tasted it, give it a try in a small quantity before adding to the entire recipe. If it's not for you, substitute chopped regular parsley or dried parsley flakes

What You Need

1 cup uncooked rice

½ medium-size white or yellow onion

1 tablespoon vegetable oil

2 medium-size tomatoes

1 ripe avocado

4 (8") flour tortillas

1 (15-ounce) can black beans, with liquid

⅛ teaspoon ground cumin

⅛ teaspoon dried minced garlic

1 cup shredded Cheddar or Monterey jack cheese

¼ cup bottled salsa

¼ cup sour cream

½ cup fresh cilantro or 2 tablespoons dried parsley flakes (optional)

What You Do

1. Cook the rice according to package directions. While the rice is cooking, chop the onion. Pour the vegetable oil into a large frying pan over medium-high heat. Add the onion and cook, stirring constantly, until lightly brown and tender. Remove from heat. Cover to keep warm. Set aside.

2. Preheat oven to 350°F. Chop the tomatoes. Set aside. Peel and slice the avocado. Set aside.

Black Bean Burritos—*continued*

3. Place the tortillas on an ungreased baking sheet. Warm in oven for 10 minutes, until softened. (Or place between damp paper towels in the microwave on high for 40 seconds.) While the tortillas are warming, place the black beans and the liquid from the can into a medium-size saucepan over medium heat. Stir in the cumin and garlic until the mixture is heated through.

4. Remove the tortillas from the oven and place on serving plates. Spoon the onions in a line across the middle of each tortilla. Sprinkle with cheese and top with rice, the black bean mixture, the salsa, avocado, sour cream, and cilantro (or parsley).

5. Fold up the bottom ⅓ of each tortilla to cover the fillings. Fold side flaps in, over each other. Fold down the top ⅓ of the tortilla. Place on the serving plate seam side down. Serve warm.

How Do I Know When an Avocado Is Ripe?

Fresh avocados should be stored at room temperature until they are ripe. Test for ripeness by gently squeezing the fruit. It should "give" to slight pressure. Most avocados remain green when ripe, although the lighter the color, the less ripe the fruit. The Hass variety turns black when ripe.

Mushroom Stir-Fry v

Hoisin is an Asian sauce. Look for it and sesame oil in the international foods section close to such Chinese foods as canned water chestnuts.

Serve with white or brown rice.

What You Need

½ pound fresh shiitake mushrooms

4 cups hot water

1 medium-size white or yellow onion

1 bunch scallions or green onions

1 tablespoon fresh ginger root

1 clove fresh garlic (or ⅛ teaspoon dried minced garlic)

2 tablespoons vegetable oil

3 tablespoons hoisin sauce

½ teaspoon sesame oil

½ teaspoon salt

½ teaspoon vinegar

1 (20-ounce) package silken tofu

1½ teaspoons cornstarch

1 tablespoon water

What You Do

1. Soak the mushrooms in the 4 cups of hot water for at least 20 minutes. While the mushrooms are soaking, cut the onion in half lengthwise. Slice lengthwise. Set aside. Drain the mushrooms over a small mixing bowl to save the liquid. Remove the mushroom stems and cut the mushrooms into slices about ¼" thick. Set aside.

Mushroom Stir-Fry—*continued*

2. Chop the scallions. Finely chop the ginger root and garlic. Heat the vegetable oil in a large frying pan on medium-high. Add the scallions, ginger root, and garlic. Stir constantly for about 5 minutes, until the scallions are just tender (if using onions, they should be translucent). Reduce heat to low.

3. In a small mixing bowl, stir together the hoisin sauce and sesame oil. Stir into the vegetables along with the salt, vinegar, and 1 cup of the soaking liquid from the mushrooms. Cook for 5 minutes, stirring occasionally.

4. Cut the tofu into 1" cubes. Set aside. Dissolve the cornstarch in the 1 tablespoon water. Stir into the vegetables until well mixed and slightly thickened. Place the tofu cubes on top of the vegetables. Cover and cook for about 5 minutes, until the tofu is heated through.

?

What Are the Ways That I Can Cook Mushrooms?

Grilling is only one of several ways you can cook mushrooms. Some recipes you may come across will specify a particular variety of mushroom for a particular cooking style, but in general, you can sauté, broil, bake, and microwave most types. To sauté, place about 1 tablespoon olive oil in a frying pan over medium-high heat, stirring constantly for about 3 minutes until tender. Before broiling, baking, or microwaving, brush mushrooms with olive oil, butter, or margarine. Broil for about 5 minutes, turning mushrooms after the first 2 minutes. Bake in a single layer in a shallow baking pan at 375°F for 12 to 15 minutes until brown. Microwave uncovered on high for 4 to 6 minutes.

Open-Face Veggie Melt   v

Here's a chance to use the broiler in your oven for hot open-face sandwiches you can serve for lunch or a dinner entrée.

Or, cut the bread slices in half and serve as an appetizer.

What You Need

½ eggplant (about 8 ounces)

1 medium zucchini

1 medium tomato

3 slices mozzarella cheese

⅓ cup bottled Italian salad dressing

4 slices Italian bread (¾" thick)

3 tablespoons mayonnaise

½ teaspoon dried basil

What You Do

1. Rinse the eggplant and zucchini. Slice eggplant into 8 slices ¼" wide. Cut the zucchini in half horizontally. Cut each half in half lengthwise. Set aside. Slice the tomato horizontally into 8 slices. Set aside. Cut each cheese slice into 4 strips. Set aside.

2. Place eggplant and zucchini on a cookie sheet sprayed with nonstick cooking spray. Brush half of the salad dressing on the tops of the slices. Adjust top oven rack so it's 4" to 6" from the broiler. Cook 5 minutes. While the veggies are cooking, place mayonnaise and basil in a mixing bowl. Stir until blended. Set aside.

3. Remove sheet from oven. Turn vegetables cooked-side down. Brush uncooked side with remaining salad dressing. Broil 5 minutes until tender and slightly browned. Remove from oven and set aside.

4. Place bread on clean cookie sheet. Broil 2 minutes until lightly browned. Remove sheet from oven. Spread ¼ of mayonnaise mixture on each slice. Top with 2 slices each of eggplant, zucchini, and tomato. Top each sandwich with 3 slices of mozzarella. Return to the oven. Broil 1 to 2 minutes until cheese melts.

Chapter 9

Side Dishes

Easy

Mashed Potatoes 210
Variation: Garlic Mashed Potatoes 210
Green Bean Casserole 211
Italian Zucchini 212
Cheesy Asparagus 213
Orange-Glazed Carrots 214
Brussels Sprouts to Die For 215

Medium

Steamed Artichokes 216
Pesto 217
Sweet Potato–Apple Bake 218
Mashed Sweet Potatoes 219
Baked Potatoes & Onion 220
Asparagus with Almond Sauce 221
Stir-Fry Parsnip Medley 222
Creamy Broccoli Broil 223
Twice-Baked Potato Casserole 224
Variation: Mashed Casserole 224
Rice Casserole 225
Hot Beans & Corn 226
Warm Red Cabbage 227
Baked Potato Latkes 228
Parsley Rice 229

Hard

Nater's Taters 230
Greek Green Beans 232

Serve with your favorite toppings: butter, sour cream, chopped chives, bacon bits, and/or shredded Cheddar cheese.

Or try sour cream mixed with ranch or French onion powdered dip mix.

Mashed Potatoes v

What You Need

4–6 medium-size red potatoes or 2 large baking potatoes

¼ cup milk

2 tablespoons butter or margarine

¼ teaspoon salt

⅛ teaspoon pepper

What You Do

1. Rinse the potatoes under cold, running water. Peel with a potato peeler or paring knife. Cut into fourths and place in a 2-quart saucepan. Cover with water. Bring to a boil over high heat. Boil for 8 to 10 minutes, until the potatoes are soft when pierced with a fork. Drain in a colander. Reduce heat, and return the potatoes to the pan.

2. Add the milk, butter, salt, and pepper. Using an electric hand mixer (or by hand using a masher), whip the ingredients together until not quite smooth. (Add more milk if needed.) Serve warm.

Variation: Garlic Mashed Potatoes v

Place mashed potatoes in an ovenproof baking pan that has been sprayed with nonstick cooking spray. Sprinkle ¼ teaspoon of garlic powder over the top. Stir in ¼ cup mayonnaise. Top with ½ cup shredded Cheddar cheese. Cover with aluminum foil. Bake at 350°F for 30 minutes or until warmed through.

Green Bean Casserole v

In a hurry? Here's a quick, easy, and attractive side dish.

French-style cut green beans look prettiest in this casserole, but you can use any style of cut beans.

You can also substitute canned cut green beans for frozen.

What You Need

1 (10-ounce) package frozen French-style cut green beans

½ (7-ounce) can sliced mushrooms or mushroom stems and pieces

½ (10¾-ounce) can condensed cream of mushroom soup

⅓ cup milk

⅛ teaspoon pepper

⅔ cup canned French-fried onions (plain or Cheddar flavor)

What You Do

1. Set out the green beans to thaw slightly so you can separate them with a fork. Preheat oven to 350°F. Spray a 2-quart ovenproof baking pan with non-stick spray. Drain the mushrooms.

2. Place the green beans and mushrooms in the prepared baking pan. Stir in the condensed mushroom soup, milk, pepper, and ½ of the French-fried onions; mix well. Top with the remaining onions. Bake uncovered for 30 minutes. Or, microwave on high for 3 to 4 minutes, until heated through.

Italian Zucchini v

Use this casserole as a vegetarian side dish or as a main course.

Use spaghetti sauce from a jar or make your own.

What You Need

4 small zucchini (about 6"–8" long)

½ medium-size white or yellow onion

2 tablespoons butter or margarine

2 cups spaghetti sauce

¼ teaspoon garlic salt

2 tablespoons canned or freshly grated Parmesan cheese

What You Do

1. Rinse the zucchini in cold, running water. Cut crosswise into ½"-thick slices. Chop the onion. Heat the butter (or margarine) in a frying pan over medium heat. Add the zucchini and onion. Cook, stirring constantly, for 1 to 2 minutes.

2. Reduce heat to medium-low. Stir in the spaghetti sauce, garlic salt, and Parmesan cheese. Cover and simmer for 6 to 8 minutes, until the zucchini is tender but still firm.

?

What Kinds of Zucchini Are There?

Zucchini, which looks a little like a cucumber, is a type of squash known as "summer squash." Despite its name, summer squash is available year-round. Summer squash, which has a soft shell and edible seeds, is distinguished from winter squash, which has a hard shell. Zucchini has a mild flavor. You can cook zucchini or eat it raw by itself or with dip or in salad. When purchasing, look for firm texture and shiny skin that is free from pits or other injury. Also avoid zucchini with yellowish areas on the skin. Smaller zucchini are more tender than large ones.

A creamy Cheddar topping adds color and flavor to the asparagus for an attractive accent to entrées without sauces.

Do not substitute canned asparagus—it will be too mushy and too salty.

Cheesy Asparagus v

What You Need

1 pound fresh asparagus

Seasoned salt, to taste

2 eggs

¼ cup evaporated milk

½ cup shredded Cheddar cheese

¼ teaspoon salt

⅛ teaspoon pepper

½ cup shredded mozzarella cheese

What You Do

1. Steam the asparagus (see Appendix C) and sprinkle with seasoned salt. Spray a shallow 9" × 12" oven-proof baking pan with nonstick cooking spray. Pre-heat oven to 350°F.

2. Place the asparagus in the prepared pan. Use a fork to stir together the eggs (break the yolks), milk, Cheddar cheese, salt, and pepper. Pour the mixture over the asparagus. Top with mozzarella cheese. Bake uncovered for 15 to 20 minutes, until the cheese melts.

What Is Evaporated Milk?

Evaporated milk, also called condensed milk, is whole milk cooked until only 40 percent of its water content remains. You can buy evaporated milk or evaporated skim milk in 5-ounce or 12-ounce cans, usually found in the baking aisle of the grocery store. Do not confuse evaporated milk with sweetened condensed milk, which has added sugar, and never substitute evaporated or condensed milk for the sweetened variety.

If you use whole carrots, clean, peel, and slice them before cooking.

You can substitute canned or frozen carrots for fresh without precooking them.

Orange-Glazed Carrots   v

What You Need

1 cup fresh baby carrots

⅛ teaspoon salt

2 tablespoons butter or margarine

1½ teaspoons white granulated sugar

¼ cup prepared orange juice

1 tablespoon dried parsley flakes

What You Do

1. Place the carrots in a saucepan. Add the salt and about ½" of water in the bottom of the pan. Bring to a boil over high heat. Cover and cook for 10 to 15 minutes, until tender. Drain.

2. While the carrots are cooking, melt the butter over low heat in a small frying pan. Add the sugar and orange juice. Stir until the sugar dissolves.

3. When the carrots are done (and drained), stir in the orange juice mixture. Cover and heat over low heat until warm. Sprinkle with parsley.

You might think you don't like these vegetables that look like little cabbages, but before you give up on them, try them this way.

Brussels Sprouts to Die For v

What You Need

16 fresh Brussels sprouts

Olive oil, as needed

Coarse sea salt, as needed

Water, as needed

What You Do

1. Preheat the oven to 375°. Rinse Brussels sprouts under cold, running water. Remove stems and outer leaves. Place sprouts in an ovenproof baking pan.

2. Generously sprinkle with olive oil.

3. Generously sprinkle with coarse sea salt or kosher salt

4. Bake uncovered 45 minutes to 1 hour until tender.

Steamed Artichokes v

Here's a side dish you can use as a fun appetizer for a small gathering.

Teach guests how to remove the petal and enjoy.

What You Need

2 artichokes

½ cup (1 stick) butter

Lemon juice, to taste (about 1 teaspoon)

What You Do

1. To begin (unless you are using a thornless variety), cut off the tips and needles of each petal. For both varieties, cut off the top 1" of the whole artichoke so steam can flow through the inside. Pull off the lowest row of petals, and cut off the bottom ½" of the stem so the remainder is about 1" long. Rinse under cold, running water.

2. Set the artichokes in a saucepan or steamer, stem-side down. Steam (see Appendix C) for 20 to 45 minutes, until tender. (Test by sticking a fork into the bottom of the stem. The fork should easily penetrate the stem.)

3. Cool for 2 to 4 minutes. In the meantime, melt the butter in a small saucepan. Stir in lemon juice to taste. Place the butter mixture in a serving dish to share. Serve warm.

How Should I Eat Steamed Whole Artichokes?

To serve a steamed whole artichoke, start from the bottom. Use your fingers to tear off a petal. Hold the tip of the petal between your thumb and index finger. Dip into butter mixture, place on tongue and pull off the flesh with your teeth. (You eat the larger end of the petal—the one that was attached to the plant.)

Pesto v

Pesto is a green sauce with lots of garlic that tastes good on almost everything.

Spoon 1 to 2 tablespoons of the sauce onto Scrambled Eggs (page 9), pasta, or steak.

Store covered in the refrigerator for up to 2 weeks.

For the best results, use a food processor to make this sauce.

What You Need

2 cups fresh basil leaves

½ cup olive oil

½ cup grated Parmesan cheese

3 cloves garlic

Freshly ground black pepper, to taste

3 tablespoons pine nuts or walnuts

What You Do

1. Rinse the basil under cold, running water. Drain. Pat dry with paper towels. Place in a food processor. (If you don't have a food processor, cut all the ingredients into very small pieces and blend in an electric blender.)

2. Add the olive oil, cheese, garlic, pepper, and pine nuts (or walnuts). Process until the sauce is well blended. Cover and refrigerate until ready to use.

For the best results, choose McIntosh, Granny Smith, or Jonathan apple varieties for this recipe.

For a different flavor, you can substitute unpeeled orange slices for the apples.

Sweet Potato–Apple Bake v

What You Need

2 sweet potatoes

2 apples

4 teaspoons margarine or butter

½ cup brown sugar

1 teaspoon salt

Shortening, vegetable oil, or nonstick cooking spray, as needed

What You Do

1. Rinse the sweet potatoes under cold, running water. Place in a saucepan and cover with water. Bring to a boil over high heat. Boil for 30 to 35 minutes. Drain and let cool. Slice crosswise into circles.

2. While the sweet potatoes are cooling, peel the apples and use a knife to remove the cores. Slice crosswise into circles. In a separate saucepan, melt the margarine over low heat. Stir in the brown sugar and salt. Set aside.

3. Preheat oven to 350°F. Grease an ovenproof baking pan with shortening or vegetable oil, or spray with nonstick cooking spray. Layer ½ of the sweet potato slices in the bottom of the prepared baking pan. Layer ½ of the apple slices on top. Drizzle ½ of the butter mixture over the apples. Repeat with another layer of sweet potato slices, apple slices, and the remaining butter mixture. Bake for 1 hour.

Mashed Sweet Potatoes   v

Using fresh potatoes (instead of canned yams) is important in this recipe with a secret. The secret is the white potato added to the mixture. (Don't tell!)

What You Need

5 large sweet potatoes

2 large baking potatoes

2 tablespoons butter or margarine

¼ cup brown sugar

⅛ teaspoon salt

¼ cup whole milk

2 cups miniature marshmallows (optional)

What You Do

1. Peel and slice the sweet potatoes and baking potatoes. Place in a large saucepan and cover with water. Boil over high heat for about 20 minutes, until tender. Drain.

2. Preheat oven to 350°F. Add the butter, brown sugar, and salt to the potatoes. Use a potato masher or electric mixer to mash. Add milk 1 tablespoon at a time until the mixture has the consistency of mashed potatoes. (Add more milk if necessary.)

3. Place the mixture in a 9" × 12" ovenproof baking pan that has been sprayed with nonstick cooking spray. Top with miniature marshmallows. Refrigerate to let flavors blend until almost ready to serve. Bake for 20 to 25 minutes, until the marshmallows are melted and slightly browned.

This potato side dish is easier and more flavorful than regular baked potatoes—in half the time.

Garnish with fresh parsley.

Baked Potatoes & Onion v

What You Need

2 baking potatoes

½ medium-size white or yellow onion

2½ tablespoons butter or margarine

¼ teaspoon garlic salt

Salt and pepper, to taste

What You Do

1. Preheat oven to 350°F. Rinse the potatoes under cold, running water. Peel and cut crosswise into slices. Place in a 9" × 12" ovenproof baking pan. Slice the onion. Separate into individual rings and mix in with the potato slices.

2. Cut the butter into pats and spread around the top of the potatoes and onions. Sprinkle with garlic salt, salt, and pepper. Cover tightly with aluminum foil. Bake for 30 minutes. Or, cover with baking pan lid or plastic wrap, and microwave on high for about 6 minutes until the potatoes are tender. (Do not use aluminum foil in a microwave oven.)

?

What is the Difference Between *Slicing* and *Dicing*?

Slice means to cut pieces of food using parallel lines. You can slice foods lengthwise or crosswise. For roasted meat, you want to slice against the grain, or crosswise. If you cut meat with the grain, you'll see long lines in the meat. Cutting crosswise makes the meat easier to chew. *Dice* means to cut into cubes. The easiest way to dice is to slice lengthwise but keep the food in place as if it were still whole. Then slice crosswise.

This sauce adds zesty flavor to fresh asparagus.

You can substitute 1 teaspoon cornstarch for the 2 teaspoons flour.

A wooden spoon works well to stir the sauce to prevent sticking or burning.

Asparagus with Almond Sauce

What You Need

¼ cup slivered almonds

1 tablespoon butter or margarine

⅓ cup water

2 teaspoons all-purpose flour

½ teaspoon chicken-flavored bouillon granules

2 teaspoons lemon juice

⅛ teaspoon pepper

1 pound fresh asparagus

What You Do

1. Cook the almonds in the butter (or margarine) in a frying pan over medium-high heat for 3 to 5 minutes, stirring constantly until golden brown. Reduce heat to low.

2. In a medium-size mixing bowl, stir together the water, flour, bouillon granules, lemon juice, and pepper until well blended. Add to the almonds in the frying pan. Cook over medium heat, stirring constantly, until the mixture comes to a boil. Boil for 1 minute. Remove from heat. Keep warm.

3. Steam the asparagus (see Appendix C). Arrange on a serving platter. Pour the sauce over the asparagus. Serve immediately.

Stir-Fry Parsnip Medley v

LEVEL **M**

SERVINGS **2**

Consider color combinations when planning your menu. This bright orange and white dish offers a nice contrast with green vegetables or salads.

You can bake the unused half of the sweet potato and serve with butter and brown sugar. Or, use it in Curried Vegetable Stew (page 63).

What You Need

1 fresh carrot

1 fresh parsnip

½ raw sweet potato

2 tablespoons olive oil

¼ teaspoon minced garlic

What You Do

1. Rinse the carrot, parsnip, and sweet potato in cold water and peel. Cut the vegetables into sticks about 3" long and about ¼" wide and ¼" thick.

2. Coat the bottom of a frying pan with olive oil and heat on medium-high. Stir in the carrots, parsnip, sweet potato, and garlic. Stirring constantly, cook until tender but still firm.

?

What's a Parsnip?

A parsnip is a specialty root vegetable that looks like a white carrot and tastes like a sweet potato. You may have to ask where they are in the produce section of your grocery store, as parsnips don't get the same shelf space allotment as other, more popular vegetables.

LEVEL **M**

SERVINGS **4**

You can substitute 1 cup each of frozen cauliflower and broccoli. If you use frozen, you don't steam them. Thaw before chopping.

Creamy Broccoli Broil v

What You Need

½ head cauliflower

½ bunch broccoli

⅓ cup sour cream

½ cup shredded Cheddar cheese

What You Do

1. Rinse the cauliflower and broccoli under cold, running water. Steam them (see Appendix C). Chop and place in an ovenproof baking pan that has been sprayed with nonstick cooking spray. Move the top oven rack into a position closest to the broiler element. Preheat broiler.

2. In a medium-size mixing bowl, stir together the sour cream and cheese. Spoon the mixture over veggies. Broil for 10 to 15 minutes until lightly browned and heated through.

Twice-Baked Potato Casserole

LEVEL **M**

SERVINGS **6**

Hot and cheesy, this yummy side dish goes well with Beef Roast (page 108), Pork Roast (page 132), or Roast Chicken (page 146).

It's a popular contribution to a potluck supper.

What You Need

6 red russet potatoes

1 cup water

2 chicken bouillon cubes

4 green onions

1½ cups sour cream

¾ cup small-curd cottage cheese

2 cups shredded Cheddar cheese, divided

What You Do

1. Bake the potatoes (see "How Do I Bake a Potato?" on page 109). Let cool. Peel and cut into 1" cubes. Place in a 10" × 15" ovenproof baking pan that has been sprayed with nonstick cooking spray.

2. Preheat oven to 350°F. In a saucepan, bring the water to a boil. Add the chicken bouillon cubes. Stir until dissolved. Pour over the potatoes.

3. Chop the green onions, including the green tops. Add to the potatoes, along with the sour cream, cottage cheese, and 1 cup of the Cheddar cheese. Gently stir until well blended. Top with remaining Cheddar cheese. Bake uncovered for 30 to 35 minutes, until the cheese melts and bubbles.

LEVEL **M**

SERVINGS **6**

Variation: *Mashed Casserole*   v

Instead of baking the potatoes, boil them until tender and mash them. Omit the chicken bouillon cubes and water. Sprinkle with paprika.

Rice Casserole   v

You can serve this cheesy rice dish as a vegetarian main course or as a side dish for non-vegetarians with beef, chicken, or pork.

It's especially good as a side dish with Vegan Enchiladas (page 200) and Mexican Corn Bread (page 248).

What You Need

1 cup uncooked rice

1 medium white or yellow onion

½ cup butter

1 (8-ounce) can sliced tomatoes with juice

2 cups shredded Cheddar cheese

1 cup water

Salt and pepper, to taste

What You Do

1. Preheat oven to 350°F. Place the rice in an ungreased 2½-quart ovenproof baking pan.

2. Chop the onion and add to the baking pan. Slice the butter into chunks of about 2 tablespoons each. Add to the pan. Stir in the tomatoes, cheese, and water. Sprinkle with salt and pepper. Cover and bake for 1 hour.

Hot Beans & Corn v

Hot! Too hot! Ya gotta love spicy to enjoy this dish.

Serve with something cheesy to balance the meal.

Keep a pitcher of ice water handy.

What You Need

1 medium-size white or yellow onion

1 tablespoon vegetable oil

1 (16-ounce) can baked beans

1 (10-ounce) package frozen corn

2 teaspoons vinegar

½ teaspoon hot pepper sauce

What You Do

1. Chop the onion. Pour the oil into a saucepan over medium-high heat. Add the onion. Cook until the onion is tender, stirring constantly. Stir in the beans and corn, and bring the mixture to a boil.

2. Reduce heat to low. Cover and cook for about 5 minutes, until warmed through. Stir in the vinegar and hot pepper sauce. Serve warm.

?

Is Corn a Vegetable?

Many people think of corn as a "yellow vegetable." Don't let the color fool you. Although it is sold in the produce department, corn is a grain, not a vegetable. Corn is a staple in many cultures, and it's a good source of vitamin C. In some American Indian cultures, corn is used for ritual and healing.

This tangy side dish goes well with sausages, Hot German Potato Salad (page 105), or other German dishes.

Warm Red Cabbage

What You Need

1 head red cabbage

1 small white or yellow onion

2½ cups water, divided

2 teaspoons salt, divided

4 slices bacon

2 tablespoons brown sugar

2 tablespoons all-purpose flour

⅓ cup white vinegar

⅛ teaspoon pepper

What You Do

1. Shred the cabbage using the large holes on the grater. Set aside. Slice the onion. Set aside.

2. Place the cabbage in a large saucepan. Add 2 cups of the water and 1 teaspoon of the salt. Bring to a boil. Cover and reduce heat to low. Cook for 5 to 8 minutes, until tender but still firm. Remove from heat. Drain and return the cabbage to the saucepan. Cover to keep warm and set aside.

3. Fry the bacon (see Makin' Bacon on page 5). Drain. Pour off ½ of the bacon fat from the pan. Reduce heat to low. Add the brown sugar and flour to the bacon fat remaining in the frying pan. Stir until well blended. Stir in the onion, remaining ½ cup water and 1 teaspoon salt, the vinegar, and pepper. Cook for about 5 minutes, until the mixture thickens.

4. Pour the dressing over the cabbage in the saucepan. Add the bacon crumbles. Cook over low heat, stirring until well coated and heated through. Serve warm.

Baked Potato Latkes v

You can make the latkes the night before, cover, and store in the refrigerator overnight. Reheat for about 10 minutes at 350°.

Serve with applesauce or sour cream and sugar.

For party appetizers, make latkes 1" in diameter.

What You Need

1 tablespoon vegetable oil

1 (20-ounce) package frozen hash brown potatoes

3 eggs

½ cup flour

2 teaspoons salt

½ teaspoon pepper

6 green onions

What You Do

1. Use 1 teaspoon of the vegetable oil to grease each of 2 cookie sheets. Preheat oven to 450°. Set out frozen potatoes to slightly thaw in a medium mixing bowl. In a separate large mixing bowl, beat eggs. Stir in flour, the remaining 1 teaspoon of vegetable oil, salt, and pepper. Set aside.

2. Cut onions into very small pieces, including about 6" of the dark green tops (to make about 1 cup). Add to the egg mixture in the large mixing bowl. Add hash browns about 1 cup at a time. Use 2 table forks to toss ingredients. Repeat until all ingredients are well mixed.

3. Pour about ⅓ cup of the potato mixture onto a cookie sheet for each latke. Use a pancake turner to spread and slightly flatten the mixture into a pancake shape.

4. Bake 10 minutes or until golden brown on the bottom. Remove from oven. Use a pancake turner to flip over latkes. Switch position of the cookie sheets, so that the one that was on the top oven rack is now on the bottom and vice versa. Bake about 5 more minutes until second side is golden brown.

Here's an attractive side dish you can make with leftover rice. Or, cook rice especially for this recipe.

The parsley adds a touch of green.

The garlic and curry powder make it taste good.

Parsley Rice v

What You Need

½ teaspoon vegetable oil

1 egg

1 cup milk

1 small onion

1 clove garlic

1 tablespoon dried parsley

¼ teaspoon curry powder

Salt and pepper, to taste

2 cups cooked rice

What You Do

1. Use the vegetable oil to grease an ovenproof covered casserole dish. Add the egg, and beat with a fork. Stir in the milk.

2. Peel and chop the onion and garlic into very small pieces. Add to the baking pan.

3. Stir in the curry powder, salt, and pepper.

4. Add the rice, and mix well. Cover. Cook 45 minutes.

Nater's Taters   v

What You Need

7 white potatoes

½ medium onion

2½ cups heavy whipping cream, unwhipped

1 stick butter

1 tablespoon coarse sea salt or kosher salt (or more, to taste)

1 tablespoon fresh ground pepper (or more, to taste)

1 whole garlic

1 teaspoon lemon zest

½ teaspoon liquid smoke

½ teaspoon Worcestershire sauce

½ teaspoon hot pepper sauce

Juice of 1 lemon

2–3 cups grated Parmesan cheese, to taste

What You Do

1. In a cooking pot, boil the whole potatoes with skin on 30 to 35 minutes over high heat until tender.

2. While the potatoes are cooking, cut the onion into 2 halves (¼ onion each), and place in a separate pot over low heat. Add the heavy whipping cream, butter, salt, and pepper.

3. Remove the natural "wrapper" of the garlic. Mash it and add to the cream mixture.

Nater's Taters—*continued*

4. Rinse the lemon in cold, running water. Use a grater or a sharp knife to scrape off 1 teaspoon of the yellow peel. Add to the cream mixture. Stir in the liquid smoke, Worcestershire sauce, hot pepper sauce, and lemon juice until well blended. Stir occasionally.

5. Drain the potatoes. Return the potatoes to the pot over high heat. Mash with a potato masher. Let sit uncovered on the hot burner for 3 minutes, until most of the moisture boils out.

6. Remove the cream mixture from the burner and turn off the heat. Reduce the heat under the potatoes to low. Use a slotted spoon to remove the onion and garlic from the cream mixture. Pour the mixture a little at a time into the mashed potatoes. Leaving the potatoes over the heat, use a portable mixer to blend to the preferred consistency. (The result will be thicker than traditional mashed potatoes.)

7. Pour the Parmesan cheese over the potatoes. Continue cooking 2 to 3 minutes until heated through.

If you're tired of green bean casserole made with mushroom soup, try this lighter side dish from the Greek Isles.

Greek Green Beans ᵛ

What You Need

1 medium onion

1 clove garlic

1 tablespoon olive oil

1 (6-ounce) can tomato paste

¾ cup water

Additional ½ cup water, as needed

Salt and pepper, to taste

1 (10-ounce) package frozen, French style green beans

What You Do

1. Peel and slice the onion horizontally about ¼" thick. Peel and chop the garlic into very small pieces.

2. Place the olive oil in a medium-size saucepan over medium-high heat. Add the onion and garlic, stirring constantly for about 1 minute until the onion is tender.

3. In a separate, small mixing bowl, stir together the tomato paste and water until smooth. Pour over the onion mixture. Sprinkle with salt and pepper.

4. Gently stir in the green beans until well coated with sauce. Cover and reduce heat to low. Cook 45 minutes, stirring several times during the cooking time. Occasionally stir in all or some of the additional ½ cup water as needed to keep the beans from burning. Beans are done when they are very soft.

Chapter 10
Snacks and Appetizers

Easy

Deviled Eggs 234
Chocolate Granola Bars 235
Cheese Biscuits 236
Apple Dip 237
S'Mores 238
Nutty Homemade Granola 238
Graham Cracker Sandwich 239
Easy Guacamole 240
Artichoke Parmesan Dip 241
Blue Cheese Veggie Dip 242
Tangy Mushrooms 243
Tangy Smoked Sausages 243
Cheese Quesadillas 244
Gouda Goodness 245
Krab with a Kick 246
Onion Bruschetta 247

Medium

Mexican Corn Bread 248
Spinach-Stuffed Mushrooms 249
Chili Cheese Dip 250
Green Chives Dip 251
Warm Pecan Cheese Dip 252
Pineapple Pepper Cheese Ball 253
Crab Cracker Spread 254
Variation: Shrimp Cracker Spread 254
Pizza on Rye 255
Sausage Swirls 256
Hummus 257
Sweet Wings 258

Hard

Easy Dinner Rolls 259
Latvian Ham and Onion Treat 260
Broccoli Cheese Dip 261
Reuben Dip 262
Spinach & Artichoke Dip 263

These picnic and potluck favorites also make a quick lunch or snack.

Because they contain mayonnaise that can easily spoil, take care to keep them cold until ready to eat—especially on a hot day.

If available, use a serving plate with depressions made especially for deviled eggs.

Deviled Eggs v

What You Need

6 eggs

¼ cup mayonnaise or mayonnaise-like salad dressing

½ teaspoon prepared mustard

Salt and pepper, to taste

Paprika, as needed

What You Do

1. Hard-boil the eggs (see Boiled Egg on page 8). Peel off the shells. Cut the eggs in half lengthwise. Remove the yolks and place them in a medium-size mixing bowl. Place the egg whites, rounded-side down, on a serving plate.

2. Mash the yolks with a fork. Stir in the mayonnaise, mustard, salt, and pepper. (Adjust measurements to taste.) Use a spoon to heap the mixture back into the holes in the egg white halves. Sprinkle with paprika. Refrigerate until ready to eat.

Grab a granola bar for breakfast or when you need a quick snack.

Tightly wrap leftovers in plastic wrap until ready to eat.

Chocolate Granola Bars v

What You Need

2½ cups crispy rice cereal

2 cups dry instant oatmeal

½ cup raisins

½ cup chocolate morsels

½ cup brown sugar

½ cup light corn syrup

½ cup peanut butter

1 teaspoon vanilla extract (or imitation)

What You Do

1. Place the rice cereal, oatmeal, raisins, and chocolate morsels in a large mixing bowl. Gently stir until well blended.

2. In a saucepan over medium-high heat, stir together the brown sugar and corn syrup until the mixture boils. Remove from heat. Stir in the peanut butter and vanilla extract until smooth.

3. Add the mixture from saucepan to the large mixing bowl. Gently stir until the all the ingredients are well coated. Place in a 9" × 13" baking pan that has been sprayed with nonstick cooking spray. Press into an even layer using the back of a spoon or your fingers. Cool. Cut into bars.

Cheese Biscuits v

Serve these biscuits as a snack any time of day.

They also make a nice accompaniment for Scrambled Eggs (page 9), Breaded Oven-Baked Fish (page 167), or soups and stews.

For best results, use ice-cold milk to make the dough easy to work with.

What You Need

Shortening, as needed

2 cups all-purpose flour

Pinch of salt

½ cup (1 stick) butter

½ cup milk

1 cup grated Cheddar cheese

What You Do

1. Preheat oven to 400°F. Grease a baking sheet with shortening.

2. In a large mixing bowl, use a fork to mix together the flour, salt, and butter. Stir in the milk until well mixed.

3. Use your hands to knead in the cheese. Press the heel of your hand into the dough, then fold over the dough onto itself. Repeat until well mixed.

4. Drop heaping spoonfuls of the dough onto the prepared baking sheet in rows. Bake for 10 to 12 minutes, until golden brown.

LEVEL **E**

SERVINGS **2**

It takes just a minute to transform an ordinary apple into a tasty snack.

This dip tastes best with tart apple varieties like Granny Smith and McIntosh.

If you have time, make the dip ahead and let it chill before eating.

Apple Dip v

What You Need

1 (8-ounce) package block cream cheese

1 cup dark brown sugar

2 teaspoons vanilla extract (or imitation)

2 apples

A few drops lemon juice

What You Do

1. Let the cream cheese soften at room temperature for about 10 minutes. Place in a small mixing bowl. Add the brown sugar and vanilla extract. Stir until well blended. Chill covered for at least 1 hour to give the flavors a chance to mingle.

2. Rinse apples in cold, running water. Pat dry with a paper towel. Cut apples in half. Remove cores. Slice apples. (Or use an apple corer.) Sprinkle a few drops of lemon juice on the apples to help prevent them from turning brown. Serve with the dip.

How Can I Keep Fruits from Turning Brown?

Fruits such as apples, bananas, and pears tend to turn brown after slicing. If you're using these fruits with dips or in salads, you can prevent this browning by sprinkling a few drops of lime or lemon juice on the fruit before serving. You can omit this step if the salad dressing includes lime or lemon juice as an ingredient.

S'Mores v

What You Need

2 graham cracker squares

½ flat-shaped chocolate bar (with or without nuts)

1 marshmallow

What You Do

If outdoors, roast marshmallow on a stick over a wood fire. Otherwise, place chocolate square on top of 1 graham cracker square. Place marshmallow on top of chocolate. Place on a microwave-safe plate. Microwave on high for 10 to 15 seconds until marshmallow softens. Remove from oven. Place second graham cracker square on top. Squish together.

Nutty Homemade Granola v

What You Need

2 tablespoons butter or margarine

2 tablespoons honey

2 tablespoons brown sugar

1 cup uncooked oatmeal (not instant)

¼ cup sunflower kernels

¼ cup sliced almonds

What You Do

In a frying pan, melt butter or margarine over low heat. Stir in honey and brown sugar until well blended. Stir in oats, sunflower kernels, and almonds. Cook and stir for 4 to 5 minutes. Spread (loose) on cookie sheet to cool. When cooled, store in an airtight container.

Graham Cracker Sandwich v

Name your favorite flavor, and it's in here.

No cooking, just stack it. The peanut butter holds it all together.

For variety substitute cinnamon-flavored graham crackers.

What You Need

4 chocolate graham cracker squares

2 tablespoons peanut butter

1 banana

2 teaspoons semisweet chocolate morsels

What You Do

1. Spread ¼ of the peanut butter on each graham cracker square.

2. Cut banana in half lengthwise. Cut in half again crosswise. Place 2 quarters of the banana on top of the peanut butter on each of 2 graham crackers. They will become the bottoms of the sandwiches.

3. Spoon chocolate morsels onto the other graham cracker squares. They will become the tops of the sandwiches. Use your fingers or the back of a spoon to press chocolate morsels into the peanut butter. Put the tops and bottoms together.

What would a party be without guacamole? Serve with corn or tortilla chips.

Or, serve it as a garnish for Tacos (see page 110), Vegan Enchiladas (see page 200), or other festive Mexican dishes.

Easy Guacamole v

What You Need

2 ripe avocados

2 tablespoons lemon juice

1–2 teaspoons cayenne pepper hot sauce, to taste

1 small tomato

1 small white onion

What You Do

1. Cut the avocados in half the long way, cutting around the seed. Remove the seed and peel. Place the avocados in a small mixing bowl. Mash with a fork. Stir in the lemon juice. Add the cayenne pepper hot sauce 1 teaspoon at a time to taste.

2. Chop the tomato and onion. Stir into the mashed avocados. Chill for 1 hour before serving.

The aroma of melting Parmesan cheese will fill the kitchen as you heat this tangy dip.

Serve with wheat crackers.

Do not substitute mayonnaise-like salad dressing in this recipe.

Artichoke Parmesan Dip v

What You Need

1 (14-ounce) can artichoke hearts

1 cup mayonnaise

⅓ cup grated Parmesan cheese

½ teaspoon garlic powder

What You Do

1. Preheat oven to 350°F. Drain the artichoke hearts. Chop into very small pieces (about ¼" square or less). Place into an ungreased 9" × 12" ovenproof baking pan.

2. Stir in the mayonnaise, Parmesan cheese, and garlic powder until well mixed. Bake for 20 minutes or until bubbly.

?

What Else Can I Do with Artichokes?

If you're unfamiliar with artichokes, don't let their unusual appearance scare you away. Some varieties of fresh artichokes have prickly points, so use the stem as a handle during purchase and preparation. Before steaming, slice off the tip and the thorn from each petal. You can steam artichokes or microwave them together with 1½ ounce water, 1 teaspoon vegetable oil, and 1 teaspoon lemon juice in a covered microwave-safe bowl for 6 to 8 minutes. Prepare several at one time. Cover and refrigerate. Leftovers will store for several days for quick snacks.

For blue cheese lovers only! This dip has a strong flavor that goes well with sliced cucumbers; zucchini; red, yellow, and green peppers; and cool, crisp chunks of celery and baby carrots.

Blue Cheese Veggie Dip v

What You Need

1 (8-ounce) block cream cheese

⅛ teaspoon garlic salt

⅛ teaspoon seasoned salt

Milk, as needed

4 ounces crumbled blue cheese

What You Do

1. Unwrap the cream cheese and place in a mixing bowl. Set aside at room temperature for 10 to 15 minutes to soften.

2. Add the garlic salt and seasoned salt to the cream cheese, and stir in by hand or beat with an electric mixer. Add the milk 1 tablespoon at a time to thin the mixture. Beat until smooth. The mixture should be smooth and thick enough for a spoon to stand up in it.

3. Stir in the blue cheese. Refrigerate for at least 1 hour before serving.

Should I Use Block or Softened Cream Cheese?

When purchasing cream cheese for a recipe, choose the block of cream cheese that comes in a box unless otherwise specified. The softened cream cheese that comes in a tub has been whipped. That means processing has added air to the product. If you use that type, your measurement will be inaccurate, especially in recipes that call for heating the cream cheese.

LEVEL E

SERVINGS 6

These tangy mushrooms add variety to your party menu. They provide a nice contrast to appetizers with cheese or meat.

Supply toothpicks for easy serving.

Tangy Mushrooms v

What You Need

2 (7³⁄₁₀-ounce) jars or 2 (8-ounce) cans of whole mushrooms

1½ teaspoons minced onion

1½ teaspoons dried parsley flakes

2 tablespoons bottled Italian salad dressing

What You Do

Drain the mushrooms and place in small mixing bowl. Add the onion and parsley. Sprinkle with salad dressing, and stir until heavily coated. (Excess dressing in the bottom of the bowl is okay.) Cover and refrigerate for at least 1 hour to let the flavors blend.

LEVEL E

SERVINGS 8

Why just add bottled barbecue sauce to mini sausages like everyone else when this recipe is almost as easy and has a special zing? You can substitute peach preserves for the apricot.

Serve with toothpicks.

Tangy Smoked Sausages

What You Need

1 cup apricot preserves

½ cup Dijon mustard

2 green onions

1 pound mini smoked sausages

What You Do

Place the preserves and mustard in a small saucepan over low heat. Chop the green onions, including about ½ of the dark green tops. Add to the saucepan, along with the sausages. Cover and cook about 30 minutes, stirring occasionally, until heated through. Keep warm until ready to serve.

Follow this recipe for a quick appetizer or snack using your favorite cheese.

For lunch or a dinner entrée, add ¼ cup cooked chicken.

For variety, top with Easy Guacamole (page 240).

Cheese Quesadillas v

What You Need

1 tablespoon butter or margarine

2 (6") flour tortillas

½ cup shredded cheese or 2 slices cheese

2 tablespoons bottled salsa or picante sauce

2 tablespoons sour cream

What You Do

1. Melt the butter in a frying pan over low to medium heat. Place 1 tortilla in the pan. Top with the cheese. Place the second tortilla on top. Heat until the bottom tortilla is golden brown.

2. Flip, as you would a pancake, to the other side. Heat until golden brown. Remove from the pan and place on a serving plate. Cut into fourths. Top with salsa or picante sauce and sour cream, or serve them on the side.

Gouda Goodness v

The aroma of freshly baked dough and warm, creamy cheese will bring your guests into the kitchen before this delightful dish is out of the oven.

You can substitute Edam, smoked Gouda, Cheddar, or any wheel-style cheese for the Gouda cheese. Provide a cheese or butter knife for cutting wedges.

What You Need

1 (7-ounce) wheel Gouda cheese

1 (8-ounce) can crescent roll dough

What You Do

1. Preheat oven to 375°F. Unwrap the cheese and peel off and discard the wax covering.

2. Open the package of dough and unroll on a cutting board or other flat surface. Use your fingers to mold the dough around the cheese, so it completely covers the cheese.

3. Place the dough-covered cheese in the center of an ungreased baking sheet. Bake for 11 to 13 minutes. Cheese should be warm and gooey, but not runny. Serve immediately.

Krab with a Kick

What You Need

¾ green bell pepper, divided

3 green onions

2 (4¼-ounce) cans crabmeat

3 cups shredded Cheddar cheese

¾ cup mayonnaise

1½ teaspoons garlic powder

¾ teaspoon dry mustard

1½ teaspoons ground red pepper

What You Do

1. Rinse the green bell pepper in cold running water. Cut in half lengthwise. Remove the stem and seeds. Cover ½ of the pepper and refrigerate for another use. Chop the remaining pepper into very small pieces. Place in a large mixing bowl. Remove the outer layer of the green onions. Slice crosswise. Add to the bowl.

2. Drain the crabmeat. Add to the bowl. Stir in the cheese, mayonnaise, garlic powder, dry mustard, and ground red pepper. Stir until well mixed. Cover and refrigerate for at least 2 hours until well chilled.

Onion Bruschetta v

What You Need

1 whole loaf Italian bread

2–3 tablespoons vegetable oil, as needed

1 cup grated mixed Italian cheese

½ cup chopped almonds (large chunks)

¼ teaspoon cumin

¼ teaspoon paprika

1 medium-size onion

What You Do

1. Use a bread slicer to slice the bread into ½"-thick slices. Brush with the vegetable oil. Place on a cookie sheet on the top shelf under the broiler until lightly toasted. Remove from oven and cover the slices with the cheese. Set aside.

2. Lightly oil a large skillet. Add the almonds. Sprinkle with the cumin and paprika. Toss until toasted. Drain the almonds on paper towel. Set aside.

3. Slice the onion into ½"-thick slices. Add 2 tablespoons vegetable oil to the skillet. Cook the onions over medium-high heat until tender. Drain on paper towel.

4. Preheat the oven to 350°. Spread the onions on the toasted bread. Sprinkle with the almonds. Reheat in the oven 20 to 30 minutes until warm.

Spice up ordinary corn bread to make a tasty snack that you can eat by itself or serve with soups or stews.

This is especially good with pork.

Mexican Corn Bread   v

What You Need

2 eggs

1 (4-ounce) can diced green chilies

1 cup yellow cornmeal

¾ cup vegetable oil

1 (14¾-ounce) can creamed corn

½ teaspoon baking soda

1 teaspoon salt

1½ cups shredded Cheddar cheese

What You Do

1. Preheat oven to 400°F. Crack the eggs into a large mixing bowl. Beat with a fork until smooth. Drain the chilies and add to the bowl. Stir in the cornmeal, vegetable oil, creamed corn, baking soda, and salt. Pour into a 9" × 12" ovenproof baking pan that has been greased with a few drops of shortening.

2. Top with the cheese. Bake for 45 minutes until the top is golden brown.

?

What Is an Easy Way to Drain Canned Foods?

If you need to drain a can of beans or other fruits or vegetables, you can open the can and dump the contents into a sieve or colander. An easier way is simply to open the can, but leave the separated lid in place. Hold it in place with your fingers as you invert the can over the sink until the liquid drains out.

Bubbly Swiss cheese adds zing to these baked appetizers that you serve fresh from the oven.

Choose any type or size of mushroom, but larger mushrooms have a more dramatic presentation than small ones.

Garnish with sprigs of fresh parsley.

Spinach-Stuffed Mushrooms   v

What You Need

1 (12-ounce) package frozen spinach soufflé

2–3 pounds fresh whole mushrooms

4–6 slices processed Swiss cheese

What You Do

1. Preheat oven to 350°F. Remove the spinach soufflé from the freezer. Unwrap and place in a small mixing bowl. Thaw for about 15 minutes.

2. Wipe the mushrooms with a damp paper towel to clean. Remove the stems. Cover the stems and refrigerate for another use. Place the mushrooms cap-side down in a 9" × 13" ovenproof baking pan that has been sprayed with nonstick cooking spray.

3. Spoon about 1 to 2 teaspoons spinach soufflé into each mushroom cap. Top with a square of Swiss cheese (about 1" square), big enough to cover the top of the mushroom without hanging over the edge. Bake for 10 to 12 minutes, until the cheese melts.

Chili Cheese Dip

This dip is sure to please the party crowd, or it's great for a case of the munchies.

For a lower-fat variation, try using ground turkey instead of beef and low-fat cream cheese.

What You Need

1 (8-ounce) block cream cheese

1 pound ground beef

1 packet taco seasoning

1 (10-ounce) jar salsa

About 2 cups shredded cheese (Mexican or Cheddar jack)

What You Do

1. Before beginning, set out the cream cheese to soften at room temperature for 10 to 15 minutes.

2. Spread the cream cheese into the bottom of a cake or pie pan.

3. Brown the meat and add the taco seasoning according to package directions. Drain off the fat. Preheat oven to 350°F. Pour the meat over the cream cheese.

4. Pour the salsa over the beef and top with the shredded cheese.

5. Bake until the cheese melts, about 15 minutes. Serve with corn or tortilla chips.

Green Chives Dip v

What You Need

Fresh chives (enough to yield 2 tablespoons chopped)

1½ teaspoons dried parsley flakes

1 cup mayonnaise

¾ cup sour cream

¼ cup plain yogurt

1½ teaspoons white vinegar

½ teaspoon dried tarragon

1–2 tablespoons lemon juice, to taste

½ teaspoon minced garlic

What You Do

1. Finely chop the chives. Place in a small mixing bowl along with the parsley flakes.

2. Stir in the mayonnaise, sour cream, yogurt, white vinegar, tarragon, lemon juice, and garlic until well blended. An electric mixer or electric blender makes this dip easier to prepare than stirring by hand, but the flavor will be the same.

Warm Pecan Cheese Dip   v

Based on appearance, your guests may expect this dip to taste spicy. Instead, it has a creamy, sweet flavor that tastes best with wheat crackers.

Because the dip is served warm, prepare and serve it in a slow cooker, if possible. (During the party, stir every 30 minutes or so to keep the surface from hardening.)

What You Need

1-pound block processed American cheese

1 cup whipping cream

1 (2-ounce) jar diced pimientos

1 (2¼-ounce) package chopped pecans

What You Do

1. Cut the processed cheese into 1" to 2" cubes and put in a slow cooker. Add the whipping cream (do not whip the whipping cream). Heat until the cheese melts. (If you don't have a slow cooker, you can complete this step in a 2-quart saucepan over low heat or in a microwave-safe mixing bowl in the microwave oven.)

2. When the cheese has melted, drain the pimientos, and add to the mixture. Stir in the pecans. Serve warm.

?

What Is Pimiento?

Pimiento is a red garden pepper often used to stuff green olives. You'll find pimiento in the canned vegetable aisle near pickles and olives. It comes in a small glass jar, so you'll have to look hard! If you can't find it, ask a grocery stocker or customer service representative.

Pineapple Pepper Cheese Ball v

Use this cheese ball for a delicious spread for club crackers, party rye bread, or Melba toast.

Garnish the serving plate with a few sprigs of fresh parsley.

What You Need

2 (8-ounce) packages boxed cream cheese (do not used whipped)

¼ green bell pepper

2 green onions

⅛ teaspoon garlic salt

2 teaspoons seasoned salt

1 (8-ounce) can crushed pineapple

1 (2¼-ounce) package chopped pecans

What You Do

1. Set out the cream cheese for 10 to 15 minutes to soften at room temperature. Place in a medium-size mixing bowl. Chop the green bell pepper. Chop the green onions. Add to the mixing bowl. Sprinkle the mixture with garlic salt and seasoned salt. Stir until well blended. Gently stir in the pineapple. Use your hands to form the mixture into a ball.

2. Place the chopped pecans in a layer on a dinner plate or a piece of waxed paper. Roll the ball in the nuts until the ball is covered. Place on a serving plate and chill for at least 1 hour before serving.

Crab Cracker Spread

Crustacean connoisseurs love this cracker spread.

Look for bottled cocktail sauce in the ketchup aisle or near the seafood department.

What You Need

½ cup bottled cocktail sauce

1 (8-ounce) package boxed cream cheese (do not used whipped)

1 (8-ounce) package imitation crab

1 sprig fresh parsley

What You Do

1. Pre-chill the bottle of cocktail sauce. Unwrap the block of cream cheese and place it in the center of a serving plate. With your fingers or a fork, separate the crab into flakes. Place the flakes on top of the cream cheese, letting some pieces fall over the side. Chill in the refrigerator for at least 1 hour.

2. When ready to serve, pour the cocktail sauce over the crab. Top with parsley. Surround with crackers. Stick a cheese knife into the top for easy serving.

Variation: Shrimp Cracker Spread

For a shrimp variation, substitute 1 (6-ounce) can of shrimp (drained) for the imitation crab, and add ¼ teaspoon garlic powder. Both variations taste best with club crackers.

Pizza on Rye

Aromatic oregano adds Italian flavor to these easy and delicious party favorites.

You may need several baking sheets. Or, heat in shifts.

Remove warm appetizers from the oven. Place on serving tray. Cool and reuse the baking sheet for the next set of "pizzas."

What You Need

1 pound ground pork breakfast sausage

1 pound shredded Cheddar or mozzarella cheese

1 loaf party rye bread

Oregano, as needed

What You Do

1. Brown the sausage in a frying pan (see "How Do I Brown Ground Beef?" on page 111). Drain off fat. Reduce heat to low.

2. Preheat oven to 350°F. Cut the cheese into 2" cubes. Add to the sausage. Stir together until the cheese melts.

3. Place the slices of party rye on ungreased baking sheets. Spoon about 1 tablespoon of the mixture onto each slice. Sprinkle with oregano. Bake for 5 to 10 minutes, until the mixture is bubbly. Serve warm.

What Can I Do with Party Rye Bread?

Look for party rye in the bread aisle. Loaves are small, and the slices are about ¼ the size of regular bread. For a quick snack, spread with softened cream cheese or spreadable Cheddar cheese. Or, make miniature bologna and cheese sandwiches to take to a potluck party.

Sausage Swirls

These appetizers look fancy, but they're easy to make, and they're sooooo good!

Refrigerate leftovers and reheat for breakfast.

What You Need

¼ cup butter or margarine

½ cup milk

2 cups biscuit mix

Flour, as needed

1 (16-ounce) package ground pork sausage

What You Do

1. Melt the butter over low heat. In a large mixing bowl, stir together the melted butter, milk, and biscuit mix.

2. Place half of the dough on a floured cutting board. Dust a rolling pin with flour. Roll the dough in each of four directions until the dough is about 7" × 10" and about ⅛" thick.

3. Spread ½ of the uncooked sausage in an even layer covering the rolled-out dough. Roll the long edge of the dough over itself until you have formed a roll about 10" long and about 3" in diameter. (The inside will alternate dough and sausage several times as you roll.)

4. Repeat steps 2 and 3 with the other half of the dough and sausage. Place both rolls in the freezer on a piece of waxed paper or aluminum foil for about 30 minutes or until the dough is hard enough to slice easily.

5. Preheat oven to 400°F. Slice the rolls crosswise into circles ¼" to ½" thick. (The dough will form a swirl through the sausage.) Lay the circles flat on an ungreased baking sheet. Bake for 15 minutes or until golden brown. Serve warm.

LEVEL **M**

SERVINGS **6**

Here's a tasty, high-protein appetizer everyone will love.

Serve with warm pita bread or in Hummus Pocket Sandwiches (page 47).

For the best results, use a food processor.

If you don't have one, use an electric blender, electric mixer, or a potato masher (this will take more elbow grease!) to make the dip smooth.

Hummus v

What You Need

1 (15-ounce) can chickpeas (also called garbanzo beans)

¼ teaspoon garlic powder

3 tablespoons tahini

½ teaspoon salt

2–3 teaspoons cumin powder

2–3 tablespoons lemon juice, to taste

¼ cup olive oil

Water, as needed (up to ¼ cup)

Additional salt and pepper, to taste

Paprika (optional)

Fresh parsley (optional)

What You Do

1. Drain the chickpeas and rinse in cold water. Place in a food processor or electric blender. Add the garlic powder, tahini, ½ teaspoon of salt, cumin, and 1 tablespoon of the lemon juice. Process until smooth, gradually adding the olive oil and water (up to ¼ cup) until the hummus reaches desired softness. Sprinkle with salt, pepper, and lemon juice, to taste.

2. Spread into a serving bowl. Drizzle a little olive oil and a few drops of lemon juice over the top. Sprinkle with paprika. Chop the parsley and sprinkle it over the hummus.

Sweet Wings

You can turn this Asian-flavored appetizer into a main dish by serving over cooked rice with a green vegetable or salad on the side.

Serve warm with lots of napkins.

What You Need

2 pounds chicken wings

¼ cup soy sauce

½ cup honey

1 tablespoon butter or margarine

What You Do

1. Rinse the chicken in cold, running water. Pat dry with a paper towel. Use a knife to separate each wing at the joint into 2 pieces. Set aside.

2. In a large mixing bowl, stir together the soy sauce and honey. Add the chicken wings to the bowl, making sure the wings are well coated with the mixture. Cover and refrigerate for at least 1 hour, or overnight.

3. Preheat oven to 400°F. Use the butter (or margarine) to grease a baking pan large enough to allow the wings to cook in a single layer. Remove the wings from the bowl and place in the pan. Spoon 2 to 3 tablespoons of the soy sauce mixture remaining in the bowl over the chicken.

4. Bake uncovered for 15 minutes. Repeat 3 times, using all of the sauce, for a total of 45 minutes cooking time. (To prevent illness, wash hands, bowl, and any surfaces that touched the raw chicken with soap and warm water.)

Easy Dinner Rolls v

What You Need

1 (¼-ounce) package active dry yeast

1 cup warm tap water

2 tablespoons white granulated sugar

1 teaspoon salt

2¼ cups all-purpose flour

1 egg

2 tablespoons solid shortening

What You Do

1. Dissolve the yeast in the water in a large mixing bowl. Stir in the sugar, salt, and ½ of the flour. Beat until smooth. Stir in the egg and shortening, then add the remaining flour. Beat until smooth. Cover with a clean kitchen towel. Set aside at room temperature (at least 30 minutes) until it rises to twice its original size.

2. Grease a muffin tin with the solid shortening. Punch down the dough until it reduces in size. Fill the muffin tin cups about ½ full. Set aside for another 20 to 30 minutes. The dough will rise again to the top of the cups. Preheat oven to 400°F. Bake for 15 to 20 minutes, until browned.

LEVEL **H**

SERVINGS **36**

Here's a traditional Latvian holiday favorite that's good any time of the year. Make the filling the night before to let the flavors mingle. Purchase refrigerated roll dough or double the recipe for Easy Dinner Rolls (page 259).

Latvian Ham and Onion Treat

What You Need

2½ pounds cooked ham

2 large white or yellow onions

Coarse black pepper, to taste

Basic roll dough for 2 dozen rolls (see Easy Dinner Rolls on page 259)

Flour, as needed

½ cup butter

What You Do

1. Cut the ham and onions into very small pieces. Place in a large mixing bowl. Add the pepper. Stir until well mixed. Cover and refrigerate overnight.

2. Make the roll dough and let rise. Dust a cutting board or rolling surface with flour. Also dust the surface of the rolling pin with flour. For each appetizer, use your fingers to pull off a piece of dough about the size of a golf ball. Roll into a ball; then roll the dough flat into a 2½"- to 3"-diameter circle.

3. Preheat oven to 400°F. Scoop a heaping teaspoon of the ham mixture onto the middle of the dough circle. Fold one side over the other. Fold the top and bottom over the sides. Pinch the dough together to seal. Turn over and place seam side down on an ungreased baking sheet. Bake for 10 to 15 minutes, until golden brown. Melt the butter in a small saucepan. Remove the appetizers from the oven and let cool. Brush with melted butter.

Broccoli Cheese Dip v

Serve this dip warm with wheat crackers or sliced party rye.

Make in a saucepan, microwave, or slow cooker.

What You Need

3 stalks celery

1 medium onion

1 (4-ounce) can sliced mushrooms

¾ cup butter or margarine

3 tablespoons flour

1 (10¾-ounce) can cream of celery soup

1 cup shredded Cheddar cheese

1 (10-ounce) package frozen chopped broccoli

What You Do

1. Thinly slice the celery. Chop the onion. Drain the mushrooms.

2. Melt the butter or margarine in a large frying pan over medium to medium-high heat. Be careful not to let the butter turn brown. Stir in the celery, onion, and mushrooms. Cook until tender. Stir in the flour.

3. Stir in the soup, cheese, and broccoli. Reduce heat to low. Cover and cook, stirring occasionally until cheese melts and broccoli is tender.

Reuben Dip

If you like grilled Reuben sandwiches, you'll love this dip—but it's not for everyone.

Serve warm with cocktail rye or triangles of pumpernickel bread.

What You Need

1 (3-ounce) package cream cheese, softened

½ cup sauerkraut

8 ounces sour cream

½ cup grated Swiss cheese

¼ pound sliced cooked corned beef

2–3 tablespoons milk

What You Do

1. Set out the cream cheese to soften (about 20 minutes).

2. Drain the sauerkraut. Chop. Place in a medium size saucepan.

3. Chop the corned beef into small pieces. Add to the saucepan.

4. Turn on heat to low. Stir in the cream cheese until mixture is warm and well-blended. Stir in the sour cream and Swiss cheese. Slowly add milk until dip is desired consistency.

LEVEL **H**

SERVINGS **8**

Your party guests will want this recipe and pass it along to all their friends.

Don't tell them how easy it is! Serve warm with blue or yellow corn chips.

Do not use fresh Parmesan cheese in this recipe.

Spinach & Artichoke Dip   v

What You Need

1 (16-ounce) bag frozen chopped spinach

1 can artichoke hearts (small can: 10 to 12 per can)

2 green onions

1 cup mayonnaise

1 cup sour cream

1 cup grated powdered Parmesan cheese

1–2 teaspoons garlic salt, to taste

Pepper, to taste

What You Do

1. Place spinach in a colander and rinse with cool, running water to thaw. Shake the spinach into a large, microwave-safe mixing bowl. Line the colander with paper towel. Return spinach to colander. With another paper towel on top, press the spinach to drain excess water. Rinse and dry the mixing bowl. Return spinach to the bowl.

2. Drain artichokes. Cut into fourths. Add to the spinach.

3. Rinse the green onions and remove outer skin and "tassels." Slice crosswise. Add to the bowl.

4. Stir in the mayonnaise, sour cream, and powdered Parmesan cheese until well blended. Add garlic salt and pepper, to taste. Microwave on high for 5 minutes, then keep warm in a slow cooker. Or, heat in a slow cooker for 2 hours on low.

Chapter 11

Desserts

Easy

Coconut Drop Cookies 266
Crispy Rice Cookies 267
Pecan Cookies 268
"Berry" Good Pudding 269
Cherry-Pineapple Pie 270
Slow-Cooked Rice Pudding 271
Easy Pumpkin Pie 272

Medium

Homemade Brownies 273
Shadow Berries 274
Baked Apples 275
Fruit Pizza 276
Chocolate Drop Cookies 277
Chocolate-Chip Cookies 278
Variation: Chocolate Chip Bars 279
Oatmeal Cookies 280
Peanut Butter Cookies 281
Kwik Kake 282
Yellow Cake 283
Chocolate Butter Frosting 284
Chocolate Peanut Parfait 285
Banana & Lemon Delight 286
Turtle Cake 287
Pink Lemonade Pie 288
Pecan Pie 289
Fresh Strawberry Pie 290
Heavenly Devil's Food Cake 291
Variation: Food for the Gods Cake 291
Fresh Peach Pie 292
Red, White, & Blue Cake 293

Chapter 11

Desserts—*continued*

Hard

Cupcake Surprise 294
Cherry Cheese Tarts à la Chalise. 296
Pineapple Pie 297
Coffee Pot de Crème 298
Honey Cake 300
Strawberry Trifle 302
Pineapple Angel Food Cake 303
Variation: Strawberry Angel Food Cake 303
Paradise Angel Food Cake. 304

These cookies—the easiest ones you'll ever make—use no flour and bake like a dream.

They make a great gift for coconut lovers.

Coconut Drop Cookies   v

What You Need

Solid vegetable shortening for greasing

1 (14-ounce) package flaked coconut

1 (14-ounce) can sweetened condensed milk

What You Do

1. Preheat oven to 300°F. Use solid shortening and a paper towel or piece of waxed paper to grease a cookie sheet. In a medium-size mixing bowl stir together coconut and sweetened condensed milk until coconut is well coated.

2. Drop spoonfuls of the mixture onto the cookie sheet. Make 3 rows of 4 drops. Bake 18 minutes until golden brown. Use a pancake turner and gently move each batch to a wire cooling rack. Cool. Repeat until all of the coconut mixture has been used. Store cooled cookies in an airtight container.

?

How Can I Sweeten Foods Besides Adding Sugar?

You can sweeten foods with corn syrup, honey, maple syrup, and molasses. But the most common sweetener used in home cooking is sugar. Sugar most commonly comes from sugar cane and sugar beet. However, some commercial sugars derive from sorghum, maple, and palm. The three types of sugar most often used in cooking are granulated sugar, brown sugar, and confectioners' sugar. Granulated sugar is the sugar you're used to seeing in a sugar bowl. Brown sugar is a mixture of granulated sugar and molasses. Brown sugar comes in light and dark varieties. Confectioners' sugar, also called powdered sugar, is fine granulated sugar mixed with cornstarch. Its texture resembles flour. When cooking, use the type of sugar the recipe specifies. Do not try to interchange them.

Crispy Rice Cookies v

What You Need

½ cup sugar

½ cup light corn syrup

1 cup peanut butter

2 cups toasted rice cereal

What You Do

1. Place sugar and syrup in a saucepan over low heat. Stir until mixture bubbles.

2. Stir in peanut butter. The mixture should have the consistency of fudge. Remove from heat. Stir in cereal until well coated. Use a tablespoon from your silverware drawer. Drop spoonfuls on waxed paper in rows. Cool.

Pecan Cookies   v

These nutty cookies are fun to make.

If you like, roll them in confectioners' sugar when they're still warm from the oven.

What You Need

¾ cup butter or margarine

½ cup brown sugar

2 tablespoons vanilla (or imitation)

1 cup pecans

What You Do

1. Place the butter or margarine in a large mixing bowl to soften for 30 minutes before beginning.

2. Stir in the sugar until creamy. Stir in the vanilla.

3. Chop the pecans into fine pieces. Add to the bowl. Blend well.

4. Preheat the oven to 250°F. Break off about 1 tablespoon of the batter and roll into a long, thin shape. Place on a greased cookie sheet. Repeat with the rest of the batter. Bake 10 minutes or until golden brown.

LEVEL **E**

SERVINGS **4**

Use your choice of strawberries, blueberries, blackberries, or raspberries for a colorful, delicious snack or dessert.

If you use strawberries, see "How Should I Clean Strawberries?" on page 274.

Slice strawberries before using as a topping.

You can substitute pressurized, canned whipped cream for the topping. Or, whip your own whipped cream.

"Berry" Good Pudding   v

What You Need

1 (3⁹⁄₁₀-ounce) package vanilla pudding (instant pudding is okay)

2 cups milk

1 cup fresh berries

¼ cup frozen nondairy whipped topping

What You Do

1. Prepare pudding according to package directions. Divide into serving bowls. Chill in the refrigerator.

2. Rinse berries under cold, running water. Drain. Top each serving of pudding with ¼ cup berries. Top each with 1 tablespoon of the whipped topping.

Rich and full of flavor, this snack is easy and delicious: it's no-crust and no-bake!

Serve with graham crackers or vanilla wafer cookies.

Cherry-Pineapple Pie v

What You Need

1 (8-ounce) can crushed pineapple

⅓ can cherry pie filling

⅓ cup sweetened condensed milk

¼ cup frozen nondairy whipped topping

What You Do

1. Drain pineapple. Place pineapple, cherry pie filling, and sweetened condensed milk in a medium-size mixing bowl. Stir together until well blended.

2. Top with whipped topping. Chill in the refrigerator at least 1 hour.

Slow-Cooked Rice Pudding v

Make this old-fashioned favorite in a modern slow cooker.

Use leftover rice, or cook rice according to package directions.

What You Need

1½ tablespoons butter

1¼ cups cooked rice

¾ cup evaporated milk

⅓ cup sugar

1 teaspoon vanilla (or imitation)

¼ teaspoon nutmeg

¼ cup raisins

2 eggs

What You Do

1. Lightly coat a slow cooker with cooking spray. Place the butter in the cold slow cooker to soften for about 30 minutes.

2. Add the rice, evaporated milk, sugar, vanilla, nutmeg, and raisins. Turn heat to low.

3. In a small mixing bowl, lightly beat the eggs. Add to the mixture in the slow cooker. Mix well. Cover and cook 1 hour. Remove cover and stir well. Cover and cook another hour.

Here's an easy recipe for the traditional Thanksgiving dessert.

Top with whipped cream, nondairy frozen whipped topping, or whipped cream in a pressurized can.

Easy Pumpkin Pie v

What You Need

1 (30-ounce) can pumpkin pie filling

1 (5-ounce) can evaporated milk

2 eggs

1 frozen 9" deep-dish pie shell

What You Do

1. Preheat oven to 425°F. Beat eggs in a large mixing bowl. Stir in pumpkin pie filling and evaporated milk until well blended. Pour into frozen pie shell.

2. Bake 15 minutes. Reduce heat to 350°F. Bake for another 50 to 60 minutes. Test for doneness by inserting a knife into the center of the pie. Pie is done when knife comes out clean. Remove from oven and place on a wire cooling rack. Cool at room temperature for 2 hours. Refrigerate at least 1 hour until thoroughly chilled.

You can make brownies from a mix, but homemade are so much better. And they're not any harder to do.

Be sure to cool completely before cutting.

Serve plain, frost with Chocolate Butter Frosting (page 284), or dust on all sides with confectioners' sugar.

Homemade Brownies v

What You Need

Shortening, as needed

4 (ounces) unsweetened baking chocolate

¾ cup butter or margarine

3 eggs

2 cups white granulated sugar

1 teaspoon vanilla (or imitation)

1 cup all-purpose flour

1 cup chopped walnuts or pecans (optional)

What You Do

1. Use the solid shortening to grease a 9" × 13" baking pan. Set aside. Preheat oven to 350°F. (If you're using a glass pan, preheat oven to 325°F.)

2. Place the baking chocolate and butter (or margarine) in a saucepan and melt over low heat. (Or, melt in a microwave on high for 2 minutes.) Stir until well blended. Pour into a large mixing bowl.

3. Lightly beat the eggs and stir them into the mixing bowl, along with the sugar and vanilla until well blended. Gently stir in the flour and nuts until all the ingredients are well mixed. Scrape into the prepared baking pan. Spread the mixture into an even layer.

4. Bake for 30 to 35 minutes. Test for doneness. Insert a toothpick into the center of the brownies and pull it out. The brownies are done if the toothpick has gooey crumbs sticking to it. Cool completely in the pan before cutting.

Shadow Berries v

Here's a fun treat to celebrate Groundhog Day. And you don't need the sun to cast a shadow over these strawberries. Make your own shadow with melted chocolate.

You can substitute chunks of banana for the strawberries.

What You Need

1 pint fresh strawberries

1 tablespoon solid vegetable shortening

1 (12-ounce) package semisweet chocolate morsels

1 (11½-ounce) bag milk chocolate morsels

What You Do

1. Rinse and clean the strawberries (see below), except leave on the stems to use as little handles for dipping.

2. In a saucepan over low heat, stir together the vegetable shortening and both packages of chocolate morsels until the chocolate melts. (Or, heat in a microwave-safe bowl in the microwave for about 2 minutes on high.)

3. Place a cooling rack on top of several thicknesses of paper towel. Use a table fork or fondue fork to "stab" each strawberry. Dip the strawberries in the melted chocolate. Place on cooling rack until the chocolate hardens.

How Should I Clean Strawberries?

Strawberries grow low to the ground, so rinse well to remove field dirt. Place strawberries in a large mixing bowl and soak several minutes in cold water. Pour into a colander. Repeat at least 3 times. With strawberries still in colander, rinse again under cold, running water. Drain. Remove the stem and green part (the large, green calyx called the hull) by cutting with a knife or using a huller, a small utensil that resembles tweezers with large flat prongs.

Baked Apples v

For the best flavor, choose such varieties as Jonathan, McIntosh, or Granny Smith. Their firm texture is best and their tartness balances the sweetness of the candy.

You can substitute 1 tablespoon cornstarch for the flour.

What You Need

2 fresh apples

3 tablespoons white granulated sugar

¼ teaspoon cinnamon

⅛ teaspoon salt

½ cup water

2 tablespoons all-purpose flour

Red-hot cinnamon candies

What You Do

1. Preheat oven to 350°F. Rinse the apples in cold, running water. Cut the apples in half and remove the cores. Place, peel-side down, in the bottom of a baking pan that has been sprayed with nonstick cooking spray.

2. In a saucepan, stir together the sugar, cinnamon, salt, water, and flour over low heat until hot and slightly thickened. Pour the mixture over the apples in the baking pan. Top with cinnamon candies. Bake uncovered for 40 to 50 minutes.

How Do I Use an Apple Corer?

If you like apples, you'll love a kitchen gadget called a corer. A corer is a circular tool with a round space in the middle and pie-shaped holes around the circle. The metal edges are sharp on the bottom side. To use, first rinse apple in cold running water. Pat dry with a paper towel (or your shirttail). Place apple on a cutting board, stem-side up. Place the circle of the corer over the stem. Push down in a single thrust. Lift tool. Apple slices will fall away, and the core will be removed.

This pizza really is a glorified cookie.

But with fresh fruit, it tastes so good that you might forget it's good for you, too.

Fruit Pizza v

What You Need

1 (18-ounce) tube refrigerated sugar cookie dough

2 (8-ounce) packages cream cheese

½ cup blueberries

½ cup green seedless grapes

½ cup strawberries

2 tablespoons confectioners' sugar

What You Do

1. Using your hands, shape the cookie dough into a circle on an ungreased cookie sheet. Or, form the dough into a ball and use a rolling pin to form into a circle. Bake according to package directions. Cool.

2. Let the cream cheese soften at room temperature for about 10 minutes. Spread the cream cheese in a thick layer over the cookie.

3. Rinse the blueberries and grapes under cold, running water. Drain. Pick the grapes off the stems. Slice in half lengthwise. Clean the strawberries (see "How Should I Clean Strawberries?" on page 274) and slice in half lengthwise.

4. Spoon the fruit over the top of the pizza. With the back of the spoon or your fingers, gently press the fruit into the cream cheese to anchor it in place. Cut into pie-shaped pieces. Sprinkle with confectioners' sugar. To serve, cut into pie-shaped pieces.

If you're in the mood for something chocolate, whip up a batch of these cookies.

Serve with a glass of cold milk or a scoop of your favorite flavor of ice cream.

Chocolate Drop Cookies v

What You Need

1 (12-ounce) package semisweet chocolate morsels

2 tablespoons butter

1 (14-ounce) can sweetened condensed milk

1 cup all-purpose flour

1 tablespoon vanilla (or imitation)

Pinch of salt

1 cup chopped pecans or walnuts

Shortening, as needed

What You Do

1. In a small saucepan over low heat, melt together the chocolate morsels and butter. Stir in the sweetened condensed milk until well blended.

2. Pour into a large mixing bowl. Stir in the flour, vanilla, and salt until well mixed. Gently stir in the nuts.

3. Preheat oven to 350°F. Grease a cookie sheet with solid shortening. Spoon a heaping teaspoonful of the mixture onto the cookie sheet. Repeat in rows. Bake for 8 to 10 minutes.

4. Use a pancake turner to remove from cookie sheet. Cool on a wire rack. Or, eat warm if you can't wait!

Chocolate-Chip Cookies   v

Chocolate chip cookies should be in every cook's repertoire, and this recipe has the added goodness and texture of oatmeal.

You can buy cookies in a package, but they're so much better homemade—especially served warm right out of the oven! You can use either regular or instant oatmeal in this recipe.

What You Need

1 cup (2 sticks) butter or margarine

1 firmly packed cup brown sugar

½ cup white granulated sugar

2 eggs

1 teaspoon vanilla (or imitation)

1½ cups all-purpose flour

1 teaspoon baking soda

2 teaspoons cinnamon

½ teaspoon salt

3 cups uncooked oatmeal

1 (12-ounce) package semisweet chocolate morsels

What You Do

1. Before you begin, set out the butter (or margarine) for about 20 minutes to soften at room temperature. In a large mixing bowl, use an electric mixer to beat together the butter, brown sugar, and white sugar until creamy. Lightly beat the eggs and add to the bowl, along with the vanilla. Beat until smooth.

2. In a separate, medium-size mixing bowl, stir together the flour, baking soda, cinnamon, and salt until well mixed. Slowly add the flour mixture to the large mixing bowl, stirring with a spoon or your hands until well mixed. Stir in the oats. Gently stir in the chocolate morsels.

Chocolate-Chip Cookies—*continued*

3. Preheat oven to 350°F. Scoop heaping tablespoons of the dough and drop onto an ungreased cookie sheet in 3 evenly spaced rows of 4 cookies each. Bake for 10 to 12 minutes, until golden brown. Remove from the oven and let cool for 1 minute. Use a pancake turner to move the cookies onto a wire rack.

LEVEL **M**

SERVINGS **48**

Variation: Chocolate Chip Bars

You can use the same recipe for chocolate chip bars instead. When the dough is ready, pour into an ungreased 9" × 13" baking pan. Bake for 30 to 35 minutes. Cool in the pan. Cut into twelve 3" × 4" rectangles.

?

What If I Can't Find the Right Ingredient Size?

What if your recipe calls for a 5⅓-ounce can of evaporated milk, but you get to the store and find only a 5-ounce can? Or, what if your recipe says a 10¾-ounce can of soup, but you find only a 10½-ounce can? Do you buy 2 cans of evaporated milk and measure out ⅓ ounce? Do you pour out some of the soup? No. Can sizes may vary by brand. If a recipe calls for a certain size can, choose the size closest to the one the recipe calls for. For example, vegetables come in sizes that are roughly 8-ounces and 15-ounces. If your recipe calls for 2 cups of green beans, use the 15-ounce can.

Here's an old-fashioned treat that's still a favorite with kids of all ages.

You can omit the raisins and/or nuts if you prefer.

The oats in this recipe are simply uncooked oatmeal.

Oatmeal Cookies v

What You Need

1 egg

¼ cup solid shortening

¼ firmly packed cup brown sugar

¼ cup white granulated sugar

¼ teaspoon vanilla (or imitation)

1 tablespoon milk

½ cup all-purpose flour

¼ teaspoon baking soda

¼ teaspoon salt

¾ cup oats

½ cup seedless raisins

½ cup chopped walnuts

What You Do

1. Lightly beat the egg. In a large mixing bowl, stir together the egg, shortening, brown sugar, white sugar, and vanilla. Stir in the milk.

2. In a separate, medium-size mixing bowl stir together the flour, baking soda, and salt. Slowly add the flour mixture to the large mixing bowl, stirring with a spoon or your hands until well mixed. Stir in the oats, raisins, and walnuts.

3. Preheat oven to 400°F. Scoop a rounded teaspoon-ful of dough onto an ungreased cookie sheet. Make 3 rows of 4 cookies each. Bake for 8 to 10 minutes. Use a pancake turner to remove the cookies from the cookie sheet. Let cool on a wire rack.

Peanut Butter Cookies v

There's nothing like warm peanut butter cookies straight from the oven. And they're quick and easy to make.

What You Need

½ cup butter or margarine

½ cup solid shortening

1 cup peanut butter

1 cup white granulated sugar

1 firmly packed cup brown sugar

2 eggs

1 teaspoon vanilla (or imitation)

2¼ cups all-purpose flour

2 teaspoons baking soda

¼ teaspoon salt

What You Do

1. Before beginning, set out the butter (or margarine) for 10 or 15 minutes to soften at room temperature. In a large mixing bowl, stir together the butter, shortening, peanut butter, white and brown sugar, eggs, and vanilla until well blended.

2. In a separate bowl, mix together the flour, baking soda, and salt. Stir into the peanut butter mixture, using a spoon or your hands, until well mixed.

3. Preheat oven to 375°F. Take 1 to 2 tablespoons of dough and use your hands to form it into balls about 1" in diameter. Place about 2" to 3" apart on an ungreased cookie sheet in 3 rows of 4.

4. Dip a table fork into flour and push down on each ball to partly flatten the cookie. Repeat to form a crisscross pattern. Bake for 10 to 12 minutes. Use a pancake turner to remove from the cookie sheet. Let cool on a wire rack.

You don't even need a mixing bowl for this easy cake you make from scratch. Just mix everything together and bake. And you don't need eggs or frosting, either. It's an almost-instant snack or dessert.

Kwik Kake v

What You Need

1½ cups all-purpose flour

1 cup white granulated sugar

6 tablespoons vegetable oil

3 tablespoons cocoa

1 teaspoon salt

1 teaspoon baking soda

1 tablespoon vinegar

1 cup cold water

1 teaspoon vanilla (or imitation)

1 tablespoon confectioners' sugar

What You Do

1. Preheat oven to 350°F. In an ungreased 9" × 12" baking pan, stir together all the ingredients except the confectioners' sugar until well blended. Bake for 25 minutes.

2. Let cool. Sprinkle with confectioners' sugar.

LEVEL **M**

LAYERS **1**

Here's a quick and easy cake you can make from scratch.

Top with Chocolate Butter Frosting (page 284) or your favorite canned or packaged frosting.

Yellow Cake v

What You Need

⅓ cup solid shortening, plus extra for greasing

½ cup all-purpose flour, plus extra for dusting

¾ cup white granulated sugar

2½ teaspoons baking powder

½ teaspoon salt

1 egg

1½ teaspoons vanilla extract (or imitation)

¾ cup milk

What You Do

1. Preheat oven to 375°F. Grease a round or square baking pan with shortening and dust lightly with flour.

2. Place the ⅓ cup shortening, ½ cup flour, the sugar, baking powder, salt, egg, vanilla, and ½ of the milk in a large mixing bowl. Beat with an electric mixer or by hand for about 2 minutes. Pour in the remaining milk and beat for another 2 minutes. Pour the batter into the prepared baking pan.

3. Bake for 30 minutes. Test for doneness by inserting a toothpick into the center of the cake. The cake is done if the toothpick comes out clean. Remove from the oven and let cool on a wire rack. Let the cake cool completely before frosting.

Chocolate Butter Frosting v

This recipe makes enough frosting for a 1-layer cake

This creamy frosting will satisfy the chocolate lover in you.

Use to frost Yellow Cake (page 283), Homemade Brownies (page 273), or your favorite cake or cupcakes.

What You Need

3 tablespoons butter or margarine

1 ounce unsweetened chocolate

2⅓ cups confectioners' sugar

¾ teaspoon vanilla (or imitation)

1–2 tablespoons milk

What You Do

1. Before beginning, set out the butter (or margarine) for 10 to 15 minutes to soften at room temperature. In a saucepan over low heat, melt the chocolate. Remove from heat. Set aside.

2. Sift the confectioners' sugar into a mixing bowl or shake through a strainer 3 times. Set aside.

3. In a small mixing bowl, beat the butter with an electric mixer or by hand until fluffy. Stir in the melted chocolate, vanilla, 1 tablespoon milk, and ½ of the sugar. Beat until well blended. Slowly add remaining sugar. If the frosting becomes too thick, add more milk a little at a time until the frosting reaches the desired consistency.

Chocolate Peanut Parfait v

Wow your guests with this frozen dessert that takes only minutes to prepare but needs to be made at least 4 hours before the party to allow for the necessary freezing time.

Cover any leftovers with aluminum foil and freeze.

What You Need

1 quart vanilla ice cream

¼ cup (½ stick) butter or margarine

1 dozen chocolate sandwich cookies

6 ounces salted Spanish peanuts

2 cups hot fudge topping for ice cream

What You Do

1. Remove the ice cream from the freezer and set aside for about 10 minutes to soften. Spray a 9" × 13" baking pan with nonstick cooking spray.

2. In a frying pan, melt the butter over low heat. Place the cookies on a cutting board. Crush between 2 sheets of waxed paper with a rolling pin. Add to the melted butter. Remove from heat and stir. Spoon the mixture into the baking pan. Use your fingers to pack the mixture in the bottom of the pan.

3. Spread the ice cream over the cookie mixture. Add a layer of peanuts. Cover with aluminum foil and freeze for at least 3 hours, until hard.

4. Top with fudge topping. Refreeze for about 1 hour. Serve directly from the freezer.

Banana & Lemon Delight v

Sweet, tangy, and salty, this dessert has something to please everyone.

Serve while the sauce is still warm, or let cool to room temperature.

You can use lemon juice concentrate, but fresh lemons taste best.

What You Need

2 eggs

1 cup sugar

1 tablespoon flour

⅛ teaspoon salt

Juice of 2 lemons

1 cup water

½ cup whipping cream or half-and-half

6 bananas

½ cup shelled peanuts

What You Do

1. Crack the eggs into a medium saucepan. Beat lightly with a fork.

2. Turn heat to medium. Stir in the sugar, flour, salt, lemon juice, water, and whipping cream or half-and-half. Cook, stirring frequently, until sauce thickens.

3. Slice the bananas lengthwise. Arrange in the bottom of a serving dish. Pour sauce over all.

4. Spill out the peanuts on a large cutting board. Cover with waxed paper. Use a hammer to crush the peanuts. Sprinkle over the sauce.

Turtle Cake v

What You Need

1 tablespoon solid vegetable shortening

1 (18¼-ounce) box German chocolate cake mix

1 (14-ounce) package caramels

½ cup (1 stick) butter

1½ cups evaporated milk

1 cup chopped pecans

1 cup semisweet chocolate morsels

What You Do

1. Preheat oven to 350°F. Use a paper towel to grease a 9" × 13" baking pan with the shortening. Dust with about 2 teaspoons of the dry cake mix. Return "extra" dry mix to the package.

2. Mix the cake batter in a large mixing bowl, according to package directions. (Check the box for egg, oil, and water requirements to be sure you have the ingredients on hand.) Pour ½ of the batter into the prepared baking pan. Bake for 15 minutes. Remove from oven.

3. While the cake is baking, stir together the caramels, butter, and milk in a saucepan over low heat. Stir constantly until the caramels melt. Be careful not to let the milk scorch the bottom of the pan. After removing the cake from the oven, pour the caramel mixture over the cake. Top with a layer of pecans and a layer of chocolate morsels. Cover with remaining batter. Return to oven and bake for 15 to 20 minutes, until a toothpick inserted in the center comes out clean.

Pink Lemonade Pie v

Served cold, this lemony dessert makes a refreshing treat on a hot summer day.

You'll need a portable hand mixer.

Also, do not substitute frozen nondairy whipped topping for the whipping cream.

Cover any leftover pie with aluminum foil and freeze.

What You Need

1 (6-ounce) can frozen pink lemonade concentrate

1 (8-ounce) package boxed cream cheese

1 (14-ounce) can sweetened condensed milk

3 drops red food coloring (optional)

½ pint whipping cream

1 (9") graham cracker pie crust

What You Do

1. Thaw the lemonade concentrate (do not dilute). Let the cream cheese soften at room temperature for about 10 minutes.

2. In a large mixing bowl, use an electric hand mixer to beat the cream cheese until fluffy. Beat in the lemonade concentrate, sweetened condensed milk, and food coloring.

3. Whip the cream (see "How Do I Whip Cream" on page 289) in a separate mixing bowl. Spoon the whipped cream onto the cream cheese mixture in the large bowl. Gently mix by stirring from the bottom and placing the mixture on top of the whipped cream. Mix until well blended.

4. Refrigerate for 30 minutes or until the mixture mounds slightly when dropped from a spoon. Pour into the crust. Freeze for 6 hours or until firm. When ready to serve, remove the pie from the freezer and let sit for 10 minutes before serving.

Pecan Pie v

What You Need

1½ cups maple syrup

¼ cup white granulated sugar

¼ cup butter or margarine

1½ cups pecan halves

1 unbaked 9" pie crust

3 eggs

1 teaspoon vanilla (or imitation)

Dash of salt

What You Do

1. In a medium-size saucepan over medium-high heat, stir together the syrup, sugar, and butter (or margarine) until the mixture boils. Continue cooking for 5 minutes, stirring occasionally. Remove from heat.

2. Place the pecans in an even layer in the bottom of the pie crust. Preheat oven to 375°F.

3. In a mixing bowl, slightly beat the eggs with a fork. Stir in the vanilla and salt. Spoon a little of the syrup mixture at a time into the egg mixture, stirring until well mixed. Drizzle over the pecans.

4. Bake for 35 to 40 minutes. Test for doneness. A knife inserted in the center should come out clean.

?

How Do I Whip Cream?

Place the mixing bowl and wire whisk or beaters for your electric mixer in the freezer to chill for about 30 minutes. Pour whipping cream into the bowl. Use a wire whisk or electric mixer to whip until the cream is stiff enough to hold a stiff peak. Be careful not to beat too long or you'll have fresh butter! Cover and refrigerate until ready to use. If the whipped cream starts to separate while sitting in the refrigerator, whip again for 1 minute.

Fresh Strawberry Pie v

When luscious fat strawberries come into season in the spring, use some of them to create this popular pie.

If strawberries are out of season, you can substitute frozen ones. Thaw them first.

Instead of frozen topping, you can make homemade whipped cream (see "How Do I Whip Cream?" on page 289).

What You Need

1 frozen 9" pie crust

2 cups fresh strawberries

1 cup white granulated sugar

2 tablespoons cornstarch

1 cup water

¼ cup strawberry-flavored gelatin (powdered mix)

1 (8-ounce) carton frozen nondairy whipped topping

What You Do

1. Bake the pie crust according to package instructions. Set aside. Clean the strawberries (see "How Should I Clean Strawberries?" on page 274). Slice about ½ of the strawberries into halves. Set aside.

2. In a large frying pan over medium heat, stir together the sugar, cornstarch, and water until the sauce is clear and thick. Remove from heat. Stir in the gelatin mix until well blended. Let cool.

3. Gently stir in the sliced and whole strawberries until well coated. Pour the mixture into the pie shell. Chill in the refrigerator. When ready to serve, top with whipped topping.

Heavenly Devil's Food Cake   v

Warning: Serve only to your closest friends. No one will leave the party until this is all gone.

Make a day ahead, so you can refrigerate overnight and let sauces soak in.

What You Need

1 (18¼-ounce) box devil's food cake mix

1 (11¾-ounce) jar caramel topping sauce

1 (14-ounce) can sweetened condensed milk

1 (8-ounce) package frozen nondairy whipped topping

What You Do

1. Bake cake in a greased 9" × 13" pan, according to package directions. (Check box for egg, oil, and water requirements to be sure you have the ingredients on hand.) Cool completely. Use the handle of a wooden spoon to poke holes all over top of cake.

2. In a saucepan over low heat, stir together caramel topping and sweetened condensed milk until well blended. Cool. Drizzle over the cake. Cover with foil and refrigerate overnight. When ready to serve, remove from refrigerator and top with frozen non-dairy whipped topping.

Variation: *Food for the Gods Cake*

Prepare as above, but substitute white cake mix for devil's food, and substitute chocolate fudge topping for the caramel sauce.

The filling for this pie cooks into a creamy custard.

You can slice the peaches instead of cutting them in half, if you like.

A "rounded" tablespoon has a small "hill" that extends above the spoon. If you scrape off the "hill," you get a "level" tablespoon.

Fresh Peach Pie   v

What You Need

6 ripe peaches

1 unbaked 9" pie crust

1 cup sugar

2 rounded tablespoons cornstarch

1 cup whipping cream (unwhipped)

What You Do

1. Peel the peaches and cut in half horizontally. Place in the pie crust, flat-side up.

2. Preheat the oven to 425°F. In a small mixing bowl, stir the cornstarch and sugar until well mixed. Sprinkle over the peaches.

3. Pour the whipping cream over the top.

4. Bake 15 minutes. Reduce heat to 375°F. Bake 40 to 45 minutes until peaches are tender and the filling bubbles.

Here's a festive, colorful dessert for your Fourth of July picnic.

Just dump in all the ingredients and bake.

Serve in bowls with vanilla ice cream

Red, White, & Blue Cake v

What You Need

1 (18¼-ounce) package white cake mix

1 (15-ounce) can blueberries

1 (20-ounce) can cherry pie filling

1 stick (½ cup) butter or margarine

What You Do

1. Preheat oven to 350°F. Grease a 9" × 13" × 2" oven-proof baking pan. Sprinkle about 1 tablespoon of the dry cake mix over the bottom and sides of the pan. Tilt the pan right, left, back, and forth until the pan is lightly coated.

2. Pour blueberries and syrup into the pan and spread evenly. Pour cherry pie filling in a layer over the blueberries. Pour dry cake mix to form a third layer.

3. Melt butter or margarine in a saucepan over low heat. Pour the butter from a spoon to drizzle all over the top of the cake mix. Bake 45 minutes, or until the top of the cake is golden brown.

Cupcake Surprise v

These easy cupcakes have a nutty cream cheese filling, so you can serve them without frosting if you like.

For easy cleanup, use paper cupcake liners.

What You Need: For the cupcakes

¼ cup butter or margarine

½ cup white granulated sugar

1 egg

½ teaspoon vanilla (or imitation)

⅔ cup all-purpose flour

¼ cup unsweetened cocoa powder

1 teaspoon baking powder

½ cup milk

What You Need: For the filling

3 ounces cream cheese

¼ cup white granulated sugar

2 tablespoons chopped walnuts or pecans

½ teaspoon vanilla (or imitation)

What You Do

1. To make the cupcakes, set out the butter (or margarine) to soften at room temperature for 10 or 15 minutes. In a medium-size mixing bowl, stir together the butter and sugar until fluffy. Stir in the egg and vanilla.

2. In a separate small mixing bowl, stir together the flour, cocoa, and baking powder. Add ½ of the flour mixture to the egg mixture, stirring until well blended. Slowly stir in the milk. Add remaining flour mixture and stir until the batter is smooth. Set aside.

Cupcake Surprise—*continued*

3. To make the filling, set out the cream cheese for 10 to 15 minutes to soften at room temperature. Place the cream cheese, sugar, nuts, and vanilla in a small mixing bowl. Stir until well mixed.

4. Preheat oven to 375°F. Grease a 12-cup muffin tin with shortening and dust with flour, or place paper baking cups in the muffin spaces.

5. Spoon 1 tablespoon of the cupcake batter into each cup. Spoon 1 teaspoon of the filling into each cup. Spoon another tablespoon of batter on top of the filling, dividing the batter evenly among all cupcakes. Bake for 20 minutes. Let cool on a wire rack.

What Is the Difference Between *Fold*, *Beat*, and *Whip*?

The term *fold* means to mix ingredients by sliding a spoon or spatula toward you along the bottom of the bowl, then up the side. In effect, you are blending ingredients by gently turning them over on top of each other. The terms *beat* and *whip* refer to rapid, circular stirring motions, using a wire whisk or portable hand mixer. Both methods add air to the ingredients. Beating makes ingredients smooth and fluffy. Whipping lightens the mixture and increases its volume.

Cherry Cheese Tarts à la Chalise   v

This recipe is responsible for at least one marriage!

You can use a 12-cup muffin tin with paper liners. Or, you can use a 9" pie pan instead if you increase the baking time by 5 minutes.

What You Need

1 (21-ounce) can cherry pie filling

1 (8-ounce) package block cream cheese (do not use whipped)

13 graham cracker squares (7½ rectangles broken in halves)

2 teaspoons white granulated sugar

2½ tablespoons butter

½ cup confectioners' sugar

1 egg

1 teaspoon vanilla (or imitation)

What You Do

1. Chill the pie filling in the refrigerator. Set out cream cheese to soften for 10 to 15 minutes. Place the graham crackers on a cutting board or other rolling surface. Crush with a rolling pin.

2. Place the crumbs in a medium-size mixing bowl. Add the granulated sugar. Melt the butter over low heat in a saucepan. Drizzle over the crumbs. Stir until well mixed. Press the mixture into the bottom of paper cupcake liners placed in a muffin tin.

3. Preheat oven to 350°F. In a small mixing bowl, stir together the cream cheese, confectioners' sugar, egg, and vanilla until well blended. Spread over the graham cracker crust. Bake for 10 to 15 minutes. Let cool.

4. Spoon the cherry pie filling over the tarts. Chill for about 1 hour (or even overnight) before serving.

Pineapple Pie v

What You Need

1 9" frozen deep-dish pie crust

8 ounces frozen cherries

1 (8-ounce) can crushed pineapple, with juice

¼ cup all-purpose flour

½ cup, plus 2 tablespoons white granulated sugar

½ (3-ounce) package strawberry gelatin dessert

1 banana

½ (2¼-ounce) package slivered almonds

4 ounces nondairy frozen whipped topping

What You Do

1. Bake the pie crust according to package directions until golden brown. Let cool.

2. While the crust is baking, place the cherries into a saucepan to thaw. When partially defrosted, stir in the pineapple with juice, flour, sugar, and strawberry gelatin. Cook over low heat until the cherries have defrosted and the pot is steaming. Remove from heat.

3. Peel and slice the banana crosswise into thin circles. When the pie crust is cool to the touch, place ½ of the banana slices in the bottom of the pie shell. Sprinkle with almonds. Pour the cooled cherry mixture over the almond layer. Top with nondairy frozen whipped topping. Chill in the refrigerator for at least 1 hour.

This sounds hard, but it really is simple! And mmmm—so good.

It's easy enough to make any day and elegant enough to impress a party crowd! Start early. The dessert needs at least 2 hours to chill.

You'll need 6 ceramic, oven-proof coffee mugs.

Instead of whipping your own cream, you can use pressurized canned whipped cream.

Coffee Pot de Crème   v

What You Need

5 eggs

½ cup white granulated sugar

½ teaspoon vanilla (or imitation)

3 tablespoons instant coffee

½ cup heavy cream

Water, as needed

¼ cup whipped cream (see "How Do I Whip Cream?" on page 289)

What You Do

1. Preheat oven to 350°F. Separate the egg yolks and whites (see "How Do I Separate Eggs?" on page 299). Cover and refrigerate the egg whites for another use. Wash your hands with soap after handling the raw eggs. In a small mixing bowl, beat together the egg yolks, sugar, and vanilla until smooth. Set aside.

2. In a medium-size saucepan, stir together the instant coffee and heavy cream. Heat over medium-low heat, stirring often until small bubbles form at the sides and a light skin forms on the cream. (Do not let the cream boil!)

3. Hold a strainer over the yolk mixture and pour ½ of the cream into it to remove any "skin" that forms. Stir until well mixed. Strain the remaining cream into the yolk mixture. Stir until smooth. Divide the mixture into 6 ceramic coffee mugs. Place the coffee mugs in a 9" × 12" baking dish. Fill the baking dish ½ full with water.

Coffee Pot de Crème—continued

4. Bake for 25 to 30 minutes. The dessert is done when the mixture is firm enough not to slosh around when slightly shaken. Remove from oven. Cool to room temperature. Chill in the refrigerator at least 2 hours. When ready to serve, top with whipped cream.

How Do I Separate Eggs?

The easiest way to separate the yolk and the white of a raw egg is to use your hands. (Be sure they're clean!) Hold one hand—palm-side up—over a mixing bowl. Crack the egg into your palm and let the white ooze through your fingers until the yolk is all you have left in your hand. Gently place the yolk in a separate bowl or coffee cup. Be sure to wash hands and mixing bowls with soap and warm water after handling raw eggs.

Another method to separate egg yolks and whites is using a gadget called (ingeniously) an egg separator. Secure the egg separator on the lip of a small mixing bowl. Crack the egg. Open the shell over the egg separator and let the yolk fall into the depression in the device. The white will run out the sides into the bowl. Place the yolk in a separate bowl or cup.

Or, use the eggshell itself. Crack the egg over a small mixing bowl, being careful to catch the yolk in half of the shell. Let the white run into the bowl. Pour the yolk into the other half shell, again letting whatever of the egg white remains fall into the bowl. Repeat as necessary.

Honey cake recipes abound. Here's a recipe to get you started. Look for other variations—or ask your mother or grandmother.

Before you begin, let all the ingredients stand on the counter until they reach room temperature (about 70°F).

Honey Cake v

What You Need

Shortening, as needed

2 cups, plus 2 tablespoons all-purpose flour

½ cup butter (or solid shortening)

½ cup white granulated sugar

2 eggs

½ teaspoon baking soda

1 teaspoon double-acting baking powder

½ teaspoon cinnamon

¼ teaspoon ground ginger

¼ teaspoon salt

½ cup honey

½ cup strong coffee, cooled

½ teaspoon vanilla extract (or imitation)

¾ cup chopped walnuts

1 tablespoon grated orange rind

1–2 tablespoons confectioners' sugar

What You Do

1. Preheat oven to 350°F. Grease a 9" × 12" ovenproof baking pan. Place the 2 tablespoons flour into the pan. Tip, tilt, and gently tap the pan until the flour dusts the sides and bottom.

2. In a large mixing bowl, use a spoon or electric mixer to blend the butter and sugar until soft and smooth. Add the eggs and continue blending until the mixture is light and fluffy. Set aside.

Honey Cake—*continued*

3. Place a piece of waxed paper on the counter. Sift together the 2 cups flour, baking soda, baking powder, cinnamon, ginger, and salt onto the waxed paper. Set aside. In a separate medium-size mixing bowl, stir together the honey and coffee until well blended. Stir in the vanilla extract, walnuts, and grated orange rind until well mixed.

4. Scoop about ⅓ of the sifted ingredients into the egg mixture. Stir. Scoop about ⅓ of the honey mixture into the egg mixture. Stir. Continue alternating ⅓ of each mixture until all the ingredients are well blended. Pour the batter into baking pan.

5. Bake for 30 minutes. Let cool. Sprinkle with confectioners' sugar.

How Do I Sift Flour?

Sifting flour adds air to a recipe. To sift, place a small amount of flour into the top of the sifter. Hold device over a mixing bowl and pull on handle several times until all of the flour passes through the screen. One way to mix dry ingredients is to sift them together. Simply place all the ingredients into the top of the sifter at the same time. Sift. If you don't have a sifter, you can create the same effect by placing flour and other dry ingredients in a strainer. Gently shake strainer until all ingredients have passed through.

Strawberry Trifle v

Creamy pudding, fresh strawberries, and moist pound cake make this dessert good enough for royalty. In fact, a trifle is a typical dessert following traditional meals in the British Isles and may well have been enjoyed by kings and queens.

Prepare in a glass salad bowl, so guests can see the layering effect.

What You Need

1 (16-ounce) package frozen, prepared pound cake

About 1 cup prepared orange juice

1 quart fresh strawberries

2 (3-9/10-ounce) packages instant vanilla pudding

2 cups milk

1 (12-ounce) container frozen nondairy whipped topping

What You Do

1. Cut cake in thirds horizontally, then into 1" cubes. Pour enough orange juice over the cake to soak it. (Pour a little at a time so you don't drench the cake.)

2. Clean strawberries. Thinly slice all but 3 strawberries. Prepare pudding and milk according to package directions.

3. In a deep glass serving bowl, repeat layers of cake, strawberries, pudding, and nondairy frozen whipped topping until mixture reaches the top of the bowl. Regardless of the last layer, end with a layer of nondairy frozen whipped topping. Use 3 whole strawberries to decorate the top. Place in the center with points facing inward and touching. Refrigerate overnight.

Pineapple Angel Food Cake v

What You Need

1 four-serving package instant vanilla pudding

1 (20-ounce) can crushed pineapple with juice

1 cup nondairy frozen whipped topping, thawed

1 (10-ounce) prepared angel food cake

10 whole fresh strawberries with stems attached

What You Do

1. Stir together the pudding mix and crushed pineapple with juice. Slowly add the whipped topping. Set aside for five minutes.

2. Cut the cake into three horizontal layers. With the cut-side up, place the bottom layer on a serving plate. Spread 1⅓ cups of the filling on top and replace the second layer. Spread 1 cup of the filling and replace the cake top.

3. Use the remaining filling to frost the top and sides of the cake. Arrange strawberries point-side out in a circle on top of the cake. Chill at least 1 hour.

Variation: Strawberry Angel Food Cake

Prepare as above, but omit the pineapple and use strawberry flavor prepared angel food cake and strawberry flavor nondairy frozen whipped topping.

You won't believe how good this tastes—or how easy it is to make.

You'll find sliced almonds in the baking aisle.

Paradise Angel Food Cake v

What You Need

1 (2¼-ounce) package sliced almonds

1 prepared angel food cake

1 pint whipping cream

⅓ cup confectioners' sugar

2 tablespoons dry hot chocolate drink mix

What You Do

1. Preheat oven to 375°F. Place sliced almonds on an ungreased cookie sheet. Roast for 3 to 5 minutes until golden brown. Remove from oven. Set aside. Place angel food cake on a serving plate, set aside.

2. In a small mixing bowl, whip the cream (see "How Do I Whip Cream?" on page 289). As it starts to look fluffy, add confectioners' sugar and hot chocolate drink mix. Continue whipping until whipped cream is stiff.

3. Spread whipped cream on the top and around the side of the cake.

4. Preheat the oven to 375°F. Spread the almonds on an ungreased cookie sheet. Bake 3 to 5 minutes until golden brown. Sprinkle almonds on top of the cake. Keep refrigerated until ready to serve.

Appendix A

Equipping the Kitchen

If you're new to the kitchen, you may not have the essentials you need to cook for yourself. Here's a list of basic utensils, herbs, spices, and other ingredients you'll want to have on hand. Those marked with an asterisk (*) are recommended for all kitchens. Purchase other items as needed.

Aluminum foil

Appliances
Coffee pot
2-quart slow cooker
Electric blender
Electric mixer
*Electric (or manual) can opener
Electric popcorn popper
Electric skillet
*Toaster or toaster oven

*Colander

*Cutting board

Gadgets
Apple corer
Bagel slicer
Egg slicer
Kitchen scissors
*Kitchen timer
Meat thermometer
Sifter
Steamer basket

Hand utensils

Cheese slicer
Grater
Huller
Ice cream scoop
*Long-handled fork
*Pancake turner
Pizza cutter
*Potato masher
Rolling pin
*Slotted spoon
Soup ladle
Spaghetti server
Spatula (flexible)
*Spoon (large)
Tongs
Wooden spoon

Knives

Bread knife
*Paring knife
*Potato peeler
*Roast slicer

Measuring cups (oven proof glass)

1 cup
*2 cup

*Measuring spoon set

⅛ teaspoon to 1 tablespoon

*Mixing bowls, set of 3

Muffin tin

Ovenproof pans

Baking pans (2) . . . . 9" × 13" × 2"
. . . . *9" × 9" × 1¾"
*Baking sheets (2)
Covered baking dishes (3). 1-quart
. . . . 1½-quart
. . . . *2-quart
Loaf pans . . . . 9½" × 5¼" × 2¾"
. . . . or 8½" × 4½" × 2½"
Pie pan . . . . 8" or 9" diameter, 1½" deep
Roasting pan . . . . *9" × 13" × 2"
Tube pan or Bundt pan

*Paper towels

Plastic wrap

Popcorn popper

*Potholders (4)

Stovetop pots and pans (with lids)
Double boiler, 1½-quart
Frying pans (2) . . . . *9" to 10" diameter
. . . . 6" to 7" diameter
1-quart saucepan
*2-quart saucepan
*4-quart Dutch oven or stewpot

Trivet, 1 or more

Waxed paper

Wire whisk

Herbs, Spices, and Other Ingredients
Baking soda
Basil
Bay leaves
Bouillon cubes, beef, chicken, and vegetable
Brown sugar
Cayenne pepper
Cayenne pepper hot sauce
Celery salt
Celery seed
Chili powder
*Cinnamon
Confectioners' sugar
Cumin
Curry powder
Double-acting baking powder
Dry mustard
*Flour, all-purpose
Garlic, minced
Garlic powder
*Garlic salt
Ginger
*Granulated sugar
Honey

Hot pepper sauce (like Tabasco)
Ketchup
Lemon juice
Maple syrup
Mayonnaise
Mustard, prepared
Nonstick cooking spray
Nutmeg
*Olive oil
*Onion flakes, chopped
Onion, minced
Onion powder
Onion salt
Oregano
Paprika
*Parsley flakes, dried
*Pepper
Poultry seasoning
Rosemary
*Salt
Seasoned salt (like Lawry's)
Sesame seed
*Solid shortening
*Sugar
Tarragon
*Vanilla extract (or imitation vanilla extract)
*Vegetable oil
Vinegar, red wine
Vinegar, white
Worcestershire sauce

à la mode: The direct translation from French is "in the fashion." Most often, this term refers to a scoop of ice cream served with a piece of pie.

al dente: Tender but still firm. Usually applies to pasta or vegetables.

au gratin: Topped with browned bread crumbs, usually blended with butter or cheese before baking.

bake: Cook in an oven with dry heat.

barbecue: Cook on a grill over hot charcoal.

baste: Spoon liquid or fat over food during cooking.

beat: Stir vigorously to add air.

blend: Mix together.

boil: Cook in steaming water or other liquid. Boiling water has large bubbles that break at the surface.

broil: Like barbecuing, broiling is cooking directly over a fire or directly under the heating element. Heat for broiling is more intense than for baking or roasting.

chill: Cool in the refrigerator until cold.

chop: Cut into small pieces.

coat: Cover with another ingredient, such as coating lettuce with salad dressing or coating a strawberry with chocolate.

colander: A bowl-like pan with holes in the bottom for draining such foods as pasta and steamed vegetables.

confectioners' sugar: Powdered sugar.

cool: No longer warm, but not yet chilled.

corer: A utensil used to remove apple cores.

cream: Stir or beat together two or more ingredients until the mixture is soft and smooth. This term usually refers to mixing fat and sugar.

crisp-tender: Food—usually vegetables or pasta—that is tender but still firm.

cube: Cut into little boxes, usually with about ½"-long sides.

dash: An imprecise measurement that means a small amount; less than ⅛ teaspoon.

deep-fry: Cook by submersing in hot fat.

defrost: Thaw.

dice: Cut into little, bitty cubes, usually with sides less than ¼" long.

dilute: Add liquid to make an ingredient thinner or less strong.

drain: Remove liquid or fat; usually done by using a sieve or colander.

dust: Lightly sprinkle, usually with flour or confectioners' sugar.

entrée: The main dish of a meal—usually meat, fish, or poultry, but may be a meat substitute or a casserole.

evaporated milk: Whole milk that has been heated to remove 60 percent of its water; no sugar is added; do not substitute for sweetened condensed milk.

fillet: Meat or fish with the bones removed.

firmly packed: A way to measure an ingredient, like brown sugar, by tightly pressing it into the measuring cup or measuring spoon. This method results in more of the ingredient than using the usual measuring method.

flake: Separate into small pieces, often by using a fork; for example, you may want to flake tuna or salmon when you remove it from a can.

fold: A method of stirring from the bottom of the bowl to the top, rather than around in a horizontal circle; start with the spoon in the center of the bowl, then plunge it down to the bottom, and back toward you up the side to the top; turn the bowl and repeat until the ingredients are well mixed together.

freeze: Chill at a cold enough temperature (32°F for water) to turn solid.

fry: Cook in hot fat.

garnish: Decorate one food with another. Parsley is a frequently used garnish that improves the appearance of food.

grate: Rub a food against the small holes of a grater.

grater: A utensil with sharp-edged holes used to shred such foods as cheese, carrots, and lettuce.

grease: Coat a baking pan with solid shortening, vegetable oil, or nonstick cooking spray to prevent sticking.

heat: Make food warmer.

hull: Remove stems from fruit.

huller: A utensil used to remove the stem and leaves from strawberries.

invert: Turn upside down.

julienne: Cut into sticks similar in shape to wooden matches. Julienne strips are like long cubes.

marinade: A liquid mixture that contains an acid, seasonings, and, often, oil. Used to add flavor to meats or vegetables before cooking.

marinate: Soak food in a marinade.

melt: Change from solid form to liquid.

mince: Cut into teeny-weeny pieces.

mix: Combine foods, usually by stirring.

mull: Heat, sweeten, and add spices.

pare: Cut off the peel of such foods as apples and potatoes.

peel: The outer skin of a fruit or vegetable; also refers to removing the outer skin of a fruit or vegetable.

pinch: An imprecise measurement term that means the amount you can hold between your thumb and forefinger.

pit: A stone that contains the seed of such fruits as avocados and cherries; also refers to removing such a stone.

poach: Slowly simmer in liquid.

powdered sugar: Confectioners' sugar.

preheat: Heat an oven, frying pan, griddle, broiler, or other cooking appliance to a specific temperature prior to cooking.

rinse: Clean something with water. (Never wash food with soap.)

roast: Cook uncovered using dry heat, usually in an oven. Roast usually applies to meat; bake, which also means to cook with dry heat, usually applies to such foods as breads, desserts, and casseroles.

sauté: Cook in a small amount of fat in a frying pan, stirring frequently.

shortening: A fat used in baking or frying; often refers to fat in solid form.

shred: Cut into long, narrow pieces; or, rub food across the large holes of a grater.

sift: Add air to a recipe by passing such ingredients as flour through a sieve.

sifter: A utensil used to sift ingredients.

simmer: Cook in water or other liquid that is not quite as hot as boiling; water that is simmering has small bubbles below the surface.

slice: Cut a thin, flat piece of such foods as tomatoes and onions; also refers to cutting meat the same way.

soufflé: A fluffy baked egg dish with a wide variety of other ingredients.

spoon: Scoop using a spoon.

steam: Cook in steam from boiling water rather than cooking in the water.

stew: Cook slowly in liquid over low temperature.

stir: Move a spoon or other utensil in a circle to combine ingredients.

stir-fry: Cook in a small amount of fat in a frying pan or wok over high heat, stirring constantly to prevent sticking or burning.

strainer: A sieve used for straining foods; can also be used to sift such ingredients as flour.

sweetened condensed milk: Whole milk that has been heated to remove 60 percent of its water and has been commercially sweetened; not a substitute for evaporated milk.

tent: A piece of aluminum foil folded in half and propped open like the roof of a house over such food as turkey to keep the food from getting too brown when baking or roasting in the oven.

thaw: Let warm up from a frozen state to an unfrozen one.

toss: Gently mix such ingredients as lettuce and other vegetables by scooping and lifting them with hands, spoons, or other utensils.

undiluted: Without added liquid; for recipes that include condensed soup, undiluted means not to add milk or water to the soup.

whip: Beat rapidly; like beating, whipping adds air.

whisk: A kitchen utensil usually made of wire used to blend such ingredients as eggs, milk, and cream; also used as a verb meaning "to whip."

wok: A large, deep skillet used to stir-fry vegetables.

zest: The outer skin of such citrus fruits as lemons, limes, and oranges. Grated zest is sometimes used as a flavoring.

Appendix C
Cooking Vegetables

If you want to cook fresh vegetables by themselves instead of in a casserole or a fancy side dish, you can boil or steam them. Generally, steaming or boiling in a small amount of water in a covered saucepan works best for cut or small vegetables, while boiling uncovered is preferred for large or whole vegetables.

1. For most vegetables, figure about 2 servings per cup.

2. Before cooking, rinse vegetables in cold running water. Drain. Cut off inedible stems or leaves.

3. You can boil vegetables with about ½" of water in a saucepan. Bring to a boil over high heat. Cover the saucepan. Reduce heat to medium for the prescribed cooking time (see chart following).

4. Steaming is easy if you use a steamer insert that keeps the vegetables up out of the water. Or, use a pot designed as a steamer.

5. For boiling green vegetables, cook uncovered for the first 5 minutes; then cover for the remaining cooking time. For other vegetables, cover as soon as the water boils. Reduce heat to medium. Cook until tender, yet still firm.

Asparagus

You can enjoy dark green asparagus spears topped with butter, lemon pepper, cheese, or special sauces. Although it is available year-round, many people associate slender new spears with spring. In fact, peak seasons stretch from January to June and August to October, depending on the growing area. Before cooking, remove the tough bottom inch or so of the stems by cutting or breaking off as if they were sticks.

Cooking time: Tips, 5 to 8 minutes; 1" pieces, 10 to 15 minutes; whole, 10 to 20 minutes

Yields 1 serving per 5 spears

Broccoli

Choose broccoli with a firm cluster of small flower buds with dark green or sage color. A purplish tone is okay. So is a yellowish tint on the sides of the floret. However, avoid broccoli that has open clusters with greenish yellow color. Before cooking, trim off the bottom of the main stem. Serve with butter, lemon juice, and oregano, or canned cheese sauce.

Cooking time: 10 to 15 minutes

Yields 1 serving per stalk

Brussels Sprouts

Brussels sprouts look like tiny cabbages. Serve with butter or margarine and salt and pepper. Herbs and spices that enhance their flavor include garlic, basil, dill, caraway, or cumin. Before cooking, remove any discolored leaves. Trim stem ends.

Cooking time: 8 to 10 minutes

Yields 1 serving per 4 sprouts

Carrots

Carrots are good for your eyes, but they won't correct your vision. Carrots are high in vitamin A, which promotes good eye health and helps prevent night blindness. Packaged baby carrots that have already been cleaned may also be steamed.

Cooking time: Sliced, 10 to 20 minutes; small (whole), 15 to 20 minutes; large (whole), 20 to 30 minutes

Yields 1 serving per medium-size whole carrot

Cauliflower

Serve cauliflower alone or in combination with broccoli and/or carrots. Tasty toppings include melted cheese, diluted lemon juice, or bottled tartar sauce. Before cooking, cut away leaves and the center core. Cut off any discolored spots. If not cooking whole, separate the florets (the "treetops") with the stems attached.

Cooking time: Florets, 8 to 15 minutes; whole, 20 to 30 minutes

Yields 5 servings per head

Corn on the Cob

Fresh corn on the cob is a Midwestern favorite. Do not add salt during cooking, as it will toughen the corn. Serve with butter or margarine and salt and pepper. Before cooking, remove husks and corn silks from the corn. For the best flavor ever, if you live on a farm or have a home garden, wait until the water is boiling before you pick the corn.

Cooking time: 5 to 8 minutes

Serves 1 per ear

Green Beans

Green beans are fat-free and a good source of fiber. They also are low in calories, with just 25 calories per serving. When purchasing, look for clean, tender beans with uniform shape. For added flavor, toss with butter or bacon fat after cooking. Or, season with basil, marjoram, dill weed, or thyme. Before cooking, cut or snap off the ends. Leave whole, or cut crosswise into 1"-long pieces or cut lengthwise (known as French cut).

Cooking time: Cut, 15 to 20 minutes; French cut, 10 minutes; whole, 15 to 20 minutes

Yields 1 serving per ¾ cup

Peas

Finding fresh peas in the pod is rare, so most people use frozen. Cook according to package instructions. If you want to shell your own, remove from the pods immediately before cooking. For either frozen or fresh, add 1 teaspoon sugar to the cooking water. You can also use thawed frozen peas in cold salads.

Cooking time: 8 to 15 minutes

1 cup yields 2 servings

Potatoes

The potato is the most popular vegetable in the United States. The easiest way to cook is to bake them. You can boil them for use in mashed potatoes, potato salads, or potato casseroles. You can use any variety, but red and russet potatoes work especially well for boiling.

Cooking time: Bake at 375°F for 1 hour or at 350°F for 1½ hours; boil, cut 20 to 25 minutes; whole, 30 to 35 minutes

1 serving per medium-size potato

Index of Cooking Questions

How Should I Measure Brown Sugar?..................................... 4

What Do I Do with Bacon Fat?.. 5

Oops! What Do I Do If There's Eggshell in My Eggs? 6

OK, So How Do I Boil Water? 8

What Do I Do If My Potatoes Sprout in Storage?........................ 14

How Can I Customize a Grilled Cheese Sandwich?...................... 30

How Do I Use an Egg Slicer?... 40

What Does "To Taste" Mean? 41

How Do I Grate Cheese?.. 46

How Do I Make Mustard Sauce? 50

How Do I Prevent Tears When I Chop an Onion? 56

How Do I Remove Avocado Seeds? 61

What Do I Do with the Remaining Frozen Vegetables? 71

How Can I Use Broccoli Stems?...................................... 86

How Do I Know What Type of Vinegar to Choose? 88

How Do I Know What Type of Olive Oil to Choose?.................... 89

How Do I Prepare a Head of Lettuce for a Salad? 90

How Do I Store Celery?... 95

How Do I Make My Own Croutons? 96

How Can I Use Peas in Other Recipes Too? 97

What Are the Cooking Times for Bone-In Roasts?..................... 108

How Do I Bake a Potato?... 109

How Do I Brown Ground Beef?...................................... 111

How Do I Prepare French Bread?.................................... 114

How Do I Choose and Store Cabbage? 119

How Do I Roast Meat and Poultry?.................................. 123

How Do I Choose Ground Beef?..................................... 131

Which Cut of Pork Should I Roast?.................................. 132

What Does Horseradish Go With?.................................... 138

How Can I Make Gravy Easily?...................................... 140

Why Do I Need to Preheat the Oven? 147

How Do I Prevent Salmonella Poisoning?............................ 149

How Can I Save Money When I Buy Chicken? 150

Index of Cooking Questions—*continued*

◇✓

Can I Safely Save Cooked Chicken and How? 153
What is a Marinade? 154
How Should I Thaw Frozen Meat and Poultry? 156
How Can I Make My Own Cocktail Sauce? 169
Why Do People Serve Lemon with Fish? 170
How Can I Tell When Pasta is Done? 181
How Can I Use a Frozen Bag of Veggies as First Aid? 188
What Is the Quickest Way to Measure Butter? 190
How Can I Cut the Hotness of Chili Peppers? 196
How Do I Make Tofu Sour Cream? 201
How Do I Know When an Avocado Is Ripe? 205
What are the Ways That I Can Cook Mushrooms? 207
What Kinds of Zucchini Are There? 212
What Is Evaporated Milk? 213
How Should I Eat Steamed Whole Artichokes? 216
What is the Difference Between *Slicing* and *Dicing*? 220
What's a Parsnip? 222
Is Corn a Vegetable? 226
How Can I Keep Fruits from Turning Brown? 237
What Else Can I Do with Artichokes? 241
Should I Use Block or Softened Cream Cheese? 242
What is an Easy Way to Drain Canned Foods? 248
What Is Pimiento? 252
What Can I Do with Party Rye Bread? 255
How Can I Sweeten Foods Besides Adding Sugar? 266
How Should I Clean Strawberries? 274
How Do I Use an Apple Corer? 275
What If I Can't Find the Right Ingredient Size? 279
How Do I Whip Cream? 289
What Is the Difference Between *Fold*, *Beat*, and *Whip*? 295
How Do I Separate Eggs? 299
How Do I Sift Flour? 301

Index

Alfalfa sprouts, in
  sandwich, 47
Appetizers. See Snacks
  and appetizers
Apples
  about: coring, 275
  in breakfast dishes,
    10, 23
  in dessert, 275
  in salad, 95
  in side dish, 218
  in snack, 237
  in soup, 75
Artichokes
  about: cooking, 241;
    eating steamed,
    216
  in salad, 102
  in sandwich, 52
  in side dish, 216
  in snacks and
    appetizers, 241, 263
Asparagus
  about: cooking, 316
  in main dishes,
    156–57
  in side dishes, 213,
    221
Avocados
  about: judging
    ripeness, 205;
    removing seeds, 61
  in main dish, 204–5
  in salads, 84, 103
  in snack, 240
  in soup, 61

Bacon
  about: cooking, 5;
    storing fat from, 5
  in breakfast dishes,
    25, 28
  in chili, 72
  in main dishes, 105
  in salads, 103, 105
  in sandwiches, 31,
    33, 37
Baked beans
  in side dishes, 226
  in vegetarian main
    dish, 199
Bananas
  in breads/muffins/
    biscuits, 16, 27
  in dessert, 286
  in salads, 80–81, 93
  in smoothie, 2
  in snack, 239
  in spread, 11
Beans. See specific beans
Bean sprouts, in
  sandwich, 39
Beef. See also Ground
  beef
  in main dishes, 106,
    108–31
  in soups and stews,
    57, 70
Bell peppers
  in main dishes, 127,
    164, 193
  in salads, 83, 87, 100,
    103

in snack, 246
in soups and stews,
  60, 63, 68, 75
Berries, in dessert, 269.
  See also specific berries
Biscuits. See Breads/
  muffins/biscuits
Black beans
  in main dishes, 180,
    204–5
  in soup, 69
Black-eyed peas, 73
Blueberries
  in desserts, 276, 293
  in muffins, 13
Bologna, in sandwich, 38
Breads/muffins/biscuits
  for breakfast, 3–4, 13,
    15–17, 20–21, 27
  in snacks and
    appetizers, 236,
    247, 259
  vegetarian and
    vegan, 197
Breakfast foods, 1–28
Broccoli
  about: cooking, 316;
    using stems, 86
  in main dishes, 116,
    136, 151
  in salads, 86, 98
  in side dish, 223
  in snack, 261
  in soup, 59
Brown sugar,
  measuring, 4

Brussels sprouts
    about: cooking, 316
    in side dish, 215
Bulgur wheat, in salad,
    101
Butter, measuring, 190
Butter beans, in main
    dish, 199

Cabbage
    about: choosing and
        storing, 119
    in main dish, 119
    in salad, 99
    in side dish, 227
Carrots
    about: cooking, 317
    in main dish, 156
    in salads, 87, 98, 102
    in side dishes, 214, 222
    in soups and stews,
        57, 59, 64, 75–76
Casseroles
    breakfast, 28
    main dish, 114–15,
        125, 159
    seafood, 166, 174–75
    side dish, 224
    vegetarian and
        vegan, 202
Cauliflower
    about: cooking, 317
    in main dish, 156
    in salads, 86, 98
    in side dish, 223
Celery, storing, 95
Cheese
    about: grating, 46
    in beef main dishes,
        111–12, 118, 126

in breakfast dishes,
    7, 19, 22, 24–26, 28
in chicken main
    dishes, 152, 155,
    160, 161
in salad, 98
in sandwiches, 30,
    33–39, 42–45, 48,
    50, 52
in seafood main
    dishes, 166, 168,
    178
in side dishes, 213,
    223–25, 230–31
in snacks and
    appetizers, 236,
    242, 244–50, 252,
    255, 261–63
in vegetarian and
    vegan main dishes,
    189, 190–191,
    195–97, 203–5, 208
Cherries/cherry pie
    filling, in desserts,
    270, 293, 296–97
Chicken
    about: buying, 150;
        cooking ahead, 153
    in main dishes,
        146–47, 149–64
    in sandwich, 40
    in snack, 258
    in soups and stews,
        65, 75
Chickpeas
    in main dishes, 193,
        198
    in salad, 94
    in snack, 257
    in soup, 59

Chili. See Soups and
    stews
Chili beans, canned
    in chili, 54
    in main dishes,
        200–201
Chilies
    about: hotness of,
        196
    in main dish, 196
    in snack, 248
    in soup, 67
Chocolate
    in desserts, 273, 274,
        277–79, 282, 284,
        287, 294–95
    in snacks and
        appetizers, 235,
        239
Clams, in snacks, 182
Cocktail sauce, 169
Coconut
    in dessert, 266
    in salad, 80
Cod, in main dish, 171
Corn
    about, 226; cooking
        on the cob, 317
    in main dish, 180
    in side dish, 226
    in snack, 248
    in soups and stews,
        62, 65
Corned beef
    in main dish, 119
    in sandwich, 43
    in snack, 262
Cottage cheese, in
    salad, 83

Couscous
  in main dish, 198
  in salad, 100
Crabmeat
  in main dishes, 174,
    178
  in sandwiches, 37, 46
  in snacks and
    appetizers, 246,
    254
Cranberry sauce, in
  main dish, 147
Cream, whipping, 289
Cream cheese
  about: buying, 242
  in desserts, 276, 288,
    294–96
  in sandwiches, 46, 49
  in snacks and
    appetizers, 237,
    242, 250, 253–54,
    262
  in spreads, 11–12
Croutons, making, 96
Cucumbers
  in salads, 85, 87, 100,
    101
  in sandwich, 49
  in soup, 60

Desserts, 264–304
Dressings, for salads,
  88–90

Eggplant, in vegetarian
  dishes, 191, 202–3

Eggs
  about: removing
    piece of shell, 6;
    separating, 299;
    slicing, 40
  in breakfast dishes,
    6–9, 17–19, 22,
    24–25, 27–28
  in salads, 92, 97, 104
  in sandwiches, 34,
    40–41
  in seafood main
    dishes, 174–75
  in snack, 234
  in soup, 69
  in vegetarian and
    vegan main
    dishes, 197, 203,
    208
Evaporated milk, 213

Flour, sifting, 301
French bread,
  preparing, 114
French toast. See
  Breads/muffins/
  biscuits
Fruits, preventing
  brownness, 237. See
  also specific fruits

Garbanzo beans. See
  Chickpeas
Graham crackers
  in dessert, 288
  in snacks and
    appetizers, 238–39
Grapes
  in dessert, 276
  in salads, 82, 93

Great Northern beans,
  in soups and stews,
  68, 76
Green beans
  about: cooking, 318
  in salad, 94
  in side dishes, 211,
    232
  in soups and stews,
    59, 63
Ground beef
  about: browning,
    111; choosing, 131
  in breakfast dish, 24
  in main dishes, 111–
    12, 115, 117–18,
    120, 127–128,
    130–31, 159
  in sandwich, 51
  in snack, 250
  in soups and stews,
    54, 58, 64, 67, 72

Haddock, in main dish,
  175
Ham
  in main dishes, 136–
    38, 144, 161
  in salad, 92
  in sandwiches, 35,
    39, 50
  in snack, 260
  in soup, 73
Honey
  in dessert, 300–301
  in spreads, 11–12
Horseradish, 138
Hummus, in sandwich,
  47

Kidney beans
  in main dish, 199
  in salad, 94
  in soups and stews,
    54, 59, 62, 67, 76–77
Kitchen, essential
  equipment and
  ingredients for,
  305–8

Lemons
  in dessert, 286
  with fish, 170
  in soup, 69
Lettuce, preparing for
  salad, 90
Lima beans
  in main dish, 199
  in salad, 92
  in soups and stews,
    63, 65

Main dishes
  beef, 106, 108–31
  pork, 107, 132–44
  poultry, 145–64
  seafood, 165–86
  vegetarian and
    vegan, 187–208
Mandarin oranges, in
  salads, 80, 91, 93
Marinades, 154
Marshmallows
  in side dish, 219
  in snack, 238
Muffins. See Breads/
  muffins/biscuits
Mushrooms
  about: cooking, 207
  in breakfast dish, 26

in main dishes, 129,
  163, 176–78, 191–
  92, 206–7
in snacks and
  appetizers, 243,
  249, 261
Mustard sauce, 50

Noodles. See Pasta

Oats/oatmeal
  in desserts, 278–80
  in snacks and
    appetizers, 235,
    238
Okra, in stew, 65
Olive oil, types of, 89
Olives, in salads, 86, 98,
  100, 102
Onions, chopping, 56
Orange juice
  in biscuits, 3
  in dessert, 302
  in side dish, 214
  in smoothie, 2
Orange roughy, in main
  dishes, 168, 184
Oranges. See Mandarin
  oranges; Orange
  juice
Oven, preheating, 147

Pancakes, 18, 23
Parsnips, in side dish,
  222
Pasta
  about: testing for
    doneness, 181
  in beef main dishes,
    112, 118, 121

in pork main dishes,
  136, 144
in poultry main
  dishes, 156, 160,
  163
in salad, 98
in seafood main
  dishes, 166, 172,
  176–78, 181–82
in soups and stews,
  74, 76–77
in vegetarian and
  vegan main
  dishes, 189–90,
  194–95, 202
Peaches
  in dessert, 292
  in stew, 57
Peach preserves, in
  spread, 11
Peanut butter
  in desserts, 267, 281
  in sandwich, 32
  in snacks and
    appetizers, 235,
    239
Peas
  about, 97; cooking,
    318
  in main dish, 188
  in salad, 97
Pecans, in desserts, 268,
  273, 277, 287, 289
Pepperoni
  on mini pizza, 44
  in soup, 68
Pesto, 217
Pimientos, in snack,
  252

Pineapple
  in desserts, 270, 297, 303
  in main dishes, 138, 142, 143
  in salad, 80
  in snack, 253
Pinto beans, in soup, 67
Pizza
  fruit, 276
  mini, 44
Pork. *See also* Ham
  about: cuts for roasting, 132
  in main dishes, 107, 132–44
Pork and beans, canned, in soups, 58, 72
Potatoes. *See also* Sweet potatoes
  about: cooking, 109, 318; removing sprouts, 14
  in breakfast dishes, 14, 24
  in main dishes, 105, 120, 130–31, 159, 200–201
  in salads, 104–5
  in side dishes, 210, 219–20, 224, 228, 230–31
  in soups and stews, 57, 65–66, 70, 76
Poultry. *See* Chicken; Turkey
Pumpkin
  in bread, 21

in dessert, 272
Quiches, 25–26

Rice
  in beef main dishes, 115, 127, 159
  in chicken main dishes, 153, 157
  in dessert, 271
  in pork main dishes, 139, 141
  in seafood main dishes, 175, 186
  in side dishes, 225, 229
  in vegetarian main dish, 204–5

Salads, 79–105
Salmon, in main dishes, 170, 185
Salmonella poisoning, 149
Sandwiches, 29–52
Sauerkraut
  in main dish, 135
  in sandwich, 43
  in snack, 262
Sausage
  in breakfast dishes, 22, 23
  in main dish, 141
  in snacks and appetizers, 243, 255, 256
  in soups and stews, 74, 77
Seafood. *See specific fish or shellfish*

Shrimp
  in main dishes, 169, 172, 176–77, 180
  in salad, 84
Side dishes, 209–32
Smoothie, 2
Snacks and appetizers, 233–63
Soups and stews, 53–78, 199
Spinach
  in main dishes, 160, 176–77, 196–97, 202
  in salad, 102
  in snacks and appetizers, 249, 263
  in soup, 78
Spreads, 11–12
Stews. *See* Soups and stews
Strawberries
  about: cleaning, 274
  in breakfast dish, 12
  in desserts, 274, 276, 290, 302–3
  in salad, 81
Sugar, sweetening without, 266
Sweet potatoes
  in main dish, 143
  in side dishes, 218–19, 222
  in stew, 63

Tofu
  about: making sour cream with, 201

Tofu—*continued*
  in main dishes, 200–
    201, 206–7
Tomatoes, canned
  in main dishes, 136,
    139, 164, 181
  in side dish, 225
  in soups and stews,
    64–65, 68, 74–77
Tomatoes, fresh
  in main dishes, 111–
    12, 116, 171, 176–
    77, 188, 191–95,
    202, 204–5, 208
  in salads, 86, 97, 100,
    101
  in sandwiches, 31,
    35, 45, 47–48
  in snacks, 240
  in soup, 60
Tomatoes, stewed
  in main dishes, 113,
    115, 163, 199, 202
  in soups and stews,
    59, 62, 67, 70
Tortillas
  in breakfast dishes,
    19, 24
  in main dishes, 126,
    196, 200–201,
    204–5
  in sandwich, 52
  in snack, 244
"To taste," 41
Tuna
  in main dishes, 166,
    173, 179, 181, 183
  in sandwiches, 40, 45

Turkey
  in main dishes, 148,
    159
  in sandwiches, 35, 37

Vegetables. *See also*
    specific vegetables
  cooking, 315
  first aid with bag of
    frozen, 188
  mixed, in soup, 70
  storing frozen, 71
Vegetarian and vegan
    main dishes, 187–208
Vinegar, types of, 88

Water, boiling, 8
Wraps. *See* Sandwiches

Zucchini
  about: kinds of, 212
  in main dishes, 193,
    208
  in side dish, 212
  in soups and stews,
    57, 62, 63

About the Author

Mary-Lane Kamberg is an award-winning professional writer and speaker who has published ten nonfiction books, including the nostalgic cookbook *Homegrown in the Ozarks: Mountain Meals and Memories*.

She is listed in Marquis *Who's Who in America* and received the 1996 James P. Immroth Memorial Award from the American Library Association's Intellectual Freedom Roundtable. She has won numerous awards for poetry, humor, newspaper, and magazine writing. Her professional activities include the Kansas City Writers Group, Kansas Authors Club, Missouri Writers Guild, and Oklahoma Writers Federation Inc. She is a frequent presenter in classrooms and educator in-services.